Language, Minority Education and Gender

THE LANGUAGE AND EDUCATION LIBRARY

Series Editor

Professor David Corson, *The Ontario Institute for Studies in Education, 252 Bloor St. West, Toronto, Ontario, Canada M5S 1V6.*

Other Books in the Series

Critical Theory and Classroom Talk
    ROBERT YOUNG
Language Policy Across the Curriculum
    DAVID CORSON
School to Work Transition in Japan
    KAORI OKANO
Reading Acquisition Processes
    G. B. THOMPSON, W. E. TUNMER and T. NICHOLSON (eds)
Worlds of Literacy
    D. BARTON, M. HAMILTON and R. IVANIC (eds)

Other Books of Interest

Attitudes and Language
    COLIN BAKER
Education of Chinese Children in Britain and USA
    LORNITA YUEN-FAN WONG
European Models of Bilingual Education
    HUGO BAETENS BEARDSMORE (ed.)
Foundations of Bilingual Education and Bilingualism
    COLIN BAKER
Language, Culture and Education
    M. BEVERIDGE and G. REDDIFORD (Eds)
Language Education for Intercultural Communication
    D. AGER, G. MUSKENS and S. WRIGHT (eds)
Life in Language Immersion Classrooms
    ELIZABETH B. BERNHARDT (ed.)
Psychology, Spelling and Education
    C. STERLING and C. ROBSON (eds)
Teaching Composition Around the Pacific Rim
    M. N. BROCK and L. WALTERS (eds)
World in a Classroom
    V. EDWARDS and A. REDFERN

Please contact us for the latest book information:
Multilingual Matters Ltd,
Frankfurt Lodge, Clevedon Hall, Victoria Road,
Clevedon, Avon BS21 7SJ England

THE LANGUAGE AND EDUCATION LIBRARY 6

Language, Minority Education and Gender

Linking Social Justice and Power

David Corson

MULTILINGUAL MATTERS LTD
Clevedon • Philadelphia • Adelaide

ONTARIO INSTITUTE FOR STUDIES IN EDUCATION
Toronto

Library of Congress Cataloging in Publication Data
Corson, David
Language, Minority Education and Gender: Linking Social Justice and
Power/David Corson.
p. cm. (The Language and Education Library: 6)
Includes bibliographical references and index.
ISBN 1-85359-210-2 (hbk). ISBN 1-85359-209-9 (pbk)
1. Language and education. 2. Language policy. 3. Minorities–Education.
4. Women–Education. I. Title. II. Series.
P40.8.C668   1993   306.4'49–dc20   93-8605

British Library Cataloguing in Publication Data
A CIP catalogue record for this book is available from the British Library.

Canadian Cataloguing in Publication Data
Corson, David
Language, Minority Education and Gender: Linking Social Justice and Power
(The Language and Education Library: 6)
Includes bibliographical references and index.
ISBN 0-7744-0406-X (pbk)
1. Language and education. 2. Language policy. 3. Minorities–Education.
I. Title. II. Series
P40.8.C67   1993   306.4'49   C93-094414-3

Multilingual Matters Ltd
UK: Frankfurt Lodge, Clevedon Hall, Victoria Road, Clevedon, Avon BS21 7SJ.
USA: 1900 Frost Road, Suite 101, Bristol, PA 19007, USA.
Australia: P.O. Box 6025, 83 Gilles Street, Adelaide, SA 5000, Australia.

Ontario Institute for Studies in Education
252 Bloor Street West, Toronto, Ontario, Canada M5S 1V6

Index compiled by Tim Corson.
Cover photograph by Tim Corson.
Printed and bound in Great Britain by WBC Print Ltd.

For Elizabeth Corson, Diana Lee and Marissa Mohammed

'The real political task is to criticize the working of institutions that appear to be both neutral and independent; to criticize them in such a way that the political violence which has always exercised itself obscurely through them will be uncovered so that people can fight it.'

Michael Foucault

Contents

Foreword

My concern in this book is to examine injustices in language policy and practice in education, and to suggest ways to remove them. In the chapters that follow I treat policies that are formal and explicit, as well as policies that are tacit but no less real. Three groups seem most affected by unfair language policies in education: women and girls; minority cultural groups; and minority social groups. In setting the background for later discussion, Chapters 1 and 2 attempt 'state of the art' accounts that deal respectively with the interplay between language policy and power, and language policy and social justice. Chapters 3 to 6 examine factors affecting the three groups. These chapters overlap their treatment wherever there is clear evidence that similar justice issues affect more than one group, or wherever clear parallels can be drawn. Chapter 7 presents recommendations for school action, integrating recommendations that address the interests of all three affected groups.

My project here tries to complement other recent work incorporating a critical approach to language policy and ideologies of literacy and pedagogy in multilingual societies (e.g. Grillo, 1989; Tollefson, 1991; Gee, 1990). It goes beyond other accounts by giving clear priority to the pursuit of social justice as an explicit social practice.

Throughout the book I distinguish informally between minority social groups and minority cultural groups. The basis for the distinction is that the latter usually possess or identify with a language which is not the majority language of the society, and which reflects a very different culture. Although social and cultural minorities are different in the definition I am offering, the one depending more on criteria related to ethnicity and racial origin, and the other depending more on matters of social class, occupation, and level of income, they often stand in a similar relationship to the more dominant groups in a society. Leaving language aside, it is possible for any single minority social group to be less like the dominant group culturally than any single cultural group. Urban African American minorities in the USA, for example, are perhaps as far removed from the dominant culture as some minority cultural groups who maintain their own language as well as English. As later discussion indicates, when gender is added as a variable, language injustices tend to multiply, whether or not the children concerned are from a social or a cultural minority.

In developing this book, I have benefited greatly from the scholarly criticism of a number of people whose names are known to me: Roy Bhaskar; Pierre Bourdieu; Jim Cummins; Viv Edwards; and Dell Hymes. I have also benefited from the criticism of many people who are not known to me, especially the anonymous referees of the seven published articles that make up large sections of the subject matter of the first six chapters. These articles appear in issues of *Language and Education, Educational Theory, The Canadian Review of Modern Languages, Journal of Education Policy, Australian Journal of Education*, and *Gender and Education*. My thanks to the editorial boards and publishers of those journals for allowing me to test my ideas against the expertise and wisdom of their reviewers. The book is no doubt much the better for it.

David J. Corson
The Ontario Institute for Studies in Education

1 Language Policy and Power

Power and Language[1]

There are many theories of power, but none seems to capture in full the range of meanings that individuals can reasonably attach to this difficult term (Wrong, 1979; Lukes, 1974). Rather than working from any single theory of power, my purposes here are better served by dealing directly with the link between 'power' and 'language'. This seems a reasonable course to follow because even including that form of power that is expressed through physical violence (in punishment, warfare, confinement, or any of the other manifestations of physical violence), all kinds of power are directed, mediated, or resisted through language. For most everyday human purposes, power is exerted through verbal channels: language is the vehicle for identifying, manipulating and changing power relations between people.

This chapter points to the ways that education and the discourse practices that it authorizes can routinely repress, dominate and disempower language users whose practices differ from the norms that it establishes. I begin with the links between language and power, arguing that language is only an instrument of domination having little power that is independent of human agencies, structures, and social institutions. I focus that discussion on the institution of education which often allocates power to favoured norms of discourse and thereby creates discrimination and injustice for many. Relevant to this point, I offer a brief and critical consideration of Pierre Bourdieu's compelling arguments about language and education. Finally I recommend an approach for finding out about human needs and interests that may help policy makers in education to know when the exercise of power through language is useful and benevolent, and when it is harmful. The challenge is to separate wanted from unwanted forms of determination, and then through policymaking to replace the unwanted with the wanted. Roy Bhaskar is a contemporary theorist who offers an approach for doing this which is already influential. He argues that structures of power have no existence separate from the activities that they

1

govern and from agents' reports [in language] of those activities. I discuss his emancipatory conception of discovery, offering an approach to policy making that seems especially relevant at this time to minority schooling.

Four lines of debate

This brief account gives only a few signposts to the many theorists who discuss the relationship between language and power. Below I present four lines of debate which are far from discrete. In general this chapter's starting ideas come from the third and the fourth lines of debate. I turn first to the oldest continuous line of debate about language and power, which has its roots in the surviving classical works of political and moralist orators, like Cicero and Demosthenes, who used language as an instrument for wielding power even while reflecting themselves upon the rhetorical force of that usage. Both were very aware that oratorical language can be almost devoid of propositional content yet still have power. It is easy to see this debate continuing in the ideas of Dewey, Hegel, and Marx who saw a connection between moral power-broking and the sophisticated human ability to wield complex vocabularies. Pierre Bourdieu (1988) extends this line of debate in his discussion of 'magisterial language', especially as it is wielded by academics in universities: the language acquires a status and authority which tends to rule out any question about the genuinely informative efficiency of the communication.

A second line of debate connects the instability of discourse with structures of power and meaning. This debate can be traced back to one of the earliest Western historians, Thucydides, who wondered why it was, after the devastations of the Peloponnesian War between the Athenian and the Spartan alliances, that 'many words had lost their meanings'. This and the first line of debate recur in contemporary hermeneutics, especially in those disciplines where the difficult ideas of post-structuralism are discussed. Post-structuralists argue that if human subjectivity is unstable, then anything that depends upon subjectivity as a base, such as discourses about social arrangements, power distributions, and structures, is inherently unstable and potentially illusory.

A third line of debate springs from the ideas of Marx & Engels (1976 [1846]) linking power and language by way of ideology.[2] That influence continues through the work of key interpreters in the Marxian tradition on this topic, such as Gramsci, Habermas, Bourdieu, and Bhaskar, who see structure and agency as key concepts in addressing the issue; and who see power over discourse as a means for elevating the needs and interests of non-elite groups above those of the system that is designed and controlled by elites. Modern ideology studies, which examine language from two vantage points, continue this line of debate. In the one approach to the study of language and ideology, questions are asked about the development of 'political narratives' and their effects. These narratives seem to take on a power of their own, so that structural relations of domination become represented as 'legitimate' through the stories that are told to justify the exercise of power by agents who hold it. For example, Brian Faye's study of narratives of National Socialism that were developed during the Weimar period in Germany shows how effective these 'stories' were when circulated within their limited sphere of operation and structured space (in Thompson, 1984). Any power in the battle of words that took place under Weimar lay with the languages of German nationalism, anti-semitism, and militarism. In the other approach to the study of language and ideology, questions are asked not so much about the discourse of the ideologues themselves as about the language of everyday life and the taken-for-granted semantic structures that mundane discourse distributes among men and women.

A fourth line, not unrelated to the third, can be traced through German Romantic ideas about any power that language has in shaping thought and world view. Extending these ideas, thinkers like Herder, von Humboldt, and Fichte were outspoken in promoting notions of linguistic nationalism, eventually with the tragic human consequences already noted. These thinkers have had their own academic impact too, in linguistic anthropology, especially through the Sapir–Whorf hypothesis and in the ideas of some feminist writers who see 'man-made language' having an Orwellian role in 'controlling' women's thought (see Chapter 6). This account of 'thought-control via malespeak' is difficult to support since meaning in language depends on context and is ultimately indeterminate; no group can fix meaning or exercise power over it (Cameron, 1984). Sapir's view too, that language is a guide to social reality and even powerfully conditions all our thinking about social problems and processes, seems overstated. However, it is clear that language is an expression of world view (Hymes, 1966): in many contexts of use it does more than just reflect social structures; it can also perpetuate existing differences in power by expressing a prejudiced view of the world. Discussion in Chapters 3, 4, 5 & 6 and recommendations in Chapter 7 follow from this conclusion.

The immanent power of language

There is a key question implicit in all these debates: Does language have power of and by itself? Certainly George Orwell in his fictional 1984 seemed worried by the immanent influence of language, especially at the mass political level. His negative-utopian account of totalitarianism at work found its factual parallel in many real-world regimes of the left and the right. It is true that key figures in these regimes have often operated as if they believed that language has power of and by itself. Yet, as Dennis Wrong notes, even the Orwellian use of language to control people at a distance depended on science fiction techniques to overcome the visibility problem: two-way television screens which projected the powerful into the setting of the controlled. Language alone was not enough. Indeed even the intensity and comprehensiveness of power itself tends to vary inversely with its extensiveness. On the other hand, as mentioned, language does reflect social patterns such as sex-role stereotypes in such a way as to reinforce and disseminate those patterns, embodying a point of view of which people are unaware, and this is a form of power without any clear agency. Perhaps we have some reason for assenting to the immanent power of language if we allow that it does fashion, reflect, and reinforce structures of domination with no apparent agents at work.

But whichever way we look at language, it is hard to ignore that language is essentially powerless on its own. It is people who have the power to use language in various ways; it is people who give discourse its form and make judgments about the status of various texts; and it is the situations in which people have power and are using language to serve some potent purpose which give language a power that it lacks when it is without such precise contexts. The debunking and resisting power of satire is a case in point. As Mikhail Bakhtin observes, by manipulating the effects of context it is 'very easy to make even the most serious utterance comical' (1981 [1975]: 340). For examples of this, we need look no further than the clever ironies and satires that are used in television comedies like 'Yes Minister' and 'Monty Python' to parody the pretensions and the pomposity of powerful figures by putting their language into contexts that are subtly but critically removed from settings that are normally pregnant with power. Again the dissident movements in East European countries, from the 1950s to the 1980s, used the language of theatre and of satirical poetry to counter power. At the same time, some uses of power are too horrific to be satirized and even this power of dissident resistance came about because the powerful allowed the dissidents their theatre and poetry as a political safety valve for dissent. Without that shrewd concession, made by auth-orities creating contexts of meaning where dissident power could be exer-cised, while remaining relentlessly totalitarian in other contexts, the language of the dissenters might have had much less influence.

Language then seems mainly an instrument of power, a claim which meshes with Michel Foucault's judgment on the matter (1972; 1977; 1980): rather than a privilege that is ascribed to the individual, power itself is a network of relations constantly in tension and ever-present in activity;

rather than possessed and localized in individual hands, power is exercised through the production, accumulation and functioning of various discourses; rather than the mere verbalization of conflicts of domination, power is the very object of human conflict; and rather than concerned with conscious intention or decision, the study of power is best located at the point where any intentions of the powerful are invested in real and effective practices. In short, the development of particular forms of language meets the needs of the powerful and depends upon a particular exercise of power through discourse practices.

Language, Education and Power

The process of schooling is a form of 'social and cultural reproduction' that is linked openly to other structures in society, especially economic structures, which reproduce social relations. Michael Apple (1982) lists some of the major social functions that schools have: they select and certify a workforce; they maintain privilege by taking the form and content of the dominant culture and defining it as legitimate knowledge to be passed on; they are agents in the creation and the re-creation of an effectively dominant culture; they legitimate new knowledge, new classes and strata of social personnel. In short, for Apple, as part of their *raison d'être*, schools allocate people and legitimate knowledge, or legitimate people and allocate knowledge. As a result, in many of its practices formal education looks after the interests of some social groups better than the interests of other social groups. As I argue below, language is the vehicle for this routine activity of power distribution through education.

Society, language and control

Although an individual's language code and styles of usage are very personal possessions, there are obvious similarities between people in the codes and styles of language that they use. It is these commonalities in language orientation that make communication possible; the degree of commonality is roughly in inverse proportion to the social distance between people. Social distance (or closeness) between individuals is maintained by aspects of social structure, by the possibilities for interaction, by constraints on social behaviour, and by a myriad of other socio-cultural processes and norms. All of these things combine to help shape the meaning and value of an individual's code and style of language. This means that in any context the prevailing constraints of social structure interact with the social behaviour and social location of individuals in such a way as to add or subtract shades of meaning or significance, so that what is said, and the way in which it is said, is heavily influenced by factors external to the individual. As post-structuralists might have it, the meaning of any item of discourse cannot be disentangled from its social context. For example, in interactions between speakers of different social, gender, or cultural backgrounds the same fragment of discourse uttered by different individuals can be given very different meanings. More than this, a different pragmatic or cultural value may be placed on that utterance, depending on the background of the utterer.

Ideology theorists are alert to the influence of these extralinguistic factors on how language is valued and used. They speak of language users having images of themselves and of their roles that make them conform in their language behaviour to dominant influences in their social environment. Antonio Gramsci (1948) highlights the non-coercive aspect of domination, comparing it with the more obvious coercive forms of power. His concept of 'hegemony' describes the organization of consent through invisible cultural dominance, rather than through visible political power. In developed modern societies, control is exercised in a modern way which gives stability by basing power on wide-ranging consent and agreement. This non-coercive 'force' is said to penetrate consciousness itself, so that the dominated become accomplices in their own domination. So it is argued that power hegemonies are reinforced from both sides of the power relationship: in their language usages, the non-dominant adhere to the linguistic norms created by dominant groups, while not recognizing that they are being 'voluntarily coerced'. I return to this point many times in later chapters; this is a point about how power operates more generally which writers like Orwell and Dostoevsky also observe.

Denis Wrong (1979) concludes that there are psychological pressures from both sides of the power equation which help the powerful by converting coercive forms of power into what is perceived instead as legitimate authority. This phenomenon has been repeatedly observed in sociolinguistic studies: the classic instance comes from William Labov (1972) who found that stigmatized features of speech are judged most harshly by the very people whose speech most exhibits those features. In legitimating norms for language behaviour, this non-coercive psychological pressure can produce conformity even among actors from different sociological categories. For example, socially powerless men use the same sorts of features of speech that women in general do in formal social settings (O'Barr, 1982: but see Chapter 6). In this instance, speech differences correlate with lack of power rather than with gender; social rank interacts with gender; and socialization into the role of an accomplice in one's own domination in social settings is manifested in a use of linguistic norms that acknowledge the legitimacy of those imbalanced social relations.

Power and the language norms of education

Education's legitimate influence on language use is clear: it seeks to capitalize on the central role of language in learning, in understanding, and in knowing. While language development is a major aim of schooling, language is also the most accessible pedagogy and form of evaluation available to schools. But a more subtle and greater influence that education has on language is its power to promote and disseminate certain ideas about the appropriateness of language, whether relating to standard or non-standard codes, majority or minority languages, gender speech styles and functions, high status forms and structures etc. This pervasive influence is institutionalized in education; it comes from the power that social institutions like education have to do things which individual human beings could never do. For instance, education has the power to enforce its linguistic demands by excluding dissenters, by rewarding conformity, by pillorying deviation, and by sanctioning the 'legitimate'. These sanctions go far beyond the benign, direct, and deliberate influences that education properly exercises in the course of providing 'an education'.

In other words, as argued in this chapter and throughout this book, education can routinely repress, dominate, and disempower language users whose practices differ from the norms that it establishes. Furthermore, it can do this while concealing the relations that underlie its power and while conveying a reality that can be highly partisan. For example, the syntax of a language offers a ready vehicle for converting power relations and for distorting perceptions of the world. Because of the role of syntax in drawing causal relationships between participants and processes, it is always available to designate the relative status of social actors by putting them in different roles in sentences — as agent, experiencer or object — or by deleting them entirely through using the passive, or a transformation, or a substitution. This kind of deception is always possible, and it is not uncommon when problems arise that involve demarcations, such as those that exist in schools between people of very different statuses and social power. Whoever has the power to define the context, and the language code that describes it, is empowered; all others who accept that definition without question accept their own disempowerment in that setting. In this way, the powerful position other social actors through their discourse so that the disempowered perceive and respond to the world in particular ways. But subtle distortions in language frequently arise when humans use language to describe reality and to create personal realities, since everyone's reality can be very different from the realities of others.

Murray Edelman (1984) observes that when it is in our interests to do so, human beings often rationalize and call this reasoning; they distort through language and call this creative and original description; and they repress others through language and call this 'being helpful'. The counselling profession seems especially adept at these practices. Norman Fairclough (1985) provides some apposite examples. He presents four expressions that belong to a particular lexicalization of young people who are perceived as misfits by their families, their schools, and their communities: they are seen as 'incorrigible'; 'defiant'; 'lacking in responsibility'; and 'delinquent'. He shows how these four expressions could be placed within an alternative lexicalization creating an 'anti-language' of matching descriptors for the same young people viewed from a different ideological position: 'irrepressible' (incorrigible); 'debunking' (defiant); 'refusing to be sucked in by society' (lacking in responsibility); and 'spirited' (delinquent). Here neither code can really capture reality, since each depends on the viewpoint of the speaker; both are ideologically loaded. However, when one ideological rationalization or another becomes dominant, the distortions and 'helpful repressions' that they contain become naturalized and win acceptance as neutral codes. Professional groups often do this when establishing the limits of their interests. Edelman notes that professionals in schools commonly engage in rationalization, distortion, and repression in their language activities and even see these practices as part of their professional duties. Indeed, an important part of those duties is to define the status of their clients in education: the underachievers; the gifted and talented; the disabled; the retarded; the discipline problems; the delinquent. By doing this, teachers also define their own status in relation to those others and thereby justify the work that they do. They use and apply many special terms as labels, in an exercise of power which would be rather meaningless or misplaced if the terms were used by non-professionals. But in the hands of the empowered professionals, the terms and the categories that they create become tools of power that shape and repress other people's destinies and legitimize professional value systems. The language becomes powerful in ways that the study of education itself still leaves untheorized.

Schooling and the language of dominant groups

There is great relevance for these matters in the ideas advanced by Pierre Bourdieu.[3] A brief and critical consideration of his compelling arguments about language and education helps to integrate language, social justice, and power more generally with education (Bourdieu & Passeron, 1977; Bourdieu, 1966; 1977; 1981; 1984). This French social theorist and anthropologist argues that all forms of power that impose meanings in such a way as to legitimate those meanings and conceal the relations that underlie the exercise of power itself, add their own specifically symbolic force to those relations of power. In this way, the dominant ideas that are given communicative meaning and force through that exercise of power reinforce the power of those same dominant forces who are exercising it. He sees the culture of the school, then, as a creation of the dominant culture.

Bourdieu's special term 'habitus' represents a system of durable dispositions that are at the core of an individual's behaviour. He argues that the 'habitus' held in common by the members of dominant groups permeates every aspect of schooling. This limits the educational opportunities of children from non-dominant groups because the school demands competence in the dominant language and culture which can only be acquired through family upbringing. While the school might not openly stress this culture, it implicitly demands it through its definitions of success. As a result, those groups who are capable of transmitting through the family the dispositions or habitus necessary for the reception of the school's messages come to monopolize the system of schooling. Those groups who have alternative dispositions, tendencies, propensities, or inclinations (i.e. alternative systems of habitus) have little purchase on the culture of schooling, or on the social reward systems that that culture makes available. Bourdieu's generative principle here, however, is not some notion of linguistic deficit that can be linked in turn to levels of syntactic or verbal complexity of utterances; rather his principle lies in the different types of relations to language that different social groups possess, relations which are themselves embedded in different sets of dispositions and attitudes towards the material world and towards other people.

'Theories of social and cultural reproduction', such as Bourdieu's, examine factors in societies and cultures that are important in maintaining and reproducing traditions and conventions in those societies and cultures. Bourdieu tries to show how the practices of a society are re-invented and perpetuated, especially through language and education. Clearly language in general is the key factor in reproducing and maintaining the conventions and traditions of cultures and societies since social reproduction is driven by interpersonal communication. We learn how to perform even the most simple conventional act, such as giving our names to new acquaintances, by observing how others do it, by using and listening to those others as models, and by noting the reactions of others to our performance and changing our behaviour accordingly. In this process of learning everyday conventional acts, each of us is a teacher as well as a learner, providing models to others, or learning from the models offered by others at different times. Traditions and conventions, including codes of language themselves, are re-invented and modified continually; no single piece of behaviour is authentic forever, even though larger patterns of convention and tradition — such as a culture or a language — may appear monolithic.

As part of this reproduction process, some behavioural traditions and conventions acquire a special status in the social system which gives their possessors status in turn. In gaining possession of them, we acquire a peculiar form of sociocultural influence. When these esteemed conventions and traditions are passed on to others, especially to our offspring, the social advantages are passed on with them. Bourdieu is much concerned with this handing on of esteemed social attributes and the allocation of social and cultural power that it implies. To give an adequate analysis of the relations between language, education, and power, Bourdieu marshals a very apt economic analogy: he presents 'culture' metaphorically as an 'economic system' and looks at the way an individual's resources of culture are used in the social system. He introduces the phrase 'cultural capital' (1966) to describe those culturally esteemed advantages that people acquire as a part of their life experiences, their peer group contacts, and their family backgrounds: such things as 'good taste', 'style', certain kinds of knowledge, abilities, and presentation of self. Related to this cultural capital inherited from the family, 'academic capital' is the guaranteed product of the combined effects of cultural transmission by the family, and cultural transmission by the school. Most germane to my theme here, Bourdieu also speaks of people possessing 'linguistic capital': the most important part of the cultural heritage.

For Bourdieu, linguistic capital is more than the competence to produce grammatically well-formed expressions and forms of language; it also includes the ability to utilize appropriate norms for language use and to produce the right expressions at the right time for a particular 'linguistic market'. In any stratified society, variations in vocabulary, syntax, and accent are socially marked, so that even a basic communicative exchange between individuals gives evidence of the social structure to which the individuals belong. For example, to people from Philadelphia a change in one aspect of a single vowel in an utterance is enough to make a White speaker sound Black, and a Black speaker sound White (Fasold, 1990). For Bourdieu, people in possession of appropriate linguistic capital in any context are favourably placed to exploit the system of differences that exists, and to do this in two ways. On the one hand, profit or advantage in general accrues most from a use of those modes of expression that are the least equally distributed. On the other hand, as we have already seen, the readiness of minority language or non-standard speakers to stigmatize their own language means that they often condemn themselves to silence in public settings for fear of offending norms that they themselves sanction (see Chapters 3 to 6). Using Bourdieu's metaphor, there are many linguistic markets in which rare or high status forms result in profit for the user, and where non-standard or low-status language use is assigned a limited value.

As a result, children from non-privileged backgrounds are often either silent within those 'markets' or they withdraw from participating in them.

Bourdieu argues that while the cultural or linguistic capital that is valued in schools is not equally available to children from different backgrounds, schools still operate as if all children had equal access to it. By basing their assessments of school success and failure and their award of certificates and qualifications on children's possession of this high status capital, which is unequally available, schools act in such a way as to reproduce the social arrangements that are favourable to some but unfavourable to other social groups. In this way, Bourdieu (1966) contends, *de facto* inequalities are translated into *de jure* ones, and the value of the cultural capital passed to the next generation is reinforced yet again. This complex social process is described by Bourdieu as the application of 'symbolic power' — the power to constitute the given simply by stating it — by dominant social groups who in this way inflict 'symbolic violence' upon non-dominant groups. This symbolic violence is a form of oppression which imposes arbitrary symbols of knowledge and expression upon those who often do not perceive the symbols as arbitrary but accept them as the way things must be. The members of some social groups, as a result, come to believe that their educational failure, rather than coming from their lowly esteemed social or cultural status, results from their natural inability: their lack of giftedness. They come to believe that social and cultural factors are somehow neutralized in the educational selection process and that the process itself is a fair one that is based on objective educational criteria — like possession of knowledge about the culture and the language necessary for expressing it.

Four points stand out in Bourdieu's analysis of the role of schools in reproduction.[4] These points link schools with parents and pupils themselves as interacting agents of complicity. First, from the well attested lower success rate of children from minority or low-income backgrounds, he argues that these children systematically adjust their expectations in schooling downwards; these adjusted expectations then become part of the way the wider culture is embodied in each individual's habitus. Second, he observes that when the latter children do experience some success in schooling, their parents make choices on behalf of their offspring which deny them access to the same kinds of social and cultural power that similarly endowed children from dominant backgrounds are encouraged to grasp. Third, he introduces the idea of 'learned ignorance': especially in its later stages, schooling tends to give recognition to those who play the game of schooling by acknowledging the legitimacy of schools in offering that recognition; the criteria on which schools judge success are largely supported by the fact that pupils agree to submit to those criteria. Fourth, he stresses the importance of credential inflation: qualifications tend to become debased if too many people gain access to them; as a result other more arbitrary factors begin to affect access to power through education, especially those aspects of cultural capital that are prized and possessed in abundance by dominant groups, such as style, *savoir faire*, and high status language forms and functions.

The academic value of high status language

On Bourdieu's account, each person is schooled in language both inside and outside schooling: the factor that creates unequal esteem for different types of linguistic capital — their academic market value — is in the distance between the practical mastery of language that is transmitted by the home and community, and the symbolic mastery that is demanded by the school. Along with the obvious properties of language, like its syntax, sounds, and vocabulary, humans acquire through socialization certain attitudes towards words and their use which provide criteria for judgments about which styles and forms of expression seem superior to others. One of the surest distinctive signs of a speaker's social position is revealed in language use that is either 'reverential or casual, tense or detached, stilted or easy, heavy-handed or well-tempered, ostentatious or measured' (Bourdieu & Passeron, 1977: 117). Captured in these relationships is the significance allotted by formally educated social groups to academic culture, to the social institutions set up to transmit it, and to the language judged to be necessary for that transmission. The theory of 'the lexical bar' (Corson, 1985) examines only a small aspect of these issues: the mediating place in educational success and failure of the high status vocabulary of the English language.

The lexical bar points to the educational significance of having a high-status vocabulary whose possession and display confers sociocultural prestige on those who know the appropriate place and the manner in which to use it. As mentioned above, the use that people make of specialist vocabularies can create disadvantage, discrimination, and deception, whether intended or not. In using the English vocabulary, with its history of lexical innovation from many sources, the rich alternatives that exist for expressing almost 'the same thing' in subtly different ways (e.g. 'retribution' and 'revenge'; 'female', 'feminine' and 'womanly' etc.) can allow a particular version of reality to appear as objective: to be taken-for-granted. At the personal level, a systematic discourse analysis of a speaker's patterned linguistic choices can provide a way into that person's particular version of reality, thus revealing something of its ideological base. For example, what might the innocent-sounding sentence 'black people are a cheerful bunch' tell us about the speaker's world view (Potter & Wetherell, 1987), and what might he or she be expected to say next?

At a more general level across societies and cultures, reality construction on a grand scale through lexical choice can legitimate inequalities, or even make nonsense seem sense. For example, in the circulating narratives of National Socialism, some social groups were marked as having fewer needs and lesser rights as human beings; later, following this repeated use of forms of language that stigmatized them, the same groups were gradually outlawed and then persecuted. Again injustice can also result when an entire language is stigmatized: the decision in pluralist societies to use one language in preference to another in contexts of unequal power can produce severe discrimination for native speakers of a non-dominant language. Finally, there are recent language-wide reforms in the admissibility within educated discourse of racist jokes, or of racist and sexist terminology: such as the invariant use of the male pronoun in official documents; or the routine official reference to the mixed racial ancestry of people that once circulated unchecked in some countries. These reforms respond to the belief that unjust realities can be constructed through norms of lexical usage that are adopted uncritically.

Unlike racist and sexist terminology, people cannot systematically investigate high status lexical use, searching for evidence of discrimination. Perhaps its influence is more insidious for that reason. It is the case that coincidences of social and linguistic history have combined to create a lexical situation in English that is unique among languages: most of the specialist and high status terminology of English is Graeco-Latin in origin, and most of its more everyday terminology is Anglo-Saxon in origin. English in this respect, relative to other languages, has a fairly clear boundary drawn between its everyday and its high status vocabularies. This creates a barrier between one form of linguistic capital and another. Although the etymology of the language does not 'cause' the lexical bar, it does offer us a means in English for recognizing this bar which is not as clear-cut in other languages. Because the children of certain social groups in their final years of schooling have unequal active access to a use of high status words, and because teachers assess their students' grasp of the culture on the basis of performance in language, we can conclude that high status word usage stands as one mediating factor between social group background and educational success or failure.

There seems to be strong support in the lexical bar studies for Bourdieu's ideas. In his *Distinction* (1984), which studies artefacts of 'taste' taken from across the spectrum of social and cultural practices, the configurations of taste that he relates to specific social fractions probably have many counterparts in configurations of vocabulary usage. More directly, because educational selection processes are based upon a long-term display of access to the high status lexicon of the language — partly on the reasonable grounds that a display of this kind indicates possession of a conceptual framework steeped in the high status and academically valued aspects of the culture — the bar serves to reproduce different attainment rates in education for children socialized into the language norms of different groups. Some might argue that there are good reasons for giving academic recognition to those who can wield complex vocabularies appropriately. Dewey, Hegel and Marx, for example, all insisted on the need to supplement moral principles with vocabularies for marking out the morally relevant features of a decision making situation, even suggesting that if we have the vocabulary we can skip the principles (Rorty, 1983). On this account, moral and intellectual sophistication is implicit in the ability to wield these complex and sensitive vocabularies, establishing moral relevance in the process. But there are major difficulties in this policy if it allows schools, as they often do, to couple recognition of powerful users of language with the rewards of power. From Demosthenes to the twentieth century, we have often witnessed power being terribly abused when harnessed to oratorical brilliance and expressed through it. By giving educational recognition and thereby a purchase on temporal power to school graduates solely on their language performance, we reinforce the influence in the culture of conventionally dominant groups, whether that influence has a benign, a neutral, or a sinister effect. In the process, alternative forms of linguistic and cultural capital delineated by social, cultural, or gender background go unrecognized and remain without influence.

A critique

Briefly what Bourdieu argues is that while schools do not explicitly give students what they demand from them, they still uniformly demand that all their students should have what the schools themselves do not give: namely a relation to language and culture exclusively produced by a particular mode of inculcation. In other words, the school passes on training and information which can only be fully received by those who have had the culturally appropriate training that it does not give. While this is clear enough, there are a few points of criticism that can be brought to Bourdieu's theories which need to be considered by those taking his ideas further. One common criticism seems little more than a misinterpretation, but it does help to clarify Bourdieu's argument. Michael Apple seems to misread Bourdieu's use of cultural capital as an allocation device by assuming that cultural and linguistic capital is only the preserve of educationally dominant groups: 'students without it are, by definition, deviant' he says (1982: 45). A similar misreading appears in Stanley Aronowitz who writes of schools as sites 'where cultural capital may be wrested from those who hold it under lock and key' (in Giroux, 1981: 4). These North American writers may be missing Bourdieu's central [anthropological] point, that *all* groups possess cultural capital and a linguistic capital of their own, but not necessarily the same form of capital that is recognized and valued in education. By moving from one cultural 'field' to another, power relationships change, as does cultural capital.

Building on Bourdieu's case, Henry Giroux (1981) argues that teachers need to understand the cultural capital of the oppressed and analyze its treatment within the dominant culture. This also seems to miss the [anthropological] point. Cultural interests, such as those discussed in Chapter 2, are developed over long periods of immersion and socialization within a culture or social group; cultural capital is not equally available to all the members of any culture. For example, there are always key members of minority cultures who have an aristocratic style of relationship with their culture which derives from their manner of acquiring it in the family. To suggest that teachers could develop a deep empathy with cultural interests, as Giroux recommends, may be to trivialize those interests or to suggest that people can put on or take off cultures at will.[5] The reality is that true biculturalism and to a lesser extent true bilingualism among human beings are rare possessions, usually only won by the members of cultural minorities in societies who are forced to put on some dominant culture and its language, along with their own, in order to lead tolerable lives. For example, in discussing the teaching of Maori culture in mainstream New Zealand schools, Graeme Hingangaroa Smith (1986) addresses an intractable problem that occurs for teachers who are unequipped by cultural interests for the task. For Hingangaroa Smith, most of these teachers need to develop appropriate attitudes and personal skills before they can *begin* to develop the culturally appropriate skills and knowledge to pass on to their pupils. This is a daunting task, as Bourdieu himself observes when discussing the working class: when teachers or other intellectuals put themselves in the place of workers, without having the habitus of workers, they apprehend 'the working-class condition through schemes of perception and appreciation which are not those that the members of the working class themselves use to apprehend it' (1984: 372–3).

Other criticisms of Bourdieu may be less transparent.[6] For example, some believe his account gives too much weight to a consensual model of social reproduction by understating the influence of 'alternative ideologies of resistance' which permeate and maintain social groups outside dominant power arrangements (e.g. Giroux, 1981). These ideologies, which non-dominant groups manifest in all societies, are a form of social power expressed through discourses of resistance. These discourses provide a form of counter-control in opposition to aspects of the cultural capital of dominant groups; they are used to interrogate that dominant culture, to marginalize its influence, and sometimes to change it. Traditionally, the school has attempted to resist the culture of subordinate groups by punishing displays of its possession: for example by proscribing the use of minority languages or the language varieties of social groups. But because cultural reproduction operates outside school, as well as through it, the cultures of resistance are never eliminated. Indeed, feigned complicity in the culture of the school can be a way of weakening the influence of the dominant culture by making use of its own tools and by going around it. At the same time, dominant groups themselves are rarely homogeneous; their values are in constant tensions of conflict and contradiction. Moreover the challenge of contrary groups is common in societies. Bourdieu's theory does not seem to give adequate weight to these things. Their ubiquitous influence argues against what some see as the rather bleak determinism of many theorists in the Marxian tradition. In addition these views underplay the possibility that schools in societies could be capable of change and could become less the agencies of dominant cultural groups and more a dynamic meeting place for cultural difference and pluralist interaction.

For an applied field such as language policy and planning in schools, there is a further difficulty to consider. If schools are to be places both of justice *and* of learning, it is important to strike some balance between a view of language which sees it as 'socially' valuable on the one hand, and a view which sees it as 'intellectually' valuable on the other. Rather than stressing meanings that are dependent upon choices among styles, modes, and settings of discourse, schools tend to stress the role of meaning as 'signification': the meanings that a language carries over time which can be established in the current state of affairs. Other theorists, who have emancipatory educational interests that are similar to Bourdieu's, insist that capitalizing on this semiotic and communicative value of language is the goal of education. Gramsci insists on this, in the hope that unjust power arrangements might eventually be affected by the elevation of members of oppressed groups through their school success. In Bourdieu's writings about language, and perhaps in my discussion here so far, there may be a risk of overemphasizing the form or the style of language used (its social value) at the expense of considering the content that language can be used to express (its intellectual utility). High status words, for example, fill up those areas of thought which are the most difficult, the most abstract, and which for these and other reasons attract high regard within the culture. But probably the most important reason these areas of thought and the words used to express them attract high status in the first place is because people from a diverse range of ideological backgrounds over time have recognized their unquestionable importance: these things give access to meanings which allow us to advance the course of civilization, to criticize and improve it, and to advance considerations of justice and equity and other humanitarian concerns that are so much at the heart of Bourdieu's own theorising. The value of the communicative function of language lies in the capacity it gives us for saying things that are 'true': true to the extent that they can be supported by reasons and evidence that have 'warranted assertibility'. Indeed without these high status areas of thought and their attendant conventions of language, Bourdieu's theorizing itself might not exist; certainly his theory would not have an adequate vehicle for express-ing its own existence.

It may be too easy to underplay the idea that linguistic expressions have a value or power other than the power derived from the authority of the social institution within which the language is used. While there is no doubt that much of the power of language derives from the institutional position of the language user, there are many everyday examples of language being used to express power relations between agents without the benefit of institutional support. John Thompson (1984) instances the use of language in casual conversation to embarrass, humiliate, silence, or subordinate others; to probe into the affairs of others; or to threaten self-harm in order to get one's way. Again too the language of a single human being always carries motivating force for that individual and to that extent affects social structures indirectly. C. Wright Mills stresses the role of 'vocabularies of motive' that have ascertainable functions in situated actions and influence their users and those around them: 'a motive tends to be one which is to the actor and to the other members of a situation an unquestioned answer to questions concerning social or lingual conduct' (1940: 907). This idea of human motive, expressed in language, anticipates discussion below of Roy Bhaskar's emancipatory conception of social action and the place of lan-guage in it.

School level language policies

The point here is that while schools need to consider wider structural questions very carefully in order to decide equitable approaches, neither schools nor individuals are inevitably the willing dupes of power forces that are outside their control. Through their language policies, schools can do much to end social injustices: they can widen children's mastery of their own code; they can widen mastery of the dominant language too, if it is a different language; and they can give access to the widest possible range of 'vocabularies of motive' that might be helpful in any situated action.

Critical language theorists, including Bourdieu, suggest that an initial step is to relate structured systems of sociologically pertinent linguistic differences to equally structured systems of social differences. There is merit in this view and it justifies the modest strength that a sociology of language manages to exert in educational matters: discourse is embedded in material power relations which need to be understood and transformed before any general change in sociologically pertinent linguistic differences is possible. Here Bourdieu counters the common criticism brought against his and other reproductive theorizing in education: that it places schools in a passive and determined role with predictable outcomes. Bourdieu does allow that schools can be active agents in altering unjust reproductive tendencies in a society. At the same time, he is not so credulous as to expect that quick social reform through school reform is possible, since he believes that in the face of impending reform dominant groups will change the rules of the game by using different criteria so as to give possessors of their own capital a renewed advantage. My argument towards the end of this chapter, integrating Bourdieu with Bhaskar, is that the very selection of criteria for judging the capital of the dominated has to be based in the cultural capital of those non-dominant people, as revealed through realist interpretations of their expressed intentions and cultural interests.

So language policy on its own is rarely enough: social institutions and ideologies have to be changed to accompany any linguistic reform if it is to be effective. Indeed well designed language policies always entail wider structural changes or are set within a context of general reform. There is support for this claim in recent successful attempts at the linguistic reform of sexist language. While there is evidence that women committed to reforming their own language do change their own images of the world in response to language forms that they meet, those who are not committed to reform have images that remain sexist in spite of the language forms encountered (Khosroshahi, 1989). The campaign against sexist language usage was a movement of committed middle class people that was clearly not launched by the disadvantaged or even by those who speak for the disadvantaged. Once launched, in Robert Cooper's view (1989), the movement was adopted and promoted by legislatures and administrators who could win popularity by changes, although those changes were essentially cosmetic. In other words, dominant groups could appear responsive to their constituencies and create an illusion of progress without embarking on any fundamental alterations to the system. This is because the language problem addressed was largely symptomatic of more general discriminatory uses of power. My point here is that language change on its own can even get in the way of genuine emancipatory activities. It can be used as a tool of power to provide cosmetic reforms which can disguise the need for real social change. As a result, non-dominant groups may settle for the cosmetic change as a small victory regardless of the fact that unwanted power forces remain in place. This is not to say that there is a lesser place for linguistic reform, only that it needs to be set within a context of wider social policymaking that brings genuine reform and improvement.

Bourdieu might support the contemporary movement for language policymaking at school level. This offers an eclectic form of planning which tries to be searching in its data collection, critical in its analysis of the school and its context, and just in its implementation processes. There are several complementary lines of action that schools can take in treating language and social justice issues in education and lessening the influence of unwanted forms of power. First, there is a need to create better patterns of communication within schools which free participants to consider planned, rational, just, and consensual action in pursuit of their educational aims. Habermas' idea of 'emancipation from domination' through communicative action (1985), as realised in his 'discourse ethic', suggests that we can go a long way towards eliminating oppressive command–obedience relationships and distorted forms of communication in institutions like schools. There are possibilities for doing this in classrooms (R. Young, 1992) and in staffrooms. The first section of Chapter 7 elaborates on these possibilities. Secondly, contemporary schools in many places are finding that they need policies for meeting the kinds of complex problems that are outlined in this chapter: language policies on gender; race and minority cultures; bilingualism; poverty and disadvantage (Corson, 1990a). The second section of Chapter 7 elaborates on the aims and scope of these policies. Thirdly, some suggest that there is a need for children in schools to acquire a form of 'critical language awareness' (Clark et al., 1990; 1991) through a language curriculum that promotes social awareness of discourse, critical awareness of variety, and consciousness of and practice for change. This approach to curriculum and pedagogy is discussed fully in the third section of Chapter 7.

Finally, we need methods for finding out about human needs and interests that will allow us to know when the exercise of power through language in any setting is useful and benevolent and when it is harmful. Obviously not all uses of power are malevolent ones: power represents both a negative and a positive moment. The challenge is to separate wanted from unwanted forms of determination and then through policymaking to replace unwanted with wanted: to replace a negative exercise of power with a positive one. Bhaskar is one contemporary theorist who offers an approach for doing this which is already influential. I introduce his emancipatory conception of discovery, based in his critical realism, for several reasons: firstly, because Bhaskar shows that human reasons and accounts provide evidence whose status is ontologically real.[7] Secondly, because social structures[8] on his account have no existence separate from the activities that they govern and from agents' reports of those activities, which seems a necessary condition for human emancipation to be possible. Thirdly, because he sees an engagement with human intentionality as central to understanding any social science area: the intentions of human agents expressed as evidence in their reasons and accounts create and shape structures of power and are reciprocally shaped by them. From understanding these relationships comes the ability to isolate oppressive forms of power and to exchange them for wanted policies.

Language, Power and Emancipation

As a critical realist, Bhaskar is interested in 'emancipatory social practice' which gives him common ground with many contemporary social theorists on the libertarian-left. In promoting this practice, his position inverts the famous dictum of Marx, who gave prominence in his programme to changing the world.[9] In Bhaskar's philosophy, the world cannot be rationally changed unless it is adequately interpreted, and this interpretation has as its prerequisite the philosophical idea of the independent existence of the natural *and* the social world. As he extends his philosophy of science into the human sciences, his theme becomes a straightforward one: the nature of and the prospects for human emancipation. Emancipation occurs when we make the move from unwanted to wanted sources of determination by changing the relations between human action and structural context (1979; 1986; 1989).

In approaching any form of social policy making or inquiry, we take as *real* entities the obvious properties of the social world: things like the reasons and other accounts in language that people use to effect social or individual behaviour and change. Reasons or accounts of one kind or another make up the generative mechanisms in our social science theories or models, so the twin tasks of any inquiry are firstly to confirm the existence and then to detail the operation of these mechanisms: to show the hypothetical reasons or accounts to be real. Inquirers in the human sciences are encouraged to locate their problems firmly in the world of social interaction, since the mechanisms (rationally compelling reasons and accounts) that produce beliefs (including attitudes, values, intentions etc.) and actions are produced, exist, and evolve in that social world. This transforming model of social activity has its analogy in the activity of a sculptor at work, fashioning a product out of the material at hand and using the tools available. Beliefs, attitudes, reasons, and other mentalistic forms of evidence are available as prime sociological data which not only guide our inquiries but also morally compel us to act on our findings by putting to work the emancipatory solutions that the inquiries uncover (Bhaskar, 1989). The link between human intentions, reasons, and accounts expressed in language, on the one hand, and the power-filled structures of the social world, on the other, is plain in Bhaskar's theorizing. Structures of power have no existence separate from the activities that they govern and from agents' reports of those activities. We might say that for Bhaskar 'vocabularies of motive' provide the prime data.

The design of emancipatory language policies for schooling

If we ignore human intentionality as a factor in the exercise of power in education, or in any other social institution, we ignore an attribute of humans that is basic to interpreting social activity of any kind: our capacity for second-order monitoring. This capacity allows us to make a retrospective commentary upon our actions; it gives special status to people's accounts of their own behaviour, and this status often equals or surpasses any status that attaches to a third person's observations. Often a third person cannot easily get to grips with the presuppositions that underlie accounts offered by socially or culturally different people, and this makes understanding the accounts difficult. For instance, those minority groups with a cultural and linguistic capital that is different from that given high status in the school often provide accounts of their own behaviour and of their own intentions in relation to the world that are very different from dominant group accounts. Often these intentions, these accounts, and the acquired life needs that they refer to (collectively what Habermas calls 'interests' [see Chapter 2]) are incompatible with the logico-mathematical and technicist views of the world that characterize high status, Western (male) modes of thought. Often they are excluded from consideration in public policy making; they are discounted or marginalized for providing a 'mentalistic'[10] form of evidence that others regard as inadmissible for use in fair and justified reports, especially when that evidence comes from minority peoples or social groups who are themselves marginalized.

Not long ago, any form of accommodation to minority group views, whether mentalistic or otherwise, was discouraged in most societies. Policy accommodations to majority group mentalistic views were regularly made, as they still are today, since one function of dominant ideology is to represent sectional group interests as universal in this way. But in the culturally pluralist societies that are becoming more common in today's world, we often accept and give weight in our social policies to reasons and accounts given by non-dominant people in support of their behaviour which are not confirmed by observed events that are public and expressible. More often these reasons and accounts are coming to take some precedence over other reasons and accounts that *are* confirmed by observed events. Policymakers increasingly accept this state of affairs on moral or political grounds; even after much reflection they usually feel justified in doing so. As well as conforming to current views in the philosophy of the social sciences, this practice is also in keeping with a nascent spirit of tolerance found in many countries. It is much influenced, in a causal way perhaps, by the success of gender theorists in the social sciences who suggest that giving priority to Western 'male' technologies of control, world view, and observation might be excluding other important forms of evidence that is not so susceptible to empirical confirmation. So, as well as acknowledging that women and girls have a range of legitimate and non-trivial values that may contrast markedly with those of men and boys, this spirit is manifested in a more enlightened treatment of minorities and in greater respect for the distinct interests of the members of minority cultures.

Education is a field where the language rights and cultural values of children can be trampled on by the routine exercise even of legitimate power. I want to conclude this chapter by referring in particular to the children of those indigenous minority cultures that survive precariously alongside invasion European cultures, such as the Indian Nations or the Inuit in North America, the Maori in New Zealand, and the Koori in Australia. These and many other cultural groups, in their surviving traditional forms, often express world views and values that do not always accord with the norms that the school legitimates, yet we are bound on grounds of social justice to find ways of accommodating the children of these groups and recognizing their linguistic capital and cultural interests in schools and school systems. In discussing these minority cultures I am also making a point about other groups whose cultural capital attracts lowly status in mainstream schooling, since the argument can be extended to other groups in societies who are marginalized from the dominant culture by language, poverty, and disadvantage, or even by different forms of socialization.

On Bhaskar's account, as far as I am able to interpret it, to recognize the capital of these groups in schools we begin with the evidence of their intentions as we find it expressed in their reasons and accounts, since these discursive practices in turn produce, shape, and are shaped by the socio-cultural structures that the groups value (the bearers of their own cultural and linguistic capital). Now it seems to me impossible to avoid the conclusion that a form of schooling that is basically incompatible in its organization, pedagogy, and curriculum with those cultural structures, and with the reasons and accounts that produce and are productive of them, will consistently act against the emancipation through education of children drawn from groups who value those unacknowledged forms of cultural capital. What is and will be absent from this form of schooling are classroom and school discourse settings that have 'validity' in their communicative arrangements for culturally different participants. I use 'validity' here in the sense that Habermas intends by that term (see Chapter 2): validity claims that are understood in ideal communication settings allow all participants to expect and receive truth, sincerity, appropriateness, and comprehensibility in the exchange of messages. In this ideal setting, power relations among and between people are brought into a modicum of balance and reciprocity. But this is not remotely possible when people from minority culture backgrounds are coerced into receiving a form of education predicated upon a different and dominant culture. In such a system, normative rightness is not possible since the norms are part of the cultural capital of the dominant. Moreover in such a system, sincerity and truthfulness give way to strategic manipulation based on the deceitful point that total exposure to the dominant culture will offer advantages and life chances that schools never extend to those who are without the habitus and the cultural capital to receive them. Lastly and obviously, for minority children who are native speakers of their culture's language, even comprehensibility itself disappears from that discourse setting.

In place of an education that disempowers in these inescapable ways, linguistic minority children require a form of schooling that recognizes and responds to the reasons and accounts that minority people offer as expressions of their intentions and as shapers of the cultural power structures that they value. On both Bourdieu's and Bhaskar's accounts, the best-placed agents for designing this form of education are members of the culture itself, who can set their reasons and accounts against the backdrop of thoroughly shared and understood cultural structures. On the argument presented here, it is hard to escape the conclusion that for minority cultures in many places, such as *te tangata whenua*[11] in New Zealand, minority culture and language immersion schools[12] offer the best avenue for reaching towards these goals. As an alternative, on practical grounds, the rare school that is thoroughly bicultural or pluralist in its organization, pedagogies and curriculum (see Cazden, 1989; May, 1994) may provide a second-to-best approach. Other approaches, especially the tried and failed methods of over a century of compulsory schooling based in dominant cultural capital, endanger the emancipation through education of those who identify with another culture. Those approaches also endanger the emancipation of those who are socialized in quite different ways.[13]

Notes to Chapter 1

1. Throughout this book, my use of the term 'language' is an inclusive one. In some places I use 'language' to mean 'a language' or 'a language variety'. Elsewhere I use it to refer to 'verbal repertoire', 'mode of discourse' or some other elements of language as organized for use. As Dell Hymes urges, in determining the role of language in human affairs one has to get down to cases and cases are always a matter of specific modes of use and specific organizations of linguistic means.

2. In trying to understand the several interpreters of Marxian ideas discussed here, there is a key distinction in the writings of Marx himself. For him 'ideology' has two manifestations and each is inseparable from language and meaning: in the one, ideology is a system of ideas that distorts reality in order to serve the interests of a dominant group (e.g. for Bhaskar, 'positivism' is a system of ideas which distorts reality in this way); in the other, ideology is a means of penetrating the consciousness of human actors and uncovering the real foundations of activities (i.e. the task of critical theory). The former is a state; the latter is a process. For other accounts see Kress & Hodge (1979), Fowler, Hodge, Kress & Trew (1979), Fairclough (1989) and Pecheux (1982).

3. Bourdieu tries to produce a genuine sociological framework for his linguistic discussions by bypassing formal linguistic theories which leave no place for the agent's language performance. He also tries to avoid the narrow focus on the details of social interaction that occurs in those sociolinguistic studies which abstract away from the structural features that interactions reproduce. In spite of its lack of formal linguistic rigour, his 'marketplace' analogy allows him to steer a difficult middle course in which individual and group language codes are not isolated from the social and historical conditions in which they are embedded, or from the dispositions and cultural backgrounds that individuals and groups possess. From Saussurean linguistics he borrows the idea of 'difference' but reapplies it with sociocultural instead of mere linguistic force: words have their real-world semantic power not simply because of the relations that they contract with one another, but because of their stylistic significance and their pragmatic value in a stratified social system.

4. Richard Harker (1990: 89ff) identifies and elaborates 'five levels of practice through which inequalities are perpetuated' that are to be found in Bourdieu's work. My discussion here collapses those five levels into four summarizing points.

5. In the United States itself, there is some evidence for the impracticality of Giroux's suggestion:

> There are other [federally funded] programmes designed to sensitize Anglo teachers to the culturally distinctive backgrounds of the children they teach or will teach. The results of this study suggest that there are some crucial aspects of culturally distinctive communicative behaviour that cannot be readily internalized by Anglo teachers. Thus the findings presented here argue in favour of giving priority to the facilitation of movement of Indian adults into teaching positions in Indian classrooms (Philips, 1983: 130–1).

6. Bourdieu advises that he addresses several of these criticisms of his work in his book co-authored with Loïc Wacquant: *An Invitation to Reflexive Sociology* (1992).

7. In other words, they are prime data that cannot be logically ignored. This is consistent with other current views in the philosophy of the social sciences, expressed by Rom Harré, John Hughes, William Outhwaite, Jonathon Potter & Margaret Wetherell, and by 'critical hermeneuticists' in general. Elsewhere, I extend discussion of Bhaskar's conception of discovery into areas of educational research, policymaking, and the sociology of educational knowledge (e.g. Corson, 1991a,b).

8. I am using the term 'structure' throughout this book to refer to the intractability of the social world: structures set limits to freedom, often in tacit ways, through a complex interplay of powers within diverse social institutions. Chapter 6 offers a fuller description.

9. 'The philosophers have only *interpreted* the world, in various ways; the point is to *change* it' (Marx, 1974). To give Marx his due, he was not suggesting that the world should be changed even before we understand it, only that mere interpretation falls well short of what is required.

10. As distinguished from 'physiological' or 'behavioural' forms of evidence which are given greater priority by W.V.O. Quine, for example. A very good example of the distinction between 'mentalistic' and the more 'materialistic' accounts is offered by Mills in his discussion of the vocabularies of motive that actors verbalize in specific situations. According to Mills, in the United States of 1940, mentalistic motives, like the religious or the spiritual or the folk, were socially suspect even when they were used by a dominant member of the establishment:

> Individualistic, sexual, hedonistic, and pecuniary vocabularies of motives are apparently now dominant in many sectors of twentieth-century urban America. Under such an ethos, verbalization of alternative conduct in these terms is least likely to be challenged among dominant groups. In this milieu, individuals are sceptical of Rockefeller's avowed religious motives for his business conduct because such motives are not *now* terms of the vocabulary conventionally and prominently accompanying situations of business enterprise (1940: 910).

However, Bhaskar's recognition of 'the mentalistic' implies no spurious form of realism since for him the task of inquiry is to go beyond mere identification and show the presumed discursive mechanisms and their effects to be real. He certainly gives experience its due, but not at the expense of things that may seem intangible and unquantifiable:

> This view does not dispute the epistemic value of experience; on the contrary transcendental realism claims, against irrealism, to uniquely sustain it. But it interprets this not as the absolute privilege of a *content*, but as dependent upon the ontological and social *contexts* within which the significant experience occurs.

Now insofar as there has been a real advance in recent analytical philosophy of the human sciences, it lies in recognition of the significance of the condition that (wo)man is a self-interpreting and self-motivating animal, a member of a story-telling species, whose language, beliefs and stories are in some manner necessary for and productive of his or her life; so that social reality faces the scientific neophyte as already *pre-interpreted*, as linguistically and cognitively 'done', prior to any scientific enquiry into it (1986: 160).

11. *Te tangata whenua* in New Zealand are the ancestral Polynesian inhabitants of the country: 'the people of the land'; the Maori.

12. In New Zealand now, *Nga kura kaupapa maori* are Maori culture and language immersion [primary] schools. See Corson (1993a) for discussion of the debate that led up to the contemporary creation of these separate minority schools; and Chapter 7 for a fuller description.

13. This point can be taken to imply a different form of schooling for many adolescent girls and for many adolescent boys, preferably within the same school setting. I remain agnostic about the need for different forms of schooling for those distinguished by other sociological variables.

2 Language Policy and Social Justice

Social Justice

Social justice has much to do with ideas about legitimacy, about fairness and impartiality, about welfare and mutual advantage, and about political and social consensus. Justice itself relates to the way that benefits and burdens are distributed and is usually said to exist when people receive that to which they are entitled (Barry, 1989; Buchanan & Mathieu, 1986). It is not easy to be clearer than that and perhaps in thinking about these matters it is important to become used to tolerating a certain amount of imprecision. While uncertain about what 'justice' might be, most would agree with John Rawls (1972) that justice is the first virtue of social institutions, in much the same way as truth is the first virtue of systems of thought. Clearly any discussion about justice falls within the moral or ethical domain and this too can only be vaguely defined. Ethics merges into matters of courtesy and etiquette on one level; it merges into aesthetic judgments on another; and on still other levels it merges into prudence and into jurisprudence. Ethics is not concerned so much with what people should do as with the way that they go about deciding what they should do. The study of social justice is also more concerned with this activity of deciding rightness than with what rightness might be in any single setting.

In traditional discussions of ethics and political philosophy, there are three broad accounts of social justice (Pettit, 1980). These share a humanist origin in that they see the individual person as the starting point for any analysis that might lead to recommendations about the criteria for a just society. In this opening section I begin by sketching these three broad accounts, including some of their strengths and weaknesses. Discussion then moves to a more recent theory that is less individualist. This account of social justice is rather more collectivist in its orientation to its subject; it gives prominence to the justice needs of social groups, alongside and sometimes ahead of the needs of individuals. I argue that considerable room must be left for collectivist accounts in any discussion of social justice and language,[1] if we are to give sufficient recognition to that most obvious

27

feature of language itself: its essential role in allowing and promoting communicative interaction between social groups of two or more people.

My general point, then, in opposition to all three individualist accounts of justice can be stated here clearly at the outset: if our purpose is to provide language arrangements in education that are just ones, while also considering the rightful needs of human individuals, then we must inevitably consider the needs of the group at the same time as the individual, since language in its literal sense has no existence outside human collectivities. A language is a set of social conventions having value and point only when it develops over time from the interactional and communicative needs of social groups. As a social institution itself, a language is not just an instrumental convenience made available by chance to the individuals who acquire it; rather it is the very means by which individual human beings are socialized and from which they develop a consciousness of themselves. This consciousness is a direct and unique reflection of the culture that comprises the many social, ethnic, class, or gender groups who share the language. In promoting social justice in language matters, there is little that can be done for the individual that does not begin with the group at the same time.

The three traditional accounts of justice all have classical origins which need not concern us here. In their contemporary forms, I am referring to them as follows: the 'natural rights account' which takes the presumed legitimacy of human natural rights as its starting point; the 'welfare account' which recognizes general utility and human happiness as its starting point; and the 'fairness account' which begins with impartial judgments for determining just social arrangements. Each of these accounts advances its own criterion of justice; each assumes that in principle human social institutions can be made perfect; and each proposes that the purpose of social institutions is to serve the interests of individuals. All three accounts are relevant to discussion in this book, as is the fourth that I add later, since the criteria that they depend upon offer principles that we cannot ignore in language policy and planning in education.

Individualist Accounts

Social justice as 'natural rights'

The 'natural rights' account recognizes the existence of universal standards of right and wrong that are prior constraints in deciding what is just. These standards are deemed as rights that all individuals can lay claim to, regardless of the form of social organization under which they live; they set limits to the kinds of social institutions that can be prescribed for individuals; and they set constraints on how people may be treated in society without their consent. Robert Nozick (1974) is a prominent contemporary advocate of this position, but his views on natural rights are much older ones matching those set forth by John Locke (1690). Indeed Nozick himself provides no clear justification for the principles that he adopts from Locke; he accepts them as givens and argues from them. Moreover he sees the right to private property as fundamental to all the other rights; it is this right which governs the interpretation of other basic principles and the role of the state itself in matters of social justice.

In Locke's utopian 'state of nature' various rights obtain: people are free to order their actions and to dispose of their possessions as they see fit; a person's life, health, liberty, or possessions may not be invaded or harmed; people have the right to defend themselves against assaults on their rights; they are entitled to recompense for any harm done; and offenders are to be punished, but not beyond the degree of their offence. If we apply this charter of Locke's within societies, then any social arrangement which infringes upon these various rights is unjust and individual members of the society are entitled to object to that arrangement.

An immediate problem for this account is that it seems to outlaw even the most minimal forms of collective action taken in behalf of the public good. If we take this account literally, taxation for the general good becomes objectionable; compulsory education becomes an intrusion on personal rights; and government instrumentalities of all kinds become agencies of impropriety and even of oppression. What this account seems to recommend is a form of anarchy reminiscent of the natural state described by Locke. Philip Pettit (1980) offers other criticisms of the theory if put into practice: he identifies problems of organization, operation, and normative output. Not least of these is the problem of the inequalities that inevitably result under *laissez faire* regimes of this kind, when claims to natural rights protect the economically or politically powerful from sharing their wealth or power with the economically or politically weak. Analogous arguments about majority language dominance can be offered, which I will return to later.

Social justice as 'welfare and mutual advantage'

Locke's natural rights account began to lose favour in the nineteenth century. The search for a criterion of justice that was more concrete and more intrinsically motivating for ordinary human beings brought forward the idea of 'human welfare' as the key principle needed in judging justice. Jeremy Bentham was the founder of this utilitarian doctrine, taking his inspiration from David Hume's formally utilitarian argument: the disposition of human beings to make moral judgments comes from our capacity to regard things that are useful for people and society with favour, and to regard with disfavour things that are harmful. On Bentham's utilitarian analysis good things produce happiness and/or human welfare (utility); bad things lead elsewhere. This utilitarianism gives not only a criterion for justice but also a moral principle by which individuals can evaluate their actions: namely, we should behave in such a way as to maximize the welfare of others and minimize the pain created by our actions.

What are the problems with this account of social justice? Clearly up to a point at least, this approach to judging justice has the support of a good deal of recent history going for it. Other things being equal, those societies that put the general welfare of their citizens ahead of all else in social planning do create stable and happy social arrangements, provided that the wants that are satisfied are genuine wants rather than frivolous desires or special interests. For example, a free education is usually defended on utilitarian grounds: people in general in a society benefit when the level of education of all members is relatively high and the talents of all people are properly tapped. But the specific task of operationalizing the utilitarian criterion of justice presents a difficulty: How can social planners identify the highest net balance of welfare satisfaction in their community? There are many answers to this, ranging from Bentham's curious 'felicific calculus' (1789) for measuring net happiness or pleasure, through to Frank Ramsey's more sophisticated method for calibrating preferences in a population (1978). None of these is an ideal instrument, since each depends in part on forecasting human emotional states, and this is one of the transparent weaknesses of the welfare principle.

A serious objection against seeing social justice as welfare rests on a distinction that Ronald Dworkin (1978) makes between treating people equally and treating them as equals. When we treat people equally, everyone gets the same regardless of need; when we treat people as equals, the claims of each are equally considered, whether or not this leads to unequal treatment. Most people may agree that the needy should get more than others; they should not be treated equally. The problem becomes one of choosing between the multitude of differences between people to identify which differences justify different treatment and which justify similar treatment. The utilitarian principle of maximizing the general welfare does not guarantee fairness in the distribution of welfare. As Pettit argues, it is quite possible that a greater aggregate level of welfare will result from a system in which a minority are relatively abused than from one in which some plausible distributive constraint determines the allocation of benefits among people. Indeed, many Western democracies have routinely oppressed their minorities, especially their indigenous peoples who may have received a form of 'equal treatment' under the utilitarian rule of nineteenth century colonial governments but who remain in economically oppressed conditions today because that 'equal treatment' amounted to inequality according to need. It is easy to extend this point and relate it to the place of minority languages in those societies where languages receive 'equal treatment' rather than differential treatment according to their need for survival, recognition, and support. Equal treatment for endangered languages usually leads to further decline and eventual extinction.

Some other criterion for social justice seems warranted beyond that offered by maximizing the satisfaction of the wants of people in general. At the very least, certain other rights must be recognised, as Dworkin (1978) proposes. He suggests a fusion of the natural rights account and the welfare account: maximizing welfare in general while protecting the natural rights of individuals. As I have already argued however, the defence of natural rights can be protective of gross inequalities and it is not easy to see that adopting Dworkin's proposal would resolve the tension between the two positions. For example, speakers of majority languages everywhere are properly sensitive to the right that they possess to use and promote their languages in every reasonable context. The public use of minority languages, which are not shared by majority language speakers, can seem a straightforward intrusion on the rights of the majority since that use can plainly get in the way of the free and open use of the majority's language. Even if we apply Dworkin's integrated model to this scenario, the majority group's language has to receive preference on both justice grounds, in spite of the clear injustice this causes for minority language users: first, the use of the majority language must be unfettered to defend the natural rights of the majority to fair use of their linguistic 'property'; and second, the very real communicative value of the majority language for meeting the myriad needs of society must be supported in every possible context to maximize social welfare in general. Dworkin is of little help to minority language users.

Social justice as 'fairness and impartiality'

Intuitive preferences about just social arrangements do seem to provide the raw material for making social justice decisions, provided that they can be expressed under conditions of fairness and impartiality for all concerned. John Rawls (1972) offers a recent account of the doctrine of social justice as 'fairness'. The basic idea to which Rawls is committed is that no individual can be merely the means to the ends of society. Rawls insists on the distinctness of persons. His theory has its roots in the Enlightenment and especially in Kant's 'universalizability principle' (Hospers, 1982). For

Kant, an act is a just one if any person who is placed in exactly the same situation would be compelled by moral suasion to act in the same way. Kant argues that what each person can will without contradiction becomes a binding universal law: it is a 'categorical imperative'. For example: Afrikaner South Africans, who support apartheid, would have to argue that they would still support these laws even if they were counted among the victims of apartheid instead of among the beneficiaries (Hare, 1963). One of the earliest statements of this impartial approach to justice is the New Testament's 'Golden Rule' which advised us to do unto others as we would have them do unto us. Yet even this cornerstone of beneficence from the scriptures has a dark underside, as George Bernard Shaw cautions: Don't do to others as you would have them do to you; their tastes might be different. There is more than humour to this rider from Shaw, however. As I suggest below, it is impossible to determine in advance what fair treatment may be in any given context when one is removed from the discursive practices of a participant in the context.

For Rawls, people's preferences about the fairness of the allocation of 'primary goods' ought to be the basis for judging that arrangement. However, these preferences must be expressed in an 'enlightened' context, free from self-interest and bias. Putting it another way, justice should be the content of an agreement that rational people would reach under conditions that do not allow for bargaining power to be translated into advantage. Rawls's formula is that people's enlightened preference is the one that they would adopt if they were concerned with their own welfare, but also in ignorance of what position they might occupy under the new social arrangement. The link between this 'veil of ignorance' formula and the idea of a contract is that participants make a contractual agreement to work out what ought to exist and to do this in a context freed of self-interest and bias. So this method for arriving at assessments of justice asks people to detach themselves from their own positions and to adopt a more impartial standpoint. But there are still several obstacles to this account.

Firstly as an ideal creation by Rawls, his model has no ready or even possible prototype in the real world of human linguistic interaction. Social policies and plans for change exist in and arise from the discourse of societies; the discourse of a society, in turn, already embeds and reflects interests, biases, ideologies, and group psychological dispositions which cannot easily or perhaps ever be disentangled from the social decision-making process in the neat and ideal way that Rawls envisages. Even the list of 'primary goods' which he offers as the basis of people's presumed expectations — 'rights and liberties, opportunities and powers, income and wealth' (1972: 92) — incorporates certain specific preferences that are clearly discourse governed and also culture bound.

Second and relevant to the first point, are criticisms from Robert Wolff (1977), Milton Fisk (1976), and Iris Young (1981). These critics point to a quandary that Rawls creates for himself: either his theory claims universal validity and applicability for its principles, while necessarily avoiding factors derived from any particular socio-historical configuration; or it really does just systematize the principles of a given social order, namely his own. Rawls acknowledges this obstacle when he stipulates that his 'well-ordered society' needs to be 'a closed system' that has 'no significant relations to other societies' (1980: 526). So how can we apply his recommendations to a social institution like education, when an outstanding feature of education is that it is a relentlessly open system (Corson, 1991a) that defies ordering in the way that Rawls suggests? Certainly Rawls does not seem to relate his model to pluralist societies, such as those which exist almost everywhere in the contemporary world. Indeed, he admits this himself: 'we are not trying to find a conception of justice suitable for all societies regardless of their particular social or historical circumstances' (1980: 518). Instead, his theory seems to abstract from institutional relations of power and production in order to derive substantive moral principles from merely formal principles of practical rationality; it does not focus on any real context where social benefits and burdens might be allocated or seem to have application in an open system. We might ask whether it is ever possible to provide a single conception of justice for application in open systems, where there are no reliably constant conjunctions between events or consistency in values?

A third difficulty for Rawls's account also affects other accounts of social justice when they are related to language and education questions: in considering language questions, it is not easy to operate in a context freed of self-interest and bias since each of us begins to weigh value questions while burdened with the bias of the language(s) that we already possess, and few if any are able to be neutral in judging the merits of their own language(s) against languages that are not their own. We cannot step outside the interests that our socialization into a language creates for us, since it is these very interests and the similar interests of those who share our language that we are obliged to defend, even through the use of the language.

Fourthly, there is a critique from gender theorists who argue that the [Western] male view of justice which Rawls represents, by manifesting as it does a concern for impartiality and fairness, overlooks a different ethic of 'care and responsibility' which women would want to include alongside or ahead of the [Western] male view (Gilligan, 1982). Clearly from my first objection above, the individual agents in Rawls's account do seem to display the attitudes and beliefs of men in modern market societies in a consistent and rather exclusive way. He even describes 'the family' as a private institution to which it is not appropriate to apply standards of justice (Okin, 1989). I return to this gender critique in a later section.

Finally there is a weakness of individualist accounts of justice in general that can be applied to Rawls's account in particular. His concept of the person seems to set the individual aside from the social being. Both Lita Furby (1986) and Michael Sandel (1982) argue that the individual person in Rawls lacks human sociality. For language and education issues, this is an especially problematic aspect of his theory of justice, since language is a creation of the social being and has its value created for the individual largely through social interaction. Even the private language in which much of our thinking is conducted is fuelled by social exchanges: to a very real extent our capacity to think depends on the many previous dialogues in which we have engaged. The sense of the collective being, who is produced and produces him or herself through interaction within and across groups in a society or culture, is missing from Rawls. Nor does he focus on the institutional relations that are part of the social being and which underlie economic classes (Macpherson, 1973; Nielsen, 1978). Instead, he seems to see class inequality, and perhaps therefore cultural, gender, and linguistic inequality, as inevitable structures even in an ideal human social system.

A Collectivist Account: Social Justice as 'Consensus in Discourse'

Not far removed in practice from Rawls's account, if well removed ideologically, is Jürgen Habermas's consensus theory of justice. Like Rawls's, his is a procedural account of justice. It depends upon the creation of dialogues that allow an accurate and full exchange of views. Unlike the three accounts so far offered, this theory is collectivist rather than individualist; it sees the needs of different groups as potentially different needs that arise from different group interests and which accordingly may require differential treatment. There are other important differences between Habermas and Rawls, especially because Habermas is more concerned to discover 'truth as consensus' rather than morality, while Rawls, as mentioned, uses his special dialogue setting as a tool for extracting the conditions necessary for ideal moral contracts to be drawn. Habermas begins with the fact that language is basic to what it means to be human. He asks what it might be about language that every human being takes for granted when language is being used for free and open communication; he asks what norms of human behaviour we might extract from that use of language which would go beyond mere personal preferences. In answering these questions he argues that we can find the foundations of all rationality in the conditions of the possibility of communication which underlie and are presupposed by any speech act.

Habermas recognizes social arrangements as just if all people with an interest in the arrangements, when brought together under ideal conditions of debate and negotiation, agree that they are in fact just. Thus as Iris Young (1981) argues, this ideal speech situation must be applied within concretely specified circumstances before it yields a substantive set of evaluative principles of justice. This is contrary to the more general view of moral philosophers that any conception of justice, as a necessary condition for its objectivity, should be held independently of particular social or historical circumstances or practices. However as Fisk (1976) and Wolff (1977) point out, every supposedly objective account of justice, including the ones already discussed above, smuggle in substantive premises that are derived from the theorist's own social circumstances, so that the resulting account merely reflects in ideal form the actual structure of the society in which the theorist resides. In contrast, Habermas takes a real setting for discourse as his context and abstracts out any institutional interests speakers might have other than an interest in discursive consensus.

Habermas (1971) believes social institutions have a pathological quality about them: they operate with the same damaging consequences that human neurotic behaviour produces; they are a collective manifestation of the 'repetition compulsion' of individuals; and they act to defend a rigid uniformity of behaviour and to remove that behaviour from criticism. Habermas was a fifteen year old citizen of the Third Reich in 1945, whose contact with malignant social institutions was first hand. This experience makes him alert to the potential dysfunctioning of even the most benign institutions. On his analysis, the primary function of institutions is the external regulation of oppression. This regulation corresponds to that instinctual repression that affects individuals and which varies depending upon the relative shortage or abundance of economic goods. To confront this apparently desperate situation for modern social institutions, he re-commends a disarmingly moderate policy of institutional modification. As a solution to the 'problem of legitimacy' that confronts modern social institutions, Habermas (1970; 1985) grounds the search for norms of human institutional behaviour in language itself.

Arguing from and against Noam Chomsky's account of 'linguistic com-petence', Habermas formulates a theory of communicative competence as a basis for social analysis.[2] He identifies the possibility of an ideal speech situation in which there are no external constraints preventing participants from assessing evidence and argument, and in which each participant has an equal and open chance of entering into discussion. Habermas abstracts from the nature of human language itself certain principles that are usually taken for granted in any communicative situation. No matter how distorted the actual conditions of communication may be, for Habermas every competent speaker possesses the means to construct a speech situation which would be free from domination in the search for truth and for rational norms. When a person says something to another, Habermas suggests that the second person is able to make the following [validity] claims:

(1) that what is said is intended to be intelligible, offering a 'meaning' which can be understood;

(2) that the propositions or factual assertions offered by the speaker as part of the speech are true;

(3) that the speaker is justified in saying what is said, not going outside social rights or norms for that context of speech;

(4) that the speaker is sincere in what is said, not intending to deceive the listener.

In ideal and undistorted communication, speakers can defend by word or deed all four of the above claims: what is said is meaningful, true, justified and sincere. These four claims are ethical codes in themselves, embodied in the structure of human language; they establish basic norms of conduct for us that are a prototype for other norms such as those to do with justice, welfare, equality etc. When all of the participants in a given speech context are able to defend these claims, when all related evidence can be brought into play, and when nothing apart from logically reasoned argument is used in reaching consensus, then the circumstances provide an ideal speech situation. This is a setting in which people can sort out their real interests from their illusory ones and agree on the things that they may have in common and on other things that may divide them.[3]

In this ideal situation, power is eliminated as much as possible from the arrangements for discussion; and individuals are encouraged to express their real interests, or at least to work towards identifying those interests. They are constrained only by a discussion in which participants acknowledge a shared aim: the norms of the ideal speech situation create a setting of reciprocity, in that each participant has the right to claim that others take account of his or her interests while a reciprocal obligation exists for him or her to do likewise. The outcome is a conception of justice that expresses the interests of all to the extent that they are compatible interests. Although it is true, as Robert Young (1992) points out, that the very interests of individuals and groups stand most obviously in the way of rational openness of this kind, it is also true that we can protect ourselves against sectional interests by taking part in dialogue between groups who have different interests. So although my first objection to Rawls's account also seems to hold for the ideal that Habermas offers us, his defence would be that while the resulting dialogue may not guarantee truth, it can minimize the biases that often distort decision-making.

Most relevant to my theme in this book, Habermas's account provides for those interests and needs that people have which are not biologically given or naturally present in all people. As presented here, individualist theories of justice look for basic human rights, welfare needs, or primary goods that are (arguably) reducible to individual biological needs that all humans have. Even when these accounts address acquired needs, they discuss such needs as derive from accidents of birth or of life that can be reduced to biological needs: the needs of sufferers from congenital handicap, of accident victims, of the deserving poor etc. Rawls's primary goods seem to be no more than means for attaining a myriad of concrete ends selected according to values based in biological needs. In discussing individualist accounts of justice, Habermas (1979) argues that primary goods of the Rawlsian variety are not compatible with all the forms of life that might be chosen as a basis for justice decisions. Instead, primary goods involve limited opportunity structures; they suggest a particular underlying form of life which centres on the private commodity relations of production and exchange, and on privatism and individualism in matters of family, occupation, and citizenship.

In contrast, Habermas tries to allow for 'new' possibilities in social relations. Later, I will argue that these are not quite the 'new' possibilities that Habermas considers them to be: for many minority language users, who come from ancestral cultures, these possibilities have often involved basic expressions of their traditional cultural values; they have been repressed only by enforced contact with modern Western cultures.[4] For Habermas though, chief among these 'new' possibilities of his is the prospect that 'the "pursuit of happiness" might one day mean something different' and that it might be concerned not so much with accumulating material objects which one disposes of privately, but with 'bringing about social relations in which mutuality predominates and satisfaction does not mean the triumph of one over the repressed needs of the other' (1979: 198–9). Implicitly, he licenses us to go beyond the limits of 'needs as opportunities' to consider those 'needs as interests' that are not naturally or equally present in individuals, in men and women, in every class, or in every cultural group. Although these interests may turn out to be incompatible across class, culture, or gender group, through his discourse ethic we may be able to bring them out into the open so that any potential that they have for compatibility can be identified and debated, and so that a compromise can be reached if needed.

The emphasis in Habermas, then, shifts from one interpretation of Kant's categorical imperative to another: from what each person can will, without contradiction, to be a universal law; to what all can will in agreement to be a universal norm. Habermas cites examples from traffic rules to basic institutional norms, which 'make it intuitively clear that increasing the scope for individual options [i.e. 'particular group interests' on my account] does not decrease the chances for agreement concerning presumptively common interests' (1982: 258–9). He continues: 'Particular interests are those that prove on the basis of discursive testing not to be susceptible of generalization and thus to require compromise' (p. 259). This means that particular group interests are not rival claims; they are just incompatible claims that require the compromise that can only come when people of good will negotiate on the basis of an agreed norm. In David Rasmussen's view, Habermas 'does not provide a basis for adjudication between alternative value systems'; rather 'his discourse ethics is open to a "pluralism" of values requiring agreement on normative principles only' (1990: 62). Questions of what 'a good life' might consist in are not normative; they belong in the realm of morality and morals which is bounded by a particular life context [*Sittlichkeit* on Habermas's account]. As Alessandro Ferrara (1985) remarks, questions about the general properties of the good life can no longer be confined to ontology and biology; we need to examine the fallibilistic kind of knowledge provided by some disciplines, including metapsychology and cultural anthropology, and work from empirically falsifiable theories about the psychic requirements of human well-being within specific contexts. These questions can be negotiated and a compromise reached after normative procedures are settled through a use of the discourse ethic.

An example may help, although in practice the construction of actual circumstances conducive to an ideal speech situation is beyond the scope of these introductory chapters. I return to it in Chapter 7. In determining the status of minority languages in a pluralist society's education system, the following hypothetical policymaking procedure might follow from Habermas's account:

> Firstly a use of the discourse ethic at system level (attending to the interests of all those with a stake in the issue) to establish any universalizable norms that could operate as principles across the system to increase the scope for optional use of any single minority language with respect to the majority language and also with respect to other minority languages (see p. 153 in Chapter 7).

Secondly a use of the discourse ethic in devolved local settings to establish more 'context-bound' universalizable norms for allotting status to minority languages, critically accepting the universalizable norms already identified at system level as givens and making use of any grounds for compatibility that follow from both sets of norms.

Thirdly a use (as often as necessary) of the discourse ethic in decision making within increasingly devolved context-specific settings, establishing sub-norms where needed to determine compatibility and eventually, if necessary, compromising on incompatible values that represent pluralist versions of 'the good life' within the life contexts of individual minority groups.

Through this process of applied discourse ethics, any particular sets of interests that are incompatible are resolved through compromise. In this way, human interests acquired through socialization and enculturation are accommodated in two ways: compatible interests provide the substantive material for constructing universalizable norms; and incompatible interests become the subject of compromise in an informed consensus.

As I have argued, for Habermas these needs as interests are more akin to the needs that cultural and class groups develop: the need to have their cultural values recognised; the need to live within social arrangements that are not hostile to those values; the need to have their languages or their language varieties valued and supported. It is easy to see why this collectivist account is relevant to this book's theme. Although it bypasses the possibility of there being universal criteria for determining social justice, it still provides socially just arrangements for selecting and allocating benefits and burdens according to needs criteria.[5] What I have not established so far is a point that can seem counter-intuitive and threatening to many Westerners: that because different groups of human beings develop radically different sets of interests, this necessitates differential policy, curriculum, and pedagogical treatment in education.

Language, Social Justice and Sociocultural Group

There is now wide evidence from many countries that cultural and class groups develop very different needs and interests which have to be addressed with different social and education policy solutions. In trying to understand the nature of these differences, I find value in two concepts introduced by Ralph Dahrendorf in his book *Life Chances* (1978). He speaks of 'options' and 'ligatures' as the two distinguishing kinds of 'life chances' that societies offer to their members. I am extrapolating in this instance from 'societies' to 'education within societies'. Put simply, options in education are the range of choices (or primary goods) that people receive as a result of their education; the wider the range of options, the greater are the life chances that individuals are deemed to possess. Ligatures are life chances of a very different kind: these are the bonds between people that they establish as a result of their membership in society or participation in that society's education in my account. The 'Harvard Project on Human Potential' borrows these ideas from Dahrendorf. It offers the example of Third World women, who seem poor in options and rich in ligatures. But because ligatures provide some of the most important benefits in life, namely support, structure and motivation, and a sense of respect and continuity, it is altogether likely that women in some Third World settings experience their lives as highly satisfying even though Western observers might think that they could not do so (Levine & White, 1986: 203).

In some societies and among some cultural groups, ligatures are seen as positive ends in themselves to be cultivated as a goal in life, and not as the instruments to other ends that Westerners sometimes hold them to be. Among the Navajo, the Cree, and the Inuit of North America, for example, even in the midst of the rich options that their countries extend to their citizens, it is often the ligatures that mean much more, even when that valuing of ligatures leads to a reduction in options. Those few educationists who see the development of ligatures as an important aim for schools often stress the use of community languages, for example, as a means of extending bonds between students; a stress on language of any kind, across the curriculum, increases the ligatures between students while also enhancing their options.

Most Western education systems are strong in providing students with options but weak in providing them with ligatures. Yet in English-speaking countries in particular, many of the clients of contemporary education come from ethnic communities where ligatures are prized. For some, such as the thousands of refugees from Indo-China or the Balkans, ligatures of one kind or another may be all that remain to them; for others, such as the ancestral Koori culture in Australia, the Maori in New Zealand, the Navaho, the Inuit or the Cree in North America, there is a cultural continuity reinforcing the preservation of ligatures that remains largely outside the understanding of people from outside those cultures. In the light of these factors, more sensitive approaches to educational organization, pedagogy, and curriculum seem warranted if schools are to provide just treatment for the children of these groups.

There is also a growing body of evidence to suggest that rather basic moral views, among people who are quite morally upright within their own societies and groups, may vary across cultures, groups and even by gender. Anthropologists, of course, have long uncovered examples of this, suggesting that while justice in its application and procedures in Western societies stresses abstract principles and is universalistic, in non-Western societies it usually reflects the importance of community ties (or ligatures) and the particular justice case under consideration (Nader & Sursock, 1986). For example: Laurence Kohlberg's staged theory of moral development (1976) asserts that all cultural groups progress fairly regularly through his stages. Yet Lita Furby (1986) discusses evidence which suggests that morally exemplary people in collectivist-oriented cultures would not fit Kohlberg's schema. Hence Kohlberg's schema, on the evidence, appears rather ethnocentric. Moreover, there seem to be conditions under which a Confucian view of morality, for example, would conflict with Kohlberg's stages: for Kohlberg, working as he does from Kant, the ability to make moral decisions in accordance with universally applied principles is the most advanced stage of moral development; for a Confucian, in contrast, universal principles of this kind conflict with the need to recognize differences between people's interests and circumstances, as Habermas might also advise, and to make appropriate compromises. As Shaw argued, 'their tastes might be different' and Habermas allows that their interests probably will be too.

Also related to my theme here is the further contention that Kohlberg's higher stages of moral development may simply reflect the abstract language used in higher education in Western societies, whose public use results in a form of higher stage reasoning that may be more apparent than real. I have already made this strong link between language and moral power when discussing Bourdieu in Chapter 1. Clearly power in moral debate does rest unequally with those individuals who have the ability to wield complex and sensitive moral vocabularies. Richard Rorty (1983) argues that this lexical ability is a way of supplementing and even bypassing the need for more universal principles for moral behaviour. But I am not convinced by this logocentric point about high level moral reasoning. The pernicious influence of certain lexically brilliant but plainly evil propagandists in the twentieth century make this point of Rorty's a cause for alarm rather than for agreement. Perhaps there are good grounds for asking whether the ultratechnical interests that have evolved in modern Western society promote a form of moral reasoning which unfairly reflects technical precision and control, or in other words 'masculine' interests rather than 'feminine' ones. It is no surprise that many female investigators of Kohlberg's system have questioned it on exactly these grounds.

The work of Carol Gilligan (1982) offers a lead in examining this integration of moral interests with reasoning and development. The flaw that Gilligan finds, in Kohlberg and by implication in Western individualist accounts of moral development more generally, is close to an objection that I have already raised against Rawls's theory of justice. It is not so much that Kohlberg is wrong in his account of moral development. Rather his account is incomplete: while it recognises 'fairness in relation to the rights of others' as the goal of moral development, it overlooks a complementary conception of justice that is captured in the phrase 'care and responsibility'. This 'ethic of care' does seem an integral part of the moral domain; indeed evidence suggests it has powerful practical outcomes. The interview studies by Samuel and Pearl Oliner (1988) into the altruism of rescuers of Jews in Nazi Europe, compared with non-rescuers, suggests that the former who were both men and women acted on behalf of others, and quite contrary to their own safety and welfare, for reasons having to do with care and responsibility: they had feelings of empathy for the pain of others; they felt pity, compassion, affection and concern; and they were oriented towards developing and maintaining attachments to others. So the forms of moral reasoning arising from the complementary perspectives offered by 'fairness' and by 'care' may be rather different. In spite of Oliner & Oliner's findings that the 'ethic of care' was common to both men and women rescuers, there may still be a gender dimension to this outlook, although it would be an error to overgeneralize it as *necessarily* more typical of women than of men.[6] But there *is* evidence of significant gender differences in reasoning about justice (Furby, 1986). Such objections have much in common with a prominent critique of social theory offered by the French school of feminists, highlighting not so much what is wrong with Western social values that have developed diachronically, as what is missing from them (Branson, 1991). Usually what is missing are those historically suppressed values that are associated more with women than with men (whether men manifest them or not), such as a concern for care, responsibility, interaction, cooperation, and avoidance of hurt: in short a concern for developing and maintaining the ligatures that are also so much at the heart of the cultural behaviour of contemporary minority groups, such as the Polynesian peoples of the South Pacific and traditional Koori peoples of Australia.

If there are dramatic across-group differences in interests, why is it that they do not surface more clearly and more often? This is not an idle question, as my discussion of power and language in Chapter 1 tries to show. The answer has much to do with the range and diversity of the ideologies that people develop, depending on their sociocultural contacts throughout life. Sometimes they are able to live out these ideologies; sometimes they need to repress them in order to fit in with those who are more able to live out their own ideologies. The power and authority held by different sociocultural or gender groups in a society or culture usually determines whether or not any single group's social justice interests will prevail or even surface. Obviously in different societies different ideologies about justice will evolve, in much the same way as different conceptions of social justice have appeared and become dominant for a time. The special justice interests of minority groups and of women are only now beginning to reveal themselves, as the power of traditionally dominant male cultural groups lessens a little, perhaps voluntarily in some places. As these distinct interests gradually become better known, the injustice of not recognizing them becomes clearer. It also becomes clear that because different groups with genuinely different justice interests exist, there are very strong reasons for offering differential forms of social treatment as a way of distributing just arrangements in a more humane way. Just language policies in education attend to these differences.

Since there are many possible sets of ethnic, gender, and class interests that are very different from one another and do require different and perhaps incompatible forms of treatment, then accounts of social justice that begin solely from individualist positions are even more seriously flawed than I have already suggested. They amount to attempts to work out in advance, from the interests of dominant groups of individuals, what arrangements would be chosen under unknown conditions by other groups of people whose interests may not readily be detectable by anyone who is not steeped in the relevant class, gender, or minority culture.[7]

Language Policy, Education and Social Justice

Are individualist theories irrelevant to questions of language and social justice? Their continuing relevance becomes clear when we move education into the social justice equation. As soon as questions are raised about learning, knowledge, and understanding, individualist accounts become important since quality education is always concerned with individual students as well as with aggregate groups. Yet educational theory, research, and practice are bedevilled by the tension that comes from the need to consider the individual and the social group often at the same time. It is no accident that the study of education involves a deep consideration of disciplines like psychology and philosophy that are typically individualist in their methods; nor is it an accident that the study of education involves deep consideration of other disciplines like sociology and anthropology that are typically collectivist in their methodology and fields of interest. It is the case that educational theory which grows only from one of these orientations risks missing important points about its real domain of inquiry.[8]

For example, in considering gender questions in education it is essential to ensure that the individual rights of girls for access to the curriculum and to appropriate pedagogies is guaranteed. These are fundamental rights that depend on claims like those made in the first three accounts above: natural rights, welfare, fairness, happiness, protection of future options. But there are also other claims about women's rights that cannot be reduced to biological needs that all human beings share. People are beginning to appreciate now that the experience of being born and socialized as a female, or as a male, can create very different orientations towards the world which can extend and modify in complex ways any given biological differences that there are between men and women. Indeed, the differences can be similar in degree and perhaps often in kind to the differences that exist between people from different social or cultural backgrounds. And all these acquired differences can promote quite different sets of interests, norms of behaviour, and claims to justice.

I have argued that a very different approach to social justice is needed if we are to allow for interests as developed needs that are not naturally present in all people. Habermas's account provides for interests of this kind: the need for recognition of group values acquired through socialisation and enculturation; the need to have social and organizational arrangements provided that are sympathetic to and supportive of group values; and the need to have special group orientations towards language and learning recognized, valued, and supported. Habermas points us in this direction through his ideal speech situation, a discourse ethic that is anticipated in every act of speech and which confirms that the human interest in matters of emancipation from injustice is a real and universal phenomenon grounded in the very mode and manner of our communication itself.[9] There is a strong link between these arguments and Bhaskar's emancipatory account discussed in Chapter 1, which gives human reasons and accounts central status in any social science theory or any social policy. In their relations with non-dominant groups, policy makers do need to develop methods for finding out about very different sets of human needs and interests. But as evidence suggests (Corson, 1993b), even when conditions of debate come close to an ideal speech situation and when participants are skilled in taking a balanced point of view, an in-group of policy makers will find it difficult to engage dispassionately with the special interests and rights of socially or culturally different people. Again even when conditions do approximate Habermas's ideal speech situation, policy makers of great goodwill cannot easily get to grips with the presuppositions that underlie the accounts offered by socially or culturally different people. Using Bourdieu's analogy, those groups with capital that is different from that given high status in the school often provide accounts of their own behaviour and of their own intentions in relation to the world that are very different from dominant group accounts and which may seem inscrutable as a result.

The task of recognizing the different interests and rights of class, cultural, and gender groups begins with the evidence of group values expressed in its members' reasons and accounts, since these in turn produce, shape, and are shaped by the structures that the groups value. Again it seems impossible to avoid the conclusion reached in Chapter 1, that any policy making that does not engage with those cultural structures through the reasons and accounts that produce and are productive of them will act against the emancipation through education of people drawn from those groups. In place of policy making that disempowers in this way, we need decision-making that sincerely responds to the evidence of the cultural structures that non-dominant groups value. In some places, this may mean a wholesale change in the control of the educational decision-making that affects the interests of non-dominant groups. In other places if just decisions are going to be reached, a thoroughly pluralist organizational arrangement may be needed, incorporating group representatives at every level.

In short, a just form of language policymaking will cover the tasks that Habermas suggests: articulating and clarifying particular standards or principles as norms; elaborating the ways in which these standards can be and are related to one another; and studying what makes different standards appropriate to different situation types. When we operate in the real world of complex policy situations, this kind of 'normative pluralism' is inevitably the way things have to be. In this real world setting, incompatible claims will often arise; but when justice is seriously debated there is often less need for compromise than we might expect.

Notes to Chapter 2

1. In this chapter my use of the word 'language' connotes a much wider set of linguistic variations than is usual, as wide in fact as the range of linguistic variation treated in this book. 'Language' here implies varieties, dialects, creoles, patois, and other subsets of language that might be notionally attached at times to both majority and minority languages. My concern is to discuss ways of determining socially just forms of treatment in education for any and all of these language varieties when they are linked to social groups determined by cultural, class, or gender backgrounds.
2. The sense in which Habermas uses the phrase 'communicative competence' contrasts markedly with other similar usages:

   I propose to use this term in a way similar to that in which Chomsky uses 'linguistic competence'. Communicative competence should be related to a system of rules generating an ideal speech situation, not regarding linguistic codes which link language and universal pragmatics with actual role systems. Dell Hymes, among others, makes use of the term 'communicative competence' in a sociolinguistically limited sense. I don't want to follow this convention (1970: 374).

3. In a school setting, attempts to create a context for discussion that replicates as far as possible the ideal speech situation also create an ideal setting for policy-making by staff and community members, especially for the kind of language policymaking needed in pluralist schools and societies (see Chapter 7 and Corson, 1990a,b).

4. It would be wrong to portray Habermas himself as a thoroughgoing cultural pluralist. For example, he does not acknowledge that many contemporary traditional cultures already manifest the very cultural values that he considers possibilities only in some utopian future. John Thompson (1984) wonders how Habermas's theory of social evolution could be applied to the developmental course of societies outside of the West, since he appears to accept most of Marx's and Weber's Western-based accounts of the changing conditions and world views necessary for social and cultural development.

5. At the same time Habermas's account could make 'positive discrimination' an unnecessary concept (see John B. Edwards, 1987).

6. Susan Okin seems on the right track when she argues that 'it is misleading to draw a dichotomy as though there were two contrasting ethics. The best theo-rizing about justice is not some abstract "view from nowhere", but results from the carefully attentive consideration of everyone's point of view' (1989: 15). This is consistent with both Habermas's and Bhaskar's accounts (see Chapter 1) if policy makers give due weight to those who have interests in the matter under debate.

7. As critics of liberalism often observe 'what defines liberalism is its disregard for the context of choice, for the way that choices are situated in cultural communi-ties' (Kymlicka, 1989: 206). Will Kymlicka makes an attempt to rehabilitate liberalism, as commonly interpreted, especially its failure to respond to people's intuitions about the importance of cultural membership. In doing so he re-examines and questions the moral ontology of liberalism itself, its individualism, and its egalitarianism, arguing that membership of a cultural community has to be a relevant criterion for distributing the benefits and burdens which are the concern of a liberal theory of justice.

8. Educational aims and matters of school success and failure can be analyzed by way of 'methodological individualism' (i.e. using the characteristics and proper-ties of individuals) or by way of 'methodological collectivism' (i.e. considering group attributes). The latter analysis provides much of the original justification for having an educational sociology or anthropology; the former is more often invoked to support the methods of educational psychology and early approaches to philosophy of education. But in education, tension arises in allotting priority to either analysis when we try to account for a given piece of data. Indeed, academic faculties of education are sometimes riven by this tension. But a sociology of language tries as it must to bridge the two methodo-logical orientations: since human language is a property of individual persons then the methodological individualism of formal linguistics and psychology recommends itself as part of the domain of a sociology of language; but since

human language also depends for its very existence on the interaction and conventions of collectivities, having no existence or dynamic outside human groups, then the methodological collectivism displayed by mainstream sociology and anthropology becomes an essential route to creating a sociology of language, especially if a philosophy of language underpins it all.

9. In discussing the private sphere of human behaviour, Alessandro Ferrara (1985) allows that moral decision-makers can have the luxury of legitimately disregarding the best available argument if their own intuitions about the good in those circumstances are not in accord with that argument. But in the public sphere of policymaking, where stakes are much higher and where unknown and unconsenting agents are likely to be affected, moral decision-makers should never go beyond what is validated by the consensus provided in an ideal speech situation, since this specifies the standards for taking decisions in the public arena of a participatory democracy.

3 Language Policy and Minority Culture

Chapter 1 discussed some of the everyday ways in which discourse discrimination is exercised through educational systems. In this chapter, I am attending more directly to language injustices that affect the members of minority cultures. Language theorists have argued for a generation that many of the difficulties in mainstream schools that confront children from minority cultures can be attributed to sociolinguistic interference (Hymes, 1971). There are other more obvious difficulties that arise for children who have a different language code and culture, but these other things are compounded because teachers overlook the subtle differences in linguistic capital and habitus that children bring to school and the impact that these things can have on school learning. In spite of their best efforts, teachers often come to regard minority children as unresponsive or disruptive. Sometimes they wrongly see them as slow learners and label them accordingly.

These problems are made worse by the limited opportunities that exist for individuals to interact with one another in large classes. Lack of positive feedback and too little use of their own productive speech means that cultural minority children can be severely disadvantaged. The evidence is clear: when minority children are compared with majority culture students, the number of productive ideas that are present in a lesson for them and their moments of interaction with teachers are reduced considerably when tallied over their school and college careers (Au, 1978; Cazden, 1987; 1990; Trujillo, 1986). This unfair situation needs policy redress involving sensitive reforms in the discursive practices of classrooms and schools before we can begin to expect changes in educational outcomes for minority culture children.

Identity, Intercultural Contacts, and Majority Culture Schooling

Defining the identity of a cultural group can be very difficult. Roy Todd (1978) makes this point when he discusses the search for an adequate

48

definition of the Gypsy (*sic*) population of Britain. He remarks on the mismatch between in-group and out-group definitions. For instance, any given feature or set of features, linked to ancestry, self-employment, travelling, cultural practices, or language is only a guide to identity, and even then only within certain contexts. What really sets Gypsies apart from non-Gypsies seems inaccessible. Yet because important cultural attachments are still involved, Todd argues that weighty social policy implications result and it is clear that they do in all such cases. In Chapter 1, I recommended a realist approach in judging cultural interests, an approach that responds to the reasons and accounts that people offer about social and cultural structures that are important to them. It seems to follow from this that in judging cultural identity, the idea of 'personal allegiance' is the central consideration: an individual's strong, voluntary attachment to a cultural group and to its values, as a result of some real link in the past, should be sufficient warrant of shared identity. When individuals claim this voluntary attachment by giving an account in language that shows that the cultural allegiance is important in their lives, this outweighs other assessments of cultural identity that might be made about the same people by a second party.

The conceptual world of a culture includes many classificatory systems and most of these are expressed or supported in the language of the culture. When the classificatory systems of two cultures come into contact, there is often a mismatch. A simple example of this is the mismatch in colour coding observed between people from very different cultures whose members divide up the colour spectrum differently, although it remains the same spectrum. But many other mismatches occur that are away from the concrete and physical world, and these can produce major intercultural misunderstandings: mismatches in greeting styles, in teasing behaviour, and in other behaviours which can and do produce mistrust, a sense of impending violence, or other general feelings of unease (McDonald, 1989). These mismatches are apprehended more keenly when they appear at a boundary between people that is already clear-cut. Often the rival classificatory system is treated ironically; it is portrayed as irrational, romantic, emotional, or comical. The caricatured and humorous ways in which the English and the French sometimes view one another is an example of this. But when cultural identities are established and recognized over a long period, as is the case in the French–English cultural divide, the differences between the two cultures usually come to be viewed with a measure of reciprocal respect, even if that respect seems lukewarm on the surface. When cultural identities are less clear, or when a minority has been forced into biculturalism through conquest or through economic and political pressure, the differences between the two cultures can become a source of mutual misunderstanding and a continual source of oppression for the less powerful. Cultural identity becomes very important to people when their culture is under constant threat, and this is more likely to affect 'involuntary' minorities.

Discussing variations among minorities in their rates of school success, John Ogbu draws a very relevant distinction between 'involuntary' and 'voluntary' minorities. He argues that 'the main factor differentiating the more successful from the less successful minorities appears to be the nature of the history, subordination, and exploitation of the minorities, and the nature of the minorities' own instrumental and expressive responses to their treatment, which enter into the process of their schooling' (1987: 317). Involuntary minorities, such as the African American and First Nations peoples in North America and ancestral minorities elsewhere, are constrained by societal, school and classroom structures that have denied them equal opportunity over many generations. Historically, they have encountered a job ceiling in the world of work, inferior forms of education, and random racism in every sphere of living. Their cultural capital has not been recognized in the institution of education, and their cultural interests have not been consulted by policy makers at system or school levels. In short, the members of these minorities have good reasons for believing that they do not have an equal chance when compared with members of the dominant cultural group.

In Ogbu's account, involuntary minorities are characterized by 'secondary cultural differences' that develop as 'a response to a contact situation, especially a contact situation involving the domination of one group by another' (1987: 322). This domination occurs in a setting from which the involuntary minority cannot withdraw, since the setting is their own home. With no chance of living their lives away from the all-intruding dominant culture, they see the differences that exist between themselves and the majority culture as insurmountable; the differences are rooted in markers of their own identity that must be maintained, since it is the very substance of a culture that exists nowhere else. This contrasts with the structures that affect voluntary minorities, who are mainly the 'new minorities' discussed in Chapter 4. These see their own cultural differences as barriers to be overcome in achieving their own long-term success in employment or lifestyle; they are able to look back on their former countries or regions as places of fewer opportunities, where education in many cases was even worse than the worst forms of schooling that they experience in their new homeland. Because their 'primary cultural differences' are so recognizable and clear, this makes it easier for voluntary minorities to adopt schooling strategies that enhance academic success and produce social adjustment.

The moment voluntary or involuntary minority children enter schools, they are expected to learn and abide by the cultural norms of the school. Almost everywhere, these same norms of behaviour match the values and traditions of the dominant culture. Pierre Bourdieu compellingly sets out the case in support of this point, and Muriel Saville-Troike (1979) echoes it: for her, the educational system is one which primarily prepares middle class children from the dominant culture to take part in their own culture. In the contemporary world, the harmful impact of this monocultural practice on individuals and groups of minority children is becoming plainer. Below I quote a poignant reminder of the cultural boundaries that are put in the way of minority group identities, even through the well intentioned practices of monocultural Western schooling. Similar quotes could be gathered from ancestral minority people in many places, but in New Zealand rapid educational change is now occurring in minority schooling. This change is in response to the belief of many Maori that the European-style school system is not appropriate for the sustenance of a Polynesian culture (see Chapter 7). The nub of the injustice for minority peoples in New Zealand and elsewhere, is captured succinctly by this Maori educationist who asks:

> Have you ever heard Maori people talking about leaving their *Maoritanga* [Maori culture] at the school gate so that they can come to school to learn their *Pakehatanga* [non-Maori New Zealand culture]? Maori people have learned to behave that way in order to survive. When Maori people have been asked what they want from the education system, they have always answered, 'the best of both worlds: *Maoritanga* and *Pakehatanga*'. They have not wanted to choose one rather than the other but both. The dualism of Pakeha thinking has made the Maori feel guilty for not preferring one over the other (Penetito, 1986: 20).

Minority Culture Values and Discourse Norms in Majority Culture Classrooms

In conventional Western schools skilled teachers have often been able to make the content of their lessons relevant to children from traditional minority cultures by interweaving the known experiences of the children themselves with the content of the curriculum. This is no small achievement in itself but it is an easy task compared with the problem of establishing a context for learning that is genuinely congruent with the culture of many minority children. Since all of schooling is mediated through discourse in one form or another, priority in establishing congruency depends on getting the discourse right; but what does this involve? John Gumperz (1977) argues that, through their interactions with others, individuals develop 'co-occurrence expectations' and 'contextualization expectations' as a part of their communicative competence. These expectations about context clues, the structuring of attention, the regulation of talk or turn-taking, are often culturally specific. When people have their expectations about these things upset by subtle variations in the speech of culturally different others, then their ability and willingness to participate in the novel context is reduced.

These ideas are not new. Many studies already confirm the prevalence of inappropriate class and school contexts of interaction for minority children. However these studies are often to be found only in recondite sources. Moreover their potential for generalizability is under-recognized since they usually deal with relatively small minority groups in single countries. In what follows I try to collate these studies, since they yield evidence about subtle differences in language norms that rarely appears in the professional training curriculum of teachers. As a result, this evidence still falls outside the taken-for-granted reality of professional practice in mainstream classrooms.

There are many aspects of language use that seem to be universal: they are shared by all human beings as a result of our biological inheritance. At the same time, other aspects of language use vary across cultures and grow from cultural learning processes that establish socially appropriate forms of communicative behaviour. In Chapter 5 I examine sociocultural differences in the ways that literacy is viewed and used (pp. 116–9). That discussion is very relevant to this chapter too. Often culturally different students will approach literacy activities in majority culture classrooms in ways that are inconsistent with school norms but consistent with their own cultural norms and values. In that later chapter, I discuss this problem as a factor in the education of children from minority social groups. The evidence confirms that teachers can and do make incorrect assessments of their students' ability because of this problem, which affects all modes of language and which is clearly more likely to occur when the distance between the teacher's culture and the child's is greater. I need not elaborate on the social justice issue involved here: more than simple miscommunication results from these misassessments; life chances are often reduced and the cultural interests of entire groups of children can go unrecognized.

Cultural values and cultural norms in language use

Ronald and Suzanne Scollon (1979; 1981; 1984) identify an ancient and enduring value in the Northern Athabaskan culture of sub-Arctic America: the people display an unusually high level of respect for the individual world views of others. This key value seems to translate into Athabaskan norms for language behaviour; it is manifested in child socialization practices and in the narrative tradition of the people. In practice, it means that at all times all individuals are entitled to make their own sense of any situation without others enforcing their perspective. Consequently there is much use of negotiation among Athabaskan participants interacting in any situation. This is a norm that governs discourse exchanges. Scollon & Scollon speak of 'focused and non-focused situations': the Athabaskan interactional preference is to operate in non-focused settings where there are few pressures of time and space, so that individual differences in world view can be properly negotiated. Implications for the schooling of Athabaskan children follow from this *cultural value* and from the *language norms* that link with it.

There seems a simple analytical relationship between the idea of a *norm* in language use and the idea of a *cultural value*. A cultural value is an attitude or an interest that people in a group cherish for its own sake, or perhaps instrumentally as something that is essential to the maintenance of the group itself. A cultural value provides a structure or a mechanism, in Roy Bhaskar's sense (1986), that affects the behaviour of members of a culture or social group. For example, the concept of *cariño*, reflecting an ethic of closeness and responsibility, is often noted as a characteristic value within Hispanic communities in the United States (Cazden, 1988). This cultural value often translates into norms for language use, notably in the discourse practices that are observed in classrooms when Hispanic teachers and pupils interact. For example, the direct use of public praise is rarely used; instead, Hispanic teachers indicate their approval with a quiet smile, perhaps accompanied with an approving nod. People from other Western cultures can identify with this value very easily since the Hispanic culture is part of the fabric of Western civilization. But as Westerners make contact with cultures that have fewer roots in the West, they encounter contrasting cultural values that may be easy to recognize but more difficult to describe. What follows is an attempt to describe some of these contrasting values.

In Chapter 2, I discussed various types of group ligatures that represent essential values binding people in minority cultures. The same values may not be ranked as highly by Western people; they may not be recognized as values at all. As an example, in many Polynesian settings it is not customary for individuals to set themselves above other group members in status or in public achievement unless the group itself first allots that status. Regardless of one's achievements earned in the wider world, the act of setting oneself above others, without some group-initiated and prior consent, infringes a complex cultural value which is only partially captured in Western values of egalitarianism, modesty, community, and humility. This most basic Polynesian value is manifested in many norms of language use:

for example, a reluctance to reveal achievement in case it is interpreted as conceit; an absence of boasting; an expressed deference to the group as the true source of one's success. For many Maori New Zealanders, to infringe this value would be to bring *whakama* (shame) on themselves.

Sometimes cultural values are similar across very different traditional cultures, but still translate into similar language norms. For example, I have observed many similarities between traditional Koori (Aboriginal) Australian values and Maori values about learning and schooling, even though the two cultures are not contiguous in any historical sense. One account of 'what Koori Australians want from education' includes the following five points (M. Christie, 1988: 5–19):

(1) attention to the harmony and unity of Koori life: individual achievement which ignores the meaningfulness of the Koori group is not wanted;
(2) preserving continuity with the past, the land and the people: progress is only good if it bolsters Koori identity;
(3) placing value on doing things in response to the total physical and social environment;
(4) personal independence, with no coercion and manipulation: unconditional acceptance of everyone;
(5) interference by White educators is the problem, not the solution.

None of the above points would be out of place in a Maori philosophy of schooling. In particular, Point 5 reiterates a basic purpose in the contemporary creation and operation of monocultural Maori primary schools in New Zealand (*kura kaupapa Maori*): the organizational arrangements of these schools aim to exclude functional interference by non-Maori New Zealanders and the structural influence of non-Maori cultural forces. For example, visitors to the *kura* must be approved in advance by the entire governing *whanau* (extended community). The *whanau* need to be confident that any visitors, including government officials should they wish to visit, have the interests of Maori at heart. This means that educational researchers, for instance, can only gain access to the *kura* if they undertake to do research that empowers the *whanau* or benefits Maori in some other way. But this is not some form of incipient separatism by Maori, since any children are free to attend the *kura* if they want to have an education shaped by Maori rather than by European values (for a further discussion, see Chapter 7: 168–70). This exclusion of non-Maori influence is linked with the Maori desire and need to work out what is basic to the integrity of Maori culture and to re-create what has been lost of the culture's values through its enforced contact, integration, and assimilation with European culture.

Again from Points 1 and 2 above, we see that the concept of 'ligatures' spans many of the enduring values of traditional peoples. This emphasis on bonding seems to permeate the set of educational ideas that is seen as important in both the Koori and the Maori cultures: bonding with one another, with the culture, and with the environment. This holistic and cooperative relationship with the universe runs throughout the Maori view of language and learning, as various authorities acknowledge (Department of Education, 1989; Gadd, 1976; Bray & Hill, 1973). The aim in Maori learning is the achievement of excellence and mastery of one's total self and the physical environment through a balanced curriculum. Maori ways of thinking and responding to experience are more concerned with the whole than with the part. Ideally then, in allowing for this Gestalt style of thinking, the curriculum will be holistic, with weak classifications between fields of knowledge and a near absence of frames (after Bernstein, 1975): frames which prevent people from learning in their own way, in their own time, at their own pace, and throughout life. This means that many conventional practices are altered: school subject boundaries reduce or disappear; anyone who has knowledge teaches; schools are open outside normal hours; and teachers fill a facilitative rather than an instructional role. Organizational and learning styles give priority to the concept of *whanau* (extended family) or group involvement, with students given opportunities to learn alongside people with skills, interacting with experts and not merely (or perhaps not at all) with a textbook. Classrooms and schools need an atmosphere that encourages a sense of belonging, a family feeling of physical closeness, where each student is given personal attention, praise, encouragement, and the daily experience of success and accomplishment. High regard is paid to differences in preferred learning approaches; and in this way the self-esteem and *whanau* of students is given high regard too. Learning is a cooperative exercise, with children, teachers, parents, and *whanau* all involved. Oral language interaction, adult to child and child to child, is the central pedagogy of the Maori school. The older children must assist and care for their younger relatives in and out of school. Competitive individualism and individual gain are secondary to collaboration, cooperation, and group benefit. This relative absence of competition constrains the forms of evaluation that are desirable: great care needs to be taken to avoid embarrassment in moments of student failure and as I have already indicated to discourage conceit in success.

These Maori learning emphases complement many of the other emphases that seem to be favoured by Koori people (Brandl, 1983: 32–7):

(6) making a mistake is worse than admitting ignorance;
(7) learning by doing, not learning to do;
(8) the importance of experience in learning;

(9) the centrality of cooperative learning;
(10) competition only to catch up, not to excel;
(11) talking and learning related to the whole culture, not just to isolated
     bits of it;
(12) reinforcing cultural learning (i.e. what it means to be Koori);
(13) allowing children to explore everything;
(14) mapping space and the environment differently from non-Koori.

These different cultural values about learning often translate in complex ways into language norms that show up in majority culture classrooms, although to try to show a direct cause and effect relationship would be to understate the complex links between sets of cultural values and patterns of language norms. However, we can see something of the impact of Koori values on classroom language norms in the categories of speech acts developed by Ian Malcolm (1979; 1982). He sees the following speech acts as characteristic of Koori child discourse in conventional classrooms:

(a) empty bidding in response to teacher questions, followed by silence;[1]
(b) declined replying, after a direct elicitation from the teacher;
(c) deferred replying to a question, after a longer than normal pause;
(d) shadowed replying to a question, in the shadow of the next speaker;
(e) unsolicited replying.

Clearly these language norms differ from those approved in conventional schooling. Many conventionally trained teachers would regard these different norms of interaction as disruptive and ill-disciplined. Yet they can be related directly to home and community values and clearly to some of the culturally preferred learning emphases listed a little above. For example, (b) & (c) reflect Point 4: 'personal independence, with no coercion and manipulation: unconditional acceptance of everyone'; and (a), (b) & (d) reflect Point 6: 'making a mistake is worse than admitting ignorance'. What is evidenced here, in Cazden's apt phrases, are 'ethnic differences' becoming 'ethnic borders' (1988: 75). The structural strength of those borders and the size of the obstacle that confronts the school reflect the strength and the difference of the cultural values that the child brings as habitus into the school.

Although the educational practices that follow from these ideas can still seem heretical to teachers in majority culture classrooms, there is much evidence available from classroom research to support both the ideas and the practices. Indeed not all of it is recent. On the Warm Springs reservation in Oregon, Susan Philips (1972; 1975; 1983) looks at the children from several tribes of Native Americans, both early and late in their primary or junior school careers. She finds that Warm Springs Indian children learn socially appropriate norms for paying attention and regulating talk encounters in home and community that are culturally distinctive from those learned by Anglo-American middle class children. Moreover, they are distinctive from the norms that are utilized in classroom interaction, but they are never really taken into account in the development of the school curriculum. She argues that this incompatibility makes it difficult for the minority children to understand verbal messages conveyed through the school's Anglo middle class modes of organizing classroom interaction.

A focus of Philips' interest is the way that humans use verbal and visual cues to designate whom they are addressing or attending to in language. This can vary cross-culturally in many ways: for instance, hearers vary in the behaviours they choose to use to focus their eyes and their ears; in some cultures it is customary to show attention by looking at the speaker and in others attention is shown by looking away, perhaps at the ground. Similarly, speakers vary in the ways that they use to recognize who is paying attention: those looking away in a conversation or in a classroom event may seem uninterested; elsewhere those staring may seem rude. As a result, people from one culture may not recognize when people from another culture are addressing or receiving them. There are many other cultural differences too: other norms for attention structuring and the regulation of talk; in dialect variation; in conventions concerning loudness while talking; in rules about using general rather than focused forms of address; or, as the Koori example suggests, in norms governing hesitation in responding to questions. Philips uncovers three sources of evidence to suggest that the Indian children misunderstand teacher talk in the classrooms observed: both young and especially older Indian children talk much less in official classroom interaction and respond less often to direct teacher questions; their responses to teacher questions are more often defined as inappropriate by the teacher; and the children's questions asked about the teacher's instructions indicate uncertainty about their own comprehension. She observes that the Indian children convey attention in different ways, and so are misrecognized on occasions as being inattentive when they are not; she also finds that they actually pay less attention than other children, being more involved in interaction with their classmates, often in 'teasing' behaviour which she describes as prevalent among American Indian societies (as it is too among traditional Koori Australians). In the unfamiliar territory of the classroom, the Indian children do not take the initiative as speakers as often as others, they do not interrupt others to 'get the floor' as much, and talk is more evenly distributed among Indian students regardless of apparent academic ability. All of these attributes match the patterned norms of communication that Philips also reports among the *adult* Warm Springs Indian communities.

Philips relates her conclusions to studies of other minorities in the United States, such as African Americans and Hispanics, who often seem disinclined to participate in official classroom interaction while still having great interest and competence in informal interactions with their peers. Teachers less often integrate the talk of children from these minority groups into the sequential structure of official classroom talk, and more often reprimand them for behaving inappropriately by not paying attention, by talking out of turn, or by failing to talk at the right time. Philips cites a 1973 government report that examines teacher interactions with Mexican American and Anglo-American children, which found that average Mexican American children spend much less time speaking in class than their peers from the dominant culture. While that report uses this evidence to argue for the existence of discrimination in the American classroom, Philips argues that 'even where teachers are well intentioned, the results are similar, because the minority students' efforts to communicate are often incomprehensible to the teacher and cannot be assimilated into the framework within which the teacher operates' (1983: 129). So while the students themselves are often marked down for not comprehending the messages of the school, it is the teachers who seem to be lacking in understanding. Indeed in Philips' study, an Anglo-American teacher describes the Indian children's approach to classroom participation as inconsistent. Rather than seeing them as the users of different language norms that they are, she sees them on occasions as disrespectful, misbehaved, and uninvolved.

I am dwelling on Philips' studies because they are seminal in this area. They are already familiar to many academic educationists, yet because they stood almost alone for so long and perhaps seemed idiosyncratic as a result, her findings have not permeated teacher knowledge systems to any great degree. However, Philips does relate her findings to other cultures, arguing that other minorities may be similarly misdefined as inadequate students through their use of different discourse norms. She cites African American students, who often interact with one another informally in loud voices and are disciplined accordingly as disruptive in conventional classrooms. This norm may develop because of everyday practice interacting in environments where there is a high noise level in their own communities; they may come to tolerate a higher noise level than other groups of children, but still manage to maintain communicative efficiency within their own group.

One of the characteristics of face-to-face interaction among adult Indians that Philips notes is that there is *more of it* than among Anglo-Americans. The Warm Springs Indians spend more time with others; they usually do things together, even doing things together that might require only a single person; talk is a common accompaniment to all work and recreational activities; and they rarely live alone. All of these features are common too in contemporary Maori communities in New Zealand and among those Koori people of Australia who maintain traditional ways of life. This richly interactive environment that they maintain is a manifestation of values steeped in ligatures of community, cooperation and collectivity. The traditional Koori group in their tribal lands, for example, often sit in close proximity to each other with many people interacting in an open space no larger than a large room in a Western house. The *marae* (meeting house and its surrounds) is the focus of Maori community life; on many occasions throughout the year, all the adults and children come together to talk, eat, and sleep in a communal environment. The constant socialization within that environment inevitably produces different norms of interaction among the children of these minority peoples, when compared with children raised in nuclear families who live in relative isolation from non-family members, and who are surrounded by diversions such as books and television that require little human interaction.

While this informal interaction is intense and continuous in many traditional cultures, few opportunities are accorded to individual children or young adults to give formal verbal presentations. This obviously affects the readiness of these young people to perform as individuals in Western oriented school contexts. When opportunities for verbal presentation do occur in the traditional community, as Philips observes, great stress is laid on economy of speech, on personal control, and on showing evidence that careful thought and planning have been given to what is discussed. So it is unusual for young adults to receive these opportunities. As in the Polynesian example cited at the beginning of this section, those who put themselves forward risk being viewed as pretentious and bold, and a diminished value is placed on their contributions. Rarely do people without ascribed status speak at ceremonies, or talk in a formal capacity on behalf of the group. Children do learn to participate singly in collective performances, but their efforts are part of the whole and are perceived as such. Like both the Koori and the Maori examples cited above, great cultural value is placed on not putting oneself above others. There is a link here with Philips' observation that even the presence of a single teacher, as the sole authority figure and regulator of talk in the classroom, is alien for Warm Springs children. They are not oriented towards a single adult authority in their community and are not accustomed to competing with one another for an adult's attention. Self-sufficiency and cooperativeness are expected from an early age.

All of these many values can translate in different ways into the language norms adopted by minority children in classrooms. Rather than behaving inappropriately in classrooms, by showing excessive 'shyness', 'reticence', 'slowness', 'non-inquisitiveness' or 'disruptiveness', the children are often acting in ways that they believe are very suitable in the circumstances.

Key Situations and School Interaction

As mentioned, the Athabaskan culture places high value on the integrity of individual world views. This value leads to language norms in the culture that favour interactions where extensive non-focused negotiations take place. Everyone can make a distinctive contribution to these negotiations about the way things are. This contrasts with the contexts of interaction that are created by teachers in conventional schooling: in classrooms there are many 'key situations' where that special Athabaskan value and its related language norms would be out of place. Scollon & Scollon (1981; 1984) note that the public school is a time-constrained, crowded, modernizing, bureaucratic institution. Through placing its central emphasis on literacy, the school creates key situations of situational focusing which contrast sharply with the non-focused situations that would suit members of the minority culture. In particular, Athabaskan children often face a paradox in acquiring literacy. Their own set of discourse patterns is very different from those needed for school literacy, so that in order to read and write, they cannot readily write 'as' Athabaskans about Athabaskan things. So in many key situations in the school, Athabaskan children have to give up their own sense of the situation and their right to negotiate, even though the fact that they possess this right has been communicated to them since infancy as a central value of their culture. Scollon & Scollon believe that Athabaskan children see this as a surrender of cultural identity and of their right to make their own sense of the world. In their turn, teachers of these children often regard them as incompetent, insecure, hostile, and lacking in understanding.

The idea of 'key situation' comes from Frederick Erickson (1975) and Gumperz (1976): while living in complex stratified societies there are certain key 'gatekeeping' encounters that are prerequisites for entering occupations, for admission to advanced educational agencies, and for receiving official services. Because of cultural differences in discourse styles and strategies, some are favoured in these key settings while others are denied the same ready access to social opportunities. A close parallel exists here with Bourdieu's idea of cultural capital: some social groups bring a different form of linguistic capital which is not highly valued in those key situations and this disadvantages them. Formal educational settings are rich in key situations of this kind. Children have to display their knowledge in many communicative settings and they are evaluated on the basis of that display. Studies in the ethnography of communication try to identify these key situations; they observe participant structures within speech events; and they offer hypotheses about ethnic or subgroup differences in discourse style that over time can lead to adverse educational outcomes.

Storytelling

Researchers have given extended attention to several key situations for formal language use. They have found that participation in structured activities, such as 'sharing time' and 'storytelling', requires both linguistic and pragmatic knowledge. While linguistic knowledge is recognizable in surface level features of language such as vocabulary and syntax, teachers often assume that children share the appropriate pragmatic knowledge when they may not. For example, the point of the familiar Western fairy stories or moral tales, and the means by which that point is realised in language, may not seem obvious to children who are not reared on a regular diet of such stories. In much the same way, the point of minority culture stories can be lost on majority culture children. Again, the significant events in a child's day that he or she may want to present to other children in a 'sharing time' session, may receive very different expression. So while broad forms of social interaction need not vary from culture to culture, more precise and specific features of social interaction can be very different. As discussed already, this difference regularly leads to misunderstanding, misperception, and conflict, and some minority children seem to be more at risk than others in accommodating their linguistic and pragmatic groundrules to the school's demands.

Although storytelling is a basic narrative form, the usual surface structure features of the story can vary from culture to culture (Taylor & Matsuda, 1988). For example, what a storyteller's audience considers a proper norm for interaction can vary. In some cultures, audience participation is expected and necessary; in others, less or no involvement is the norm. The degree to which a culture is oral or literate in its orientation to the world seems to signal differences in narrative approaches. While everyone, given adequate exposure to that mode of language use, can adapt his or her language use to perform at any point on an oral or literate continuum, people's cultural values and socialization will influence their decisions about which orientation is a preferable and comfortable way of interacting with the world. Polynesian children, for instance, may tell stories that bring other children in the classroom right into the events of the story as participants; they may even hand the narration of the story over to these others for a time. This can be threatening to culturally different teachers and pupils. Discrimination in the classroom can arise when a culturally different child uses an orientation to narrative use which the teacher dislikes or which confuses other children.

Very young children, of course, are not free agents in choosing their narrative styles. There is no single way to tell stories and we begin with the rules for storytelling that our unique socialization provides: the environment outside the school determines to a large extent the things that children are prepared to do inside the school. Rich exposure to books and literacy in early childhood seems to dispose many Western children towards using narrative modes that are more like the ones that are valued in the school. Jerome Bruner's views on this point are echoed by others: 'The focused activity of book reading — even in relatively limited amounts and without the development of complex interactional scaffolding — provides a "playful setting" in which children learn to use language in "daring" and "advanced" ways' (Heath & Branscombe, 1986: 32). Shirley Heath and her colleague discuss the difference between books on the one hand, and comics, television, or routine conversation on the other. Books force adults and children to focus on saying what things are and what they mean, thus developing skills that are critical for meeting the demands of schooling. This does not mean that children with less exposure to books outside school are less ready to use narratives than other children; however, the narrative forms that they do use may be very different from the narratives used by children who are exposed to book reading. Along a continuum of narrative types, each social or cultural group may select only a few combinations from the range of possibilities available. For instance, Heath & Branscombe identify four broad categories of narrative — recounts, accounts, eventcasts and stories. Within each of these there are variations whose selection is affected by power relations, by context, and by the rules for narrative that are favoured in the culture. For example, in some cultures the narration of stories is an adult function dignified by its association with the role of an elder in the community; children may hear many stories but never narrate them themselves nor develop skill in doing so.

'Sharing time'

Differences in discourse norms that second language minority culture children bring to schools are often similar in effect to discourse differences brought to school by children from minority social groups, who speak a non-standard variety of the majority language. For example, many studies examine the contrasting discourse norms that African American children manifest in school and community (e.g. Heath, 1982; Smitherman, 1977; and Michaels, 1981: see Chapter 5). Sarah Michaels examines the key classroom activity of 'sharing time'. Philips (1983) also refers to this, under the heading of 'show and tell', a participant structure that teachers are rarely able to use with Warm Springs Indian children since the minority children are reluctant to participate fully in the activity, even when they reach the senior years of schooling. Consistent with earlier studies, Michaels reports that the African American children in her research, especially the girls, use a 'topic associating' or episodic style, in which a series of personal anecdotes makes up the discourse, often linked only by 'and'. The point or theme of these strings is not made explicit to the listener; and its relevance to the teacher's understanding of the topic often seems obscure, since it has no end, no middle, or any clear beginning. However, further analysis by Michaels shows that the same contributions are coherent and thematically focused. She argues that this kind of discourse has other attributes which give it independent narrative status: it is rhythmically chunked, with pauses, holding pitches, and vowel elongation between anecdotes; and it is not prosodically marked with sharp rising and falling contours. Cross-cultural misunderstanding is often linked to differences between groups in prosodic conventions. Gumperz (1982) lists features like intonation, pitch, and tempo which provide contextual clues that are especially helpful in comprehension and in discerning breaks and turn-taking points in spoken exchanges.

The teacher in Michaels' study is much more successful in working with other American children who use a topic centred style. The shared sense of topic and a synchronization of exchanges enables the teacher and students to collaborate in producing a coherent account, even of a complex event. The teacher provides an 'adult-like' model of literate discourse through her questions, encouraging precision, clarity, and explicitness in an oral preparation for literacy. In contrast, with the African American children, the teacher seems to have trouble seeing the point and predicting the speaker's direction; she mistimes questions and makes thematically inappropriate interruptions which disorient the children's flow of words and their train of thought. More specifically, the teacher asks that their contributions be 'important' and insists that they deal with 'one thing only'. In response to the first requirement, one child replies: 'I don't know if it is [important] or not but I want to say it anyway' (Michaels & Collins, 1984: 226). Other children also express their frustration with the teacher's demands.

Michaels & Cazden (1986) replicate and extend Michaels' research into this key situation of 'sharing time'. They believe that a study of this one activity provides a window into the larger problem of equity in education, since in many classrooms teachers approach sharing time as an oral preparation for literacy and some children get more practice and informal instruction through sharing time than others. In these replication studies, Michaels & Cazden deliberately sought out highly esteemed teachers, expecting that there would be contrasts with the earlier findings. However, they too find that children's narratives which favour a topic-associating or episodic style are perceived more negatively than narratives that are topic-centred, and they find that the former are more often used by African American children, particularly the girls, in every classroom studied. Teacher responses to these narrative styles are similar to those in the earlier study and are based on adult notions of literate discourse. Teachers tacitly assume that the children understand how to give their account in such a way as to match the quite inexplicit model that is in each teacher's mind. Moreover Cazden (1988) reports that graduate teachers in the United States who are not from the minority group, and educationists in New Zealand, are more likely to perceive the episodic accounts negatively and to erect upon them pessimistic expectations about the children themselves than are African American graduates. Michaels also finds that an African American teacher's aide is more helpful in rounding out and organizing the topic associating children's accounts. Since they find that even excellent teachers have difficulties collaborating with African American children in their classrooms, Michaels & Cazden conclude that the problems are not due to teacher incompetence or lack of good will. They cite other research (Heath, 1982; Smitherman, 1977) confirming that African American children frequently produce narratives that are stylistically different from those of majority group children and from the norm that is valued in the mainstream classroom. They wonder what other classroom speech events might provide similar problems in establishing collaboration between teachers and minority students.

Again, Frederick Erickson's study (1984) of African American discourse structures also reveals a system far removed from the literate style of linear sequencing that is valued in educated discourse. Instead the logic and systematic coherence is organized by audience/speaker interaction and by the consistent application of public aesthetic criteria for persuasion, often based on prosodic devices. It seems that the minority culture students are disadvantaged by their distance from the accepted norm at two points: in the sharing time activity itself, where they do not use the discourse style favoured by teachers and are criticized for this; and later in their literacy-related work, where the same children rely on these prosody cues as cohesive devices and are less likely to provide the explicit lexical and syntactic connections needed in writing.

Group reading narration

Other researchers study the socialization of Polynesian children at home and the lives of the same children at school in Hawaii (Vogt, Jordan &

Tharp, 1987). Native Hawaiian children who are not middle class and not acculturated into the majority culture, do not do very well in Hawaiian schools. The research looks for generalizable adaptations in early childhood classrooms that could suggest better instructional practices, better methods of classroom organization, and better techniques for providing motivation. It reports several successful strategies that seem compatible with the children's lived culture outside the school. For example, the researchers relax the usual stress on very high rates of teacher praise to individuals, replacing it with more indirect methods of praise or with praise directed at the group as a whole; they give a greater emphasis to the search for meaning in comprehension lessons, in preference to drilling in skills; and they introduce vertical grouping of children to create settings where the more advanced are able to assist less advanced students.

These researchers focus on one key situation: an approach to work in group reading narration which matches a communication strategy known in the Hawaiian community as 'talk story' (Au, 1978; Watson, 1975). This narrative form has some distinctive characteristics: contrapuntal and overlapping speech; voluntary turn-taking used as a major structuring device, often carried over from one setting to another; co-narration in a form similar to responsive reading; and joint construction of the story using a speech contour which resembles chanting. By structuring reading lessons in this way for periods of two or more years, lasting reading achievement scores result even when the minority children join majority culture reading programmes (Au, 1978). This improvement is thought to occur because the innovation is more consistent with communicative contexts created by Polynesian adults for their children, where there is less direct parental intervention and where children learn in groups which only rarely provide positive reinforcement for individuals. In the Hawaiian research, this innovation replaces the regular pattern for reading group teaching which was based on the teacher isolating individual students (Vogt, Jordan & Tharp, 1987). Students seem to be liberated by these changes; they begin to contribute freely in a speech style that is familiar to them. Teachers in turn begin to adapt their own responses to the more natural styles manifested by the children. These changes in the classroom encourage teachers to perceive the minority children differently. They abandon certain stereotypes held about the children, no longer seeing them as lacking motivation or as hard to manage. These new participation structures become formal class techniques as part of the regular language curriculum.

The researchers go on to implement the same innovative Hawaiian programme in a collaborative project working with Navajo children at Rough Rock in the United States (Vogt, Jordan & Tharp, 1987; Cazden, 1988). But in this replication study there are only mixed results. Vertical grouping promotes little peer tutoring at first among the Navajo children, but among smaller groups of the same sex it is more successful, and this is consistent with the separation of the sexes that is common in Navajo culture. Like their Hawaiian peers, Navajo children seem comfortable when responding to questions directed to the group, but they seem uncomfortable in chopping a story into small segments. Instead, they prefer a holistic approach to stories as complete units, which is consistent with the holistic approach to problem solving that the Navajo favour. The Navajo children also speak longer, volunteering questions as well as opinions that are not linked as much to other contributions but which are more complex and fully developed. The differences between the Polynesian and the Navajo cultures in their norms for learning and language, seem to affect successful implementation in different ways. While the Hawaiian programme is educationally effective for the children of the Polynesian culture, it is not completely so for the Navajo. The not too surprising lesson here is that differences in discourse norms between different minority cultures can be as great or greater than those that distinguish any single minority culture's norms from those that are favoured in the majority culture.

Cazden remarks that the cultural contrasts between the Hawaiian and the Navajo may be extreme. On this point, observing that the Navajo culture is historically related to the Athabaskan culture of sub-Arctic America, Scollon & Scollon draw attention to a unique and significant similarity between children from these two cultures in their scores on reading miscue retellings: the scores for both groups become poorer the older the children become. The researchers interpret this coincidence in scores as evidence that the two cultures share a similar value that respects individual differences in world view and which is manifested in non-focused patterns of interaction that show up in their similar language norms for miscue retellings.

The Effect of Classroom Context and Teacher Practices

The evidence from Cherokee, Sioux, Warm Springs, Athabaskan, Odawa and Hawaiian children (Au, 1978; Philips, 1983) suggests that the relative lack of responsiveness of all these children in classrooms is highly context specific; it appears in key situations. For example, all these groups of minority children respond less well in certain activities: when they are singled out as individuals before the group in a formal context; when they have to raise their hands to indicate willingness to answer; and when their personal responses are assessed publicly. Similar responses are reported from children disadvantaged by poverty or whose minority group is discriminated against on the basis of skin colour. However, among children from ancestral minority cultures such as the Navajo and Maori, the pattern seems a common one. It derives not from some psychological reticence or shyness displayed in institutional contexts in the presence of people from a dominant culture, but from broadly different patterns of childrearing and socialization that seem to produce discourse norms that are inconsistent in certain settings with the practices of formal schooling. Indeed, it is very easy to find evidence that shyness and reticence in the presence of majority culture people is by no means a ubiquitous feature of Indian and Polynesian children's behaviour.

For example, Philips reports greater competence among the same Indian students in maintaining interaction over longer periods with larger culturally-mixed groups of children. This occurs without the teacher's supervision both in formal project group work and in informal playground interaction, and reflects the great deal of practice that they receive in their own communities interacting without the help or hindrance of a dominant individual. In New Zealand playgrounds and communities, I have observed Maori boys interacting with their European friends and regularly taking the lead in informal language activities. They display a command of discourse styles that is obviously effective in those informal settings; they are often better at attracting attention to their utterances, in focusing interest on their topic, and in responding to interruptions. The model for this language role may be the formal one that they encounter when witnessing community ceremonies from their earliest years. Although it is a male model, it is gradually extending to females as well as the leadership roles on Maori formal occasions become a little more shared. Yet the same children are often rather silent in formal classroom interactions with teachers. This silence seems to express complex Polynesian cultural values which are nowhere more evident than in whole class teacher–pupil interactions and which remain influential in later childhood and in settings far removed from the speaker's cultural home.

Alison Jones (1987) reports a study of fifteen year olds in mixed ability classes in a New Zealand girls secondary school. Pacific Island students born in New Zealand speak and are spoken to much less in these classes than their European classmates; they avoid eye contact with the teacher; they decline to speak up; and they mutter more often. They explain their reluctance to engage in the verbal competition of whole class interactions as due to their fear of being singled out. They mention the cultural value of *ma* (shame) and their dislike of becoming the centre of attention. In turn, the teachers react by becoming sensitive to the discomfort their questioning causes. While they reduce the public demands that they make on the minority children, they do not substitute alternative pedagogies to encourage differential treatment. As a result in a complicated way, schooling simultaneously rewards European cultural norms for discourse use and learning, so as to reproduce successful patterns in those students who have the disposition and the capital to receive them; but 'conversely, the school is active in penalising the cultural patterns of communication of the Pacific Island girls, at the same time reproducing those very patterns it penalises' (p. 151). The actual practices of teachers seem to be both the source of the problem and the means for removing it.

Some evidence with new entrant children in New Zealand suggests that there is psychological reluctance and inability on the part of teachers and perhaps on the part of the minority pupils themselves, to promote extended interactions, even when the same teachers do have much more extended interactions with other children (Cazden, 1990). There are indications elsewhere that it is mainly a failure on the teachers' part to create appropriate discourse conditions that produces these contrasts in interaction. In their study of Panjabi new entrant children in Britain, Netta Biggs and Viv Edwards (1991) report that while there are no differences in the patterns of interaction initiated by culturally different children themselves with their teachers, there are significant differences in the patterns of interaction initiated by teachers. For example, the Panjabi children seek the teachers' advice and assistance in much the same way as other children, but the teachers spend less quality time interacting with the minority children. The researchers argue that because different amounts of time and different kinds of teacher interaction are associated with different groups of children, then the reluctance must lie with the teacher. Indeed, if we generalize the effect of this reluctance on the teachers' part to the whole school day, or to schooling as a whole or to other school systems, we see a greatly diminished engagement by certain groups of minority children with the subject matter of the curriculum, and with school learning itself. Cazden (1990) reports that by missing four teaching opportunities each per school morning, New Zealand new entrant Maori pupils may miss out on as many as 300 teaching interactions over a school term.

Changes in Educational Practice

In studies of bilingual classrooms for minority pupils in the USA, the only accommodation that seems to be made by teachers to the cultural difference of the children is the use of the children's native language for some of the instruction (Iglesias, 1985). In summary, the same research concludes that none of the recommendations put forward by sociolinguists for matching participation styles with appropriate cultural structures and styles are actually put into practice (for example, recommendations made by Au & Jordan, 1981, and Heath, 1983). Likewise, Cazden (1990) reports a reluctance by teachers in New Zealand to assimilate into their pedagogical approaches with Maori children the applied findings of research. For all these groups of minority children and doubtless for the many others like them whose circumstances may not be the subject of research, there seems to be a cultural discontinuity in norms for language use between the home and the school that goes beyond the major discontinuities that children from minority social groups often experience (see Chapter 5). Wrongly perhaps with many culturally different children, this discontinuity is often put down to language differences alone. But the factors discussed in this chapter are not simply linguistic issues that can be dealt with by topping up children's knowledge about the interaction styles used by majority language speakers. These are clearly language-related factors, but they are due to structural variations in cultural values that often show up in the different conventions for discourse that operate across different cultures. Since differing cultural values and interests come into play in all the matters treated here, important matters of social justice are also at stake. Indeed in discussing the Hawaiian studies, Kathryn Au and Jane Mason (1983) talk about the need to achieve 'a balance of rights' in participation structures to facilitate academic learning by culturally different children.

As argued, the members of a culture share an understanding of the culture's own norms for participant interaction and these norms are expressions of the culture's values. They provide informal rules that may not be explicitly known by the members of a culture but which govern speaking, listening and turn-taking behaviours. Au & Mason argue that interactants have certain reciprocal communication rights on the basis of these rules. When a classroom's participant structures are congruent with the rights recognized in the children's home culture, then a balance of rights obtains. When there is little sharing of control over significant areas of interaction because the teacher sets rules for turn-taking or other aspects of participation which make the children feel that they have little control over the interaction, there is an imbalance of rights. On justice grounds alone, this is an unwanted exercise of power. But as Au & Mason argue, a lesson that is culturally incongruent in the participation structures it uses causes students to react in ways that seriously interfere with academic goals. Kathryn Au gives the example of seven-year-old Hawaiian students, for whom the balance of rights seems to depend on the teacher controlling either the topic itself or the role and number of student speakers, but not both. When this balance of rights is achieved, much higher levels of productive student behaviour result.

As a partial explanation for the New Zealand findings that she reports, Cazden suggests that the type of individualized instruction that is used in New Zealand schools may itself contribute to differential treatment. The form of individualization may fail to take advantage of the abilities or interactional preferences of Polynesian children. She adds however that 'each intersection of philosophy and social organization is presumably vulnerable to particular forms of differential treatment' (1990: 298). The main point that comes from the research to date is that there needs to be a measure of compatibility between children's home cultural values and the pedagogical styles and organizational arrangements adopted in schools. I suspect that in linking cultural values with language norms and school practices, we may discover classroom discourse incompatibilities that are beyond the present resources of Western schools and teachers to overcome without major policy changes involving careful modifications in pedagogy, changes in school organization, and a more serious professional engagement with minority cultural knowledge. Chapter 7 takes up these points.

Note to Chapter 3

1. One important feature of Milingimbi yolngu discourse norms is that for them it is socially acceptable to ignore questions. Michael Christie (1985) also reports that this tribal group of Australians rarely use hypothetical questions to clarify and explain in the way that Westerners do; they find it confusing to answer teacher questions when they sense that the teacher already knows the answers.

4 Bilingual Education, Social Justice and Power

Perhaps the most critical policy decision to be made in any school system is the choice of the language that is to be used as the medium of instruction for children. In 1951, a UNESCO 'committee of experts' ruled that 'it is axiomatic that the best medium for teaching a child' is the child's mother tongue (UNESCO, 1953: 11). The committee claimed that this was the case on psychological, sociological and educational grounds. In this chapter I examine the justice and the accuracy of this claim. I also look at several specific justice-related issues in the bilingual education policy area. As recently as the early 1980s hard evidence for or against the above UNESCO claim had not appeared. Part of the reason for this was the difficulty of devising true experimental conditions for comparing (minority) mother tongue schooling with schooling for minority mother tongue children conducted in the majority language. Controlling other variables while excluding the Hawthorne Effect and other intruding factors, proved too difficult for any of the many early studies. From the lack of firm evidence many were ready to conclude that minority mother tongue medium instruction might not really be a substantial pedagogical advantage to children (Fasold, 1984).

In the absence of this firm evidence, the conventional policy in education for dealing with speakers of minority languages has been to ignore the minority language and to replace it with the language of education. Often educational authorities have gone beyond simply ignoring the minority language and there are many documented accounts of injustices regularly inflicted upon linguistic minorities in an attempt to eradicate their languages through schooling. Many of these accounts are quite recent and they make harrowing reading (Skutnabb-Kangas, 1981; Baker, 1988; Skutnabb-Kangas & Cummins, 1988; Tollefson, 1991; Romaine, 1989; 1991). Contemporary school policymakers could claim that these injustices of the past no longer have any currency. However, when a language spoken by a minority is not used in schooling, either as a means of instruction or as a curriculum subject, then it is clear to all concerned that that language is not valued in

71

the school. Moreover if everything that is valued in schooling can be linked to the dominant language, and if this link is legitimated in the discourses of power that operate in the school, then those past unjust policies of eradication continue in a tacit but recognizable form.

Following on from the accounts of power and social justice presented in Chapters 1 and 2, my concern in this chapter is to recommend directions that policy makers in education might take either to eliminate these continuing injustices or at least to soften their effects. I will argue that an educational system serving a multilingual society but providing only monolingual schooling exercises power unjustly, or is being used to exercise power unjustly. It is true that the degree of that injustice will vary in line with the Kantian principle that 'ought implies can'; that is to say, schools cannot be held to account for their actions or inactions if they lack the power to act in any other way. But this is only a technical defence for schools themselves and it cannot be used to defend the inactions of those who do have power to change things. In urging the latter to take policy action that redresses injustice and in line with my argument so far in this book, there are three broad social justice components that are missing from a monolingual system of schooling serving a multilingual society. Firstly following Bourdieu, the schools in that system unjustly require all children to possess the dominant language as cultural capital but fail to guarantee that children can acquire that language to an equal degree. Secondly following Habermas, the system makes no compromise in respect to the acquired cultural group interest that the minority language represents. As argued in Chapter 2, in order to support the individual's language rights the group's language must be supported at the same time. Finally following Bhaskar, an unwanted form of determination is at work in the system since it participates in tacitly suppressing a minority language without consulting the interests expressed by its speakers. As argued in Chapter 1, this unwanted policy needs to be identified and following consultation replaced by the wanted practices that a just language policy would offer.

The General Social Justice Issue in Bilingual Education

Although relatively few children arrive in the world's schools with only a background in the majority language that is used in their society, it would be wrong to conclude from this that 'balanced' bilingualism is common around the world. Most bilingual speakers are able to use the weaker of their languages to serve only limited functions, often to do with specialized activities of commerce, education, or work. Balanced bilinguals who are able to operate with ease in both languages in all everyday settings, are relatively exceptional. Complementing this situation, quality bilingual schooling is a recent phenomenon which even now is in its early stages of evolution. Bilingual education programmes are developing rapidly in pluralist nation states and they can serve very different national needs: as a step in moving towards a single or several national languages; as an instrument in developing ideological solidarity; as a way of making national contact with a world language; and as a way of extending language rights and social justice to minorities. A helpful definition of bilingual education contrasts it with second language learning: 'Bilingual education is distinguished from foreign or second language education, including the study of community languages, in that bilingual education is the use of a non-dominant language as the medium of instruction during some part of the school day' (Nemetz Robinson, 1978: 8).

In this opening section I address the general policy issue that pluralist countries need to resolve in providing bilingual education: What place should minority languages have in schools if language education policies are to be based on principles of social justice? Later sections address specific social justice and pedagogical issues in bilingual education that logically follow discussion and conclusions in this first section.

Language minorities

Language policies are now receiving world-wide attention because of the great population shifts that occurred over the last two or three generations. These shifts highlight language issues that were formerly unnoticed, even in those countries where there were always significant language minorities. Reporting from his studies of OECD countries, Stacy Churchill (1986) sees major changes occurring everywhere in national attitudes to minorities. He sees the most potent factor in this move to be the recent development of an international climate of opinion favouring the more open and tolerant treatment of minorities. He uses his own country as a case study on this point: improvements in the treatment of the Francophone minority in Canada can be linked with changes in the structures of social life brought about by increased prosperity and by urbanization.

Broadly speaking in modern societies there are three main types of language minorities: ancestral peoples; 'established' minorities; and 'new' minorities. The first of these, the ancestral peoples, includes those groups long-established in their native countries such as the Sami (Lapps), the Maori, the Inuit, American Indians and Koori or Aboriginal Australians. Increasingly in places where ancestral minority peoples are to be found, racist attitudes are becoming socially unacceptable and people of mixed ancestry are identifying more readily with the ancestral minority than once was the case. In Tasmania, for example, whose ancestral people all but disappeared a century ago following a clumsy policy of protection that was tantamount to genocide (Chalk & Jonassohn, 1990), a vigorous minority action group has surfaced which takes its lead from larger minority groups elsewhere, like the New Zealand Maori whose vigorous presence as a cultural force has never been in doubt.

Examples of 'established' minorities are the Catalans in Spain, the Acadian French in North America, the Bretons in France, or the Canadian Francophones in Ontario who are also a majority in Quebec where the Canadian Anglophones are an established minority. 'New' minorities are more recent arrivals, including those who are immigrants in the legal sense; refugees such as the boat people fleeing from Indo-Chinese countries; foreign workers living semi-permanently in their new home; and expatriates serving in countries that are tied in a loose community with one another such as the British Commonwealth, the Nordic States or the European Community.

Classifying Minority Language Policies in Education

There are many possible ways of comparing and evaluating the treatment that minorities receive from country to country in respect to their languages. The authorities cited throughout this chapter offer many classificatory schemes that are useful in certain contexts of debate. One method of comparison and evaluation is to rank the official policy responses to the issues of minority language rights which are made at national and regional level. Stacy Churchill (1986) locates OECD countries at various points on an ascending ladder of Stages. His ranking depends on each country's policy response in recognizing minority group language problems and on their success in implementing educational policies to meet those problems. The most primitive level of development is when a nation simply ignores the existence of special educational problems for language minority groups. Although most countries were located at this pre-*Stage 1* level in their very recent past, according to Churchill all OECD countries now have some policies reflecting at least *Stage 1* or *Stage 2* in the list below.

Stage 1 (Learning Deficit): sees minority groups as simply lacking the majority language. The typical policy response is to provide supplementary teaching in the majority tongue (e.g. ESL) with a rapid transition expected to use of the majority language.

Stage 2 (Socially-Linked Learning Deficit): sees a minority group's deficit as being linked to family status. An additional policy response is to provide special measures to help minority peoples to adjust to the majority society, such as aids, tutors, psychologists, social workers, career advisers etc. in concert with majority language teaching.

Stage 3 (Learning Deficit from Social/Cultural Differences): sees a minority group's deficit linked to disparities in esteem between the group's culture and the majority culture. Additional policy responses are to include multicultural teaching programmes for all children in order to sensitize teachers and others to minority needs, and to revise textbooks and teaching practices to eliminate racial stereotyping.

Stage 4 (Learning Deficit from Mother Tongue Deprivation): sees the premature loss of the minority tongue as inhibiting transition to learning the majority tongue because of cognitive and affective deprivations. An additional policy response is to provide some transitional study of minority languages in schools, perhaps as a very early or occasional medium of instruction.

Stage 5 (Private Use Language Maintenance): sees the minority group's language threatened with extinction if it is not supported. The policy response is to provide the minority language as a medium of instruction, mainly in the early years of schooling.

Stage 6 (Language Equality): sees the minority and majority languages as having equal rights in society, with special support available for the less viable languages. Policy responses include recognizing a minority language as an official language, providing separate educational institutions for language groups, offering opportunities for all children to learn both languages, and extending further support beyond educational systems.

Examples of the six stages

According to Churchill's case studies, only the very old bilingual or multilingual OECD states (Belgium, Finland and Switzerland) have reached *Stage 6*. There is some ambiguity in other countries, notably in Canada where policies differ across provincial boundaries and where responses to the Francophone minority can vary from *Stage 6* down to *Stage 2* level. Sweden provides the only *Stage 5* enrichment programme in the world for its Finnish immigrant labour force (Skutnabb-Kangas, 1988), although in Sweden educational practice in some places may be lagging well behind educational policy. In other respects it may still be at a *Stage 4* level. In New Zealand, the Maori Language Act of 1987 declared Maori to be an official language of the country and anyone now has the right to speak in Maori in legal proceedings. Largely because of the efforts of the Maori people themselves, New Zealand has begun to move towards the enrichment *Stage 5* and perhaps ultimately to *Stage 6*, at least in relation to its Maori minority. However in relation to its very large Pacific Island and other smaller minorities it is still located variously at *Stage 1*, *Stage 2* or *Stage 3*.

The USA's Bilingual Education Act locates that country officially at a *Stage 4* level, although the responses of many schools and school systems themselves seem to be at a much lower stage. That Act deals with 'limited English proficient' students of three types: persons born outside the United States or persons whose native language is not English; persons in whose environment a non-English language is dominant; and American Indians and Alaskan Natives in whose environment a non-English language has significantly affected their proficiency in English. These three categories are similar to the three types of linguistic minorities mentioned above. In dealing with these three types of students, the major goal of all school districts surveyed by Anna Chamot (1988) has been to develop students' English proficiency so that they can participate successfully in all-English instruction. Nearly all districts report that their goal is the development of the academic skills needed for school achievement, while only a small minority of schools indicate that the development or maintenance of the students' first language is a goal. One reason for the transition-to-English policies has been the belief that they would provide bilingual children with equal access to the educational system and give them achievement scores equal to monolingual children. Achievement score disparities have not been removed however (Philips, 1983).

In practice then the USA is located at *Stage 1* or *Stage 2*. There may be obstacles to producing much advance on this, given the fact that English has been repeatedly fostered there to create an 'American ethnicity' (Fishman, 1967; Romaine, 1991), even though there have always been high concentrations of people using languages other than English to conduct their affairs: Spanish in the South West, in Puerto Rico and in New York; French in some parts of Louisiana and Maine; German in Pennsylvania and Ohio. USA Census figures reveal more than 65 languages spoken, in addition to the many ancestral tongues, yet although a presidential commission has created a National Council on Foreign Language Teaching and International Studies, the image of a rigorous monolingualism is still promoted in the USA. But much the same was said of Australia before the 1970s and the changes that have occurred there in the last generation offer some hope of development in rigorously monolingual societies elsewhere.

Its major Celtic areas apart, Britain has much in common with the United States in its policies. Britain is at *Stage 3* in the attitudes to multiculturalism that curriculum specialists advocate but it is only at *Stage 1* in its treatment of new settler minority language users. Arturo Tosi (1988) finds it paradoxical that bilingualism is discussed in British schools and colleges as a subject of multicultural interest yet is still regarded as educationally undesirable. The Swann Report (DES, 1985) rejects bilingual education or mother tongue maintenance at an official school level. Instead schools are urged to teach community languages where possible as subjects in the wider curriculum and equal in status to foreign languages; schools are also urged to allow communities to use schools as a resource for the transmission of community languages. At least 28 different languages are being taught in over 500 community language schools. Local Education Authorities differ in their policies, with some stressing transition to English and others allowing for some pluralism. Euan Reid (1988) reports that local authorities have begun the practice of mainstreaming minority language students, using ESL teachers in support roles focusing on the standard curriculum.

New settler community languages in Britain do receive some recognition but only in the very early stages of schooling to ease transition to English. True bilingual education has no status; nor is there official recognition of the cultural resource represented by large numbers of speakers of non-indigenous languages. Ancestral minorities are much better provided for in Britain than new settler groups, but these provisions have been won after a long struggle by the speakers themselves. In the 1991 UK Census, 18.7% of people in Wales regarded themselves as Welsh-speaking and this resource has led to major bilingual programmes. There is also an increase in the number of young people identifying with Welsh. In Scotland, less than 2% of the population speak Gaelic and bilingual education is underdeveloped in comparison to Wales (OPCS, 1992). In Ireland, as in Wales, the language rights of the Celtic community are guaranteed and extensive research has been carried out to remove inequalities at the school level (Baker, 1988). Ireland is at *Stage 5* or *Stage 6*.

Australia, as its 'National Policy on Languages' recognizes, is located at several Stages of development at once. On the evidence of the treatment of many users of Aboriginal languages and some community language users, Australia is at *Stage 4* or *Stage 5*. However policies of multiculturalism in some Australian states as a response to the needs of other minority groups fit the *Stage 3* pattern. I return to the Australian example below.

Social justice bases for the six stages

Stages 1 to *4* are all based on the premise that the minority should seek the same social outcomes and educational objectives as the majority. *Stages 1* and *2* are clearly assimilative in that the tacit aim of the policies is the short to medium term loss by the child of the minority language and the minority culture. Clearly these policies are unjust since the minimal language rights of individuals are not guaranteed and minority children are expected to perform equally well in an educational setting without the linguistic wherewithal necessary for competing on an equal footing. Although the policies of *Stage 1* and *Stage 2* could be justified by selective reference to the pre-1960s research evidence about the negative effects of being bilingual (see below), it is difficult to escape the conclusion that a form of disguised racism is working through these policies. I say 'disguised' since it is rarely the blatant racism that supported total policy inactivity in the past.

At the most primitive level of policy development, nations simply ignored the existence of special educational problems for language minority groups. Perhaps total inactivity at this pre-*Stage 1* level was influenced at times by misunderstandings and ignorance about the place of minority languages in the lives of their speakers. More often, however, policy inactivity was rationalized and supported by robust narratives of racism (see Chapter 1) that circulated unchecked in countries with minority communities. In New Zealand for example, this endemic racism directed towards the Maori minority can be traced back to many sources: ignorance and fear of a very different culture, which even today is little understood or valued by non-Maori people; habitual ideological opposition to a proud and once warlike people; ideological opposition to the revival of a long-term subject people who have been excluded from a voice in New Zealand's affairs for much of its history and who are now often blamed for their exclusion; and other vague fears that have their roots in prejudices that are particularly strong in an isolated country like New Zealand, as in many European countries and other places that were once the colonies of European countries.[1] Other narratives of racism with different roots but similar policy consequences, circulated in other places and they continue almost unchecked in some of them.

Stages 3 and *4* respond to more recent research evidence. *Stage 3* recognizes the unjust effect of not valuing the minority child's culture; it develops approaches for placing more value on that culture. *Stage 4* recognizes the cognitive and linguistic effects of not supporting the minority child's first language; it develops approaches for using that language in transition to the dominant language. But neither Stage offers a fully just response to the difficulties of minority language groups: firstly, neither stage recognizes the culturally acquired interests of minority peoples (cf. Habermas), since they do not consult minority preferences concerning the maintenance of their languages and concerning their use as media of instruction in schools. The need for transition to the majority tongue outweighs these other considerations. Secondly, neither stage gives recognition to the linguistic capital that minority children bring to schools (cf. Bourdieu), since its possession is awarded no intrinsic value: i.e. the child's minority language has only an instrumental value in *Stage 4* for learning the dominant language. Thirdly, the policies covered in both stages have the effect of suppressing minority languages; in most instances, policy makers would discover that this exercise of power is not wanted by the minorities themselves, if the reasons and the accounts of the people themselves were consulted.

The fact that most schools in most OECD countries are operating under policies that fall within *Stage 3* or *Stage 4* highlights the difficulties that school systems and schools themselves have in pursuing the alternatives offered by later stages. For example, Australia's language situation is very complex: it is a country where more than 100 community languages are in regular use, where 50 Aboriginal languages still survive, and where English is not the mother tongue of a very large minority of the population. In the face of this social and cultural complexity, Australian schools would be hard-pressed to maintain and develop the first languages of even a fraction of their minority pupils, since in Australia it is not customary for minority groups to congregate in single areas to quite the same degree as elsewhere and each school as a result may have a sprinkling of many different minority language speakers. So on the Kantian principle again ('ought implies can'), many schools in Australia and in other similarly pluralist places cannot in justice be held to account for not providing the enrichment policies entailed by higher stages. At the same time, there are many schools in Australia, especially those serving large remote Aboriginal communities and other closely knit minority groups, that do have a clear obligation to provide language maintenance and development. In a small number of Australian schools, bilingual methods are in use and 'the effect of these programmes has extended well beyond their still limited reach' so that bilingual education has become 'a serious proposal in policy discourse, raising often controversial questions of methodology and educational priority' (Ozolins, 1991: 338).

Stages 5 and *6* involve objectives and outcomes that differ from the earlier stages. These are of a relatively minor enrichment kind in *Stage 5* (enhanced private use of the minority language and the enhanced cultural esteem associated with it), and of a major kind in *Stage 6* (participation in a minority culture, which has equal status in the society with the majority culture, with the added possibility of biculturalism and bilingualism). Only in these later stages is there any necessary abandoning of the values of a strictly monolingual society; only in these later stages is there recognition of the value of 'additive bilingual education' in contrast to the routine eradication of the minority language that is a widely practised policy. In both stages, there is emphasis on modifying the school to suit the child, rather than modifying the child to suit the school. Some attempt is made in *Stage 5* to recognize the value of the minority child's linguistic capital; in *Stage 6*, that linguistic capital and the interests of the minority culture itself are given full recognition. The unwanted forms of policy determination that appear in *Stages 1 to 4*, would probably disappear from policies in *Stage 6* if the interests of the minority peoples themselves were consulted by policy makers.

We would look in vain for perfect examples of *Stage 6* policies in operation, outside the very old multilingual states mentioned above. However the educational provisions now evolving in New Zealand at least for the Maori minority, seem to go much of the way towards this end. In Chapter 7, I outline those developments in some detail since they provide a real world context for the argument that I have developed so far.

Specific Social Justice Issues in Bilingual Education

The many unresolved issues in contemporary bilingual education mean that there is a problem separating social justice issues that schools are obliged to address, from other more general questions that schools might reasonably attend to in pursuing general educational effectiveness. In the education of minorities, the basic social justice problem is to decide where and when we should provide a form of language learning and development that will protect the life chances of children who would otherwise have limited access to social contexts where their mother tongue is used. For those children, opportunities to master varieties, styles, registers and functions of their mother tongue may be too few to allow them to function as fully competent speakers of their first language. Consequently as outlined below, the same children will be placed at risk in learning and using the majority language and in their cognitive/academic activities generally. Much of what follows in this section attends to aspects of that basic problem.

Policies of transitional or maintenance bilingual education?

The bilingual education policy issue is complicated by sharp differences in the value placed on minority languages in the schooling process. The middle stages in the development of minority language policies regard the minority language as having mainly an instrumental value in learning the majority language; but later stages see it having value for its own sake as well. According to Wallace Lambert (1975), the aims of schooling in relation to bilingualism fall into two distinct categories: 'additive bilingualism' when a second language is acquired with the expectation that the mother tongue will continue to be used; and 'subtractive bilingualism' when a second language is learned with the expectation that it will replace the mother tongue (i.e. the minority language). The former is a 'maintenance' form of bilingual schooling, which sets out to use both languages as media of instruction for a reasonable amount of the child's school career. The latter is a 'transitional' form of bilingual schooling which only lasts for the early years of schooling, with the majority tongue taking over as the means of instruction after that.

In adjudicating between these two positions an important social justice issue is at stake, hinted at by Barbara Horvath (1980) when she says that the United States Office of Civil Rights supports the maintenance approach (which is consistent with seeing cultural groups forming a broad mosaic across the nation), while the United States Office of Education supports the transitional approach (which is consistent with seeing cultural groups eventually shedding their identity in the melting pot of the American nation). No doubt there are major financial considerations that inform the Office of Education's view. However for reasons of both pedagogy and justice, subtractive (transitional) bilingualism is not a policy that should be routinely favoured in contemporary schools in pluralist societies.

A radical change in attitude and approach in education to bilingualism has accompanied the recent growth in information about the links between language, culture, identity, thinking prowess, and educational success. In many places, the transitional bilingual education that early research supported has given way to enrichment and maintenance programmes. As new evidence accumulated, a near reversal occurred in beliefs about the effects of bilingualism on the individual. In the majority of the many early studies, the overwhelming trend identified in research was that being bilingual had negative consequences for the individual. Minority pupils' lower performance on verbal IQ tests, their poor academic performance in general, and their lack of adjustment in schooling were all linked in the research with their bilingualism. Some investigations even suggested that bilinguals were untrustworthy (Cummins, 1984).

In most of these early studies, variables other than the minority language itself were discounted. Little attention was paid to those other aspects of high status cultural capital that minority children often do not bring to school and which produce the inequalities in school performance that were measured but never explained by the tests of researchers.[2] As a result, wherever there was a problem with minorities, in line with the ideology of the time schools were licensed by the research to equip their minority students with the majority language as quickly as possible. In English-speaking countries, transitional ESL programmes became the standard solution to the minority language problem, if anything at all was done. For most of the twentieth century, even the most progressive educational systems have pursued this harmful policy. For example, the following observation comes from a Toronto study of the problems of new Canadians in schools in the 1960s and early 1970s: 'The implications of seeing the entire problem of immigrant adaptation as a language problem were that undue emphasis was laid on the teaching of the English language itself, with almost no appreciation of the cultural cost to the immigrant or to the greater Canadian society' (Masemann, 1984: 354). Also commenting on this study, Thomas Greenfield, an educational administration theorist, adds some insightful summarizing points. He argues that educational policymakers approach second language and cultural programmes 'technocratically, with little concern for what they are to do' as long as they can convince themselves 'that the programmes are "effective", acceptable to taxpayers, and good for children. Whether the programmes meet any of these criteria is seldom known, for they rarely receive searching analysis in terms of their relationship to the language and cultural questions which so obviously beset Canadian society' (1976: 112). Greenfield adds that ESL alone may be a less efficient method pedagogically than teaching in two languages (p. 118). A generation later, Canada is beginning to complement its official language policies with anti-racist ones to meet the interests of children from new, established and ancestral minorities (Ministry of Education and Training, 1993).

There is a transparent and taken-for-granted ideology at work in the early bilingual research studies from 1910 to 1960. Responding to robust narratives of racism and in order to remove the threat to social cohesion and national solidarity that widespread linguistic diversity was deemed to represent, efforts were made almost everywhere through schooling to replace minority languages with the dominant language or languages. Policymakers selectively preferred research evidence detailing the negative effects of bilingualism as justification for established practices; other research, such as that from George Sanchez (1934), became marginalized. Following Pierre Bourdieu's account, the victims were blamed for possessing linguistic capital that had low status in the setting of the school, and evidence was traduced to justify this act of symbolic violence. Although recent research no longer allows this ideology to be taken-for-granted, it is hardly absent from policymaking in education in contemporary times. For example in Britain, reactionary attempts are still made to understate social and cultural diversity and to keep schools at a distance from the issues.[3]

In the contemporary world, that ideology has lost its research justification. Since Elizabeth Peal and Wallace Lambert's study in 1962, powerful evidence has been accumulating to confirm a logical point that may not need empirical evidence: proficient bilingual children have much more exposure to using and manipulating language, and this inevitably translates into improved performances in most of the areas of activity where language and thought converge. Even physiological research now supports this claim: bilinguals are said to mature earlier than monolinguals both in the development of cerebral lateralization for language use and in acquiring skills for linguistic abstraction (Albert & Obler, 1979). On other grounds too, maintaining the minority mother tongue is said by many to develop a desirable form of cultural diversity in societies, to promote ethnic identity, to lead to social adaptability, to add to the psychological security of the child, and to develop linguistic awareness (Crystal, 1987).

While the bilingual research as a whole allows a favourable conclusion linking quality bilingual schooling with cognitive advantages for the learner, Colin Baker (1988) advises us not to overestimate these advantages, especially in relation to everyday mental functioning. However, there is certainly compelling evidence to suggest that bilinguals are superior to monolinguals on divergent thinking tests; bilinguals have some advantage in their analytical orientation to language; bilinguals also show some increased social sensitivity in situations requiring verbal communication; and bilinguals may have advantages in thinking clearly and in analytical functioning. Increasingly, maintenance bilingual education curricula are bearing out the promise extended by the research on bilingualism itself.

The Curriculum Evidence

There is much evidence from studies of programmes where majority language speakers have been taught using a minority language as the medium of instruction, but this is not relevant to the subject of this chapter: the bilingual education of minorities. Studies of bilingual schooling for majority language speakers, such as the Schools Council Bilingual Education Project in Wales and the St Lambert Project in Canada, are outside my scope here since the provision of bilingual schooling to first language speakers of a dominant language is not as high a priority on social justice grounds as the provision of bilingual schooling to minorities. Those in immersion programmes for children from majority language backgrounds usually live in communities where the idea of their contact with second language immersion curricula is supported, or at least tolerated. Parental approval of the programmes and their keen support of the children's development in both languages is an accepted part of the arrangements that schools make. So while this evidence offers very positive support to bilingual immersion policies, it is not really helpful here.

Maintenance bilingual programmes for minority language children are the subject of extensive studies in recent years, and the evidence comes from many places. In Holland, a bilingual maintenance approach to the education of minority children is favoured, not just for reasons of social justice and self-esteem, but because it proves as effective in promoting majority language learning as other assimilation and transition approaches, and even requires less time to be devoted to the teaching and learning of the majority tongue (Vallen & Stijnen, 1987). Other programmes in Leyden and Enschede for the primary age children of Turkish and Moroccan immigrant workers, suggest that minority language teaching for children from these backgrounds has no negative educational or social effects (Appel, 1988). In short, these Dutch maintenance programmes achieve only good results. Another review deals with programmes over the last twenty years in Mexico, the USA, Sweden, and Canada, where children began school speaking a minority language or dialect and where that language was used as the main or only medium of instruction. Later for all these children, there was a gradual transition to instruction in both the minority and the majority language. Academic progress achieved in each case was much better than in programmes where minority language children were taught entirely in the majority language. Student self-esteem, pride in their cultural background, and group solidarity also increased in each case (Moorfield, 1987). In other settings, where the needs for bilingualism and biliteracy are so obvious that the question of desirability is never even raised, initial and advanced literacy in two languages becomes possible and full bilingualism becomes a natural and necessary acquisition for all children (Garcia & Otheguy, 1987).

In the USA, a long-term comparison study examines three approaches to bilingual schooling for Hispanic children (Chamot, 1988):

(1) immersion strategy, in which content subjects are taught through simplified English;
(2) early-exit or short term transitional bilingual programmes of 2 to 3 years;
(3) late-exit or long-term transitional bilingual programmes of 5 to 6 years.

Researchers report that long term bilingual curriculum programmes are most effective in promoting progress in both Spanish and English, and that immersion programmes promote a greater use of English by students in school itself. Elsewhere in the United States, Spanish dominant children attending schools in California benefit both academically and in their English language acquisition by having their mother tongue used as the language of instruction in the early junior school years (Campos & Keatinge, 1988).

In Sweden, a policy of 'active bilingualism' has been the goal for immigrant pupils' language learning since 1975, and it has been a legal right since 1977. The official Swedish policy of 'freedom of choice' extended to its immigrants in their decisions about maintaining their own cultures and languages is consistent with the justice criteria derived from Bhaskar, Bourdieu and Habermas. It means in practice that every immigrant child, from any minority group which is large enough, must have the opportunity to attend a mother tongue medium class. Classes for the large Finnish minority in suburban Stockholm segregated into classes using Finnish as the medium of instruction, with Swedish taught as a second language, are among the longest established (Hagman & Lahdenperä, 1988). After nine years of operation, researchers base their conclusions on extensive comparisons with other Finnish children and with other immigrant groups who have not had a rich history of instruction in their mother tongues. By the end of their compulsory schooling, the segregated Finnish maintenance children have still managed to integrate themselves into their Swedish comprehensive school, while building up their academic self-confidence, identity, and their proficiency in Swedish. Moreover the students from the Finnish maintenance classes show much higher figures for entry into further education.

In Britain, the MOTET project in Bradford (Fitzpatrick, 1987) reports the effects of bilingual education in a one year experimental programme with infant children whose home language was Panjabi. The class programme aims to preserve a 'parity of esteem' between English and Panjabi by allotting equal time and space to each language across the curriculum. The study concludes that there are no negative effects from bilingual education. Instead, there are the positive effects of mother tongue maintenance, as well as a level of progress in English that is equivalent to a matched control group who have not received a bilingual programme.

Finally the special needs of the French Canadian minority provide a spur to research and to changes in practice in Anglophone areas of Canada, where more than 288,000 children were in French immersion classes in 1990 and 58% of the population endorsed the 'two official languages' policy.[4] Francophone minority children in Ontario schools who receive most of their education in French, tend to succeed much better in education and in the world of work than those submerged in English or in only nominally bilingual schools (Churchill, Frenette & Quazi, 1986). Jim Cummins and Merrill Swain (1986) provide a general guide to the research in bilingual education currently taking place in Canada. In doing so, the authors overturn many of the prejudiced views that are widely held about bilingualism and education:

- they show that the research base for bilingual education is sophisticated and growing;
- they offer strong evidence that quality bilingual programmes have been influential in developing language skills and in contributing to broader academic achievement;
- they deny the conventional view that immersion programmes can only be effective with the very young;

- they suggest that in some respects older learners have advantages over younger ones;
- they report evidence that lower ability children also benefit from immersion programmes;
- they conclude that a quality bilingual programme will support and aid development in the first language.

This international survey of curriculum research and the conclusions that follow from it, raise difficult issues that have profound justice implications for language policy making. In the following sections, I try to present and resolve those issues.

How much first language maintenance is needed?

Following ideas first expressed by the Finnish researchers, Pertti Toukomaa and Tove Skutnabb-Kangas, Jim Cummins and Merrill Swain (1986) put forward a 'threshold hypothesis': there may be threshold levels of language competence which bilingual children must attain in their first and second languages in order to avoid cognitive disadvantages and to allow the potentially beneficial aspects of becoming bilingual to influence cognitive functioning. While the researchers cannot define threshold levels in absolute terms, since these will vary as the cognitive levels of children and the academic demands of the school vary, this hypothesis explains many different phenomena. At the same time, it still needs strong empirical support, especially at the level of language itself. Jim Cummins, for example, assumes that language proficiency is an important mediating variable between bilingualism and education, but some criticize him for not saying much about the specific linguistic advantages that being bilingual brings: such as the preconditions for literacy in speech, as distinct from the more obvious educational advantages that he spells out rather vaguely as 'literacy related skills'. In her critique of the threshold hypothesis, Suzanne Romaine (1989) warns against a compartmentalizing of language skills removed from other knowledge-related factors. I believe that research has not yet broached the major epistemic questions about the two cultural worlds to which bilinguals have access, and the effect of this access on their linguistic and intellectual development. It may turn out that young bilingual children bring intellectual skills to school that are not recognized or used in the curriculum only because the present excessively structured and normative view of child development insists that the onset of those sophisticated skills occurs much later in childhood, and even in adulthood.

Cummins & Swain do provide evidence to show that there are aspects of language proficiency that are common to both first and second languages: aspects that are interdependent. This evidence suggests why less instruction in the second language often results in higher second language proficiency scores for minority students, while for majority language students more instruction in the second language results in higher second language proficiency scores. They also argue that in some aspects of second language learning, older learners are more efficient learners; and they offer guidance to curriculum policy makers interested in producing bilingual proficiency. Three key points about bilingualism and schooling follow from their discussion:

(1) a high level of proficiency in both languages is likely to be an intellectual advantage to children in all subjects across the curriculum, when compared with their monolingual classmates;

(2) in social situations where there is likely to be serious erosion of the first (minority) language, then that language needs development and maintenance if intellectual performance is not to suffer;

(3) high level second language proficiency depends on well developed first language proficiency.

From these three points it seems that children from disadvantaged or oppressed minority groups generally profit from bilingual programmes in which their first language plays the major role, because this lays a language foundation which cannot otherwise be guaranteed. This conclusion contrasts with the findings for children from dominant or majority language groups who benefit from bilingual programmes in which the second language is used more frequently (Appel & Muysken, 1987). In the latter case, a firm foundation in the first language develops naturally because it is the language of wider communication in the society.

The third point above that learning a second language well depends on developing prior proficiency in the first, is broadly consistent with the findings of educators in the former USSR whose experience in these matters may outstrip experiences elsewhere (McLaughlin, 1986). Also, research in Germany strongly links high level development in conceptual information and discourse strategies in the first language with high level second language development (Rehbein, 1984). From all this research comes a general conclusion that seems to have great explanatory power: for more than a century of compulsory schooling in English-speaking countries, the stress on teaching only English as a second language to young minority language speakers early in their schooling has been a misplaced emphasis that has probably brought tragic consequences to many of the recipients of that schooling. In many educational systems, the tragedy continues.

There seems to be great relevance in all this for the education of large minority language groups in the countries of North America, Australasia, Britain, and Southern Africa. Firstly, because their languages are not the languages of wider communication, ancestral minority language-speaking children whose languages and cultures have been marginalized by invasion cultures, may arrive in schools with their first languages relatively under-developed in certain contexts, styles, and functions of use. At the same time, their grasp of the majority language may be limited to a relatively small range of functions, often related to passive activities such as television viewing and the like. Secondly, because there may be only occasional uses of their first languages outside the home, children from some new settler minority backgrounds may similarly arrive in school with their first languages relatively under-developed in certain school-linked ways and with less than optimum development in the majority language. For all these children intensive early exposure in school to the majority language, accompanied by school neglect of their first language, may result in low achievement in the majority language as well as a decline in mother tongue proficiency. The recommendation for policymakers seems a straightforward one: mandatory bilingual programmes that maintain the minority language are needed to avoid the routine injustice of widespread and discriminatory minority school failure.

Research on the best age for introducing the majority or dominant language

Very young children (under five), given a suitable environment, such as that offered by Maori 'language nests' in New Zealand or French immersion pre-schools in Canada, acquire a second language quickly and seem to pick up two languages simultaneously and without much difficulty. Although most theorists agree that there is some advantage in a very early start in second language learning, the causes and the nature of that advantage are far from clear. The situation becomes more complex for older children.

Swedish research (Skutnabb-Kangas, 1981) reports that Finnish children moving to Sweden and learning Swedish early in their school careers lose much of their proficiency in Finnish. Others who move later (at ten years) maintain a level of Finnish very close to their age mates in Finland, while also acquiring proficiency in Swedish. Even allowing, as Birgitt Harley (1986) suggests, that different social influences in Sweden could have influenced the younger children's academic performance arriving as they did so young in a new culture where they were negatively stereotyped, it is the case that similarly adverse social factors often affect young language learners in a new culture. I believe that the age related results of the Swedish study are significant, whether we explain them in purely linguistic or in sociocultural terms as well. Support for this view comes from Canadian studies of immigrant Japanese children; and there is evidence from Holland and Indo-China too that older children manage to maintain and develop cognitive and academic skills in their first language to a greater extent than younger immigrant children (Cummins *et al.*, 1984), while children between nine and twelve years also make more rapid progress in academic aspects of their second language than do children between five and eight years (Appel & Muysken, 1987).

Two points stand out in the above which allow firm policy conclusions. Firstly, it seems very important that the minority child's first language is given maximum attention up to the stage of middle schooling, so that skill in using it to manipulate abstractions develops and so that it can be used to perform the cognitive operations necessary for acquiring the second language. As my discussion of Churchill's Stages suggests, this is not happening in many places: in most public school systems in North America, in Australasia, and in Britain. Nor is it happening in very different places like Hong Kong, where English-medium schools in an overwhelmingly Cantonese-speaking city seem to hinder many Cantonese mother tongue students' educational attainment (Yu & Atkinson, 1988). Secondly in learning the majority language as a second language, older students up to early adolescence at least seem to have a cognitive advantage in performing academic tasks in the language that are context reduced (e.g. abstract and difficult) (Harley, 1986). Combining these two conclusions, there seems a strong case for deferring formal bilingual programmes until quite late in schooling, and concentrating instead on first (minority) language development. In all of the English-speaking countries mentioned above, ESL programmes could come later, since the majority language is widely available and constantly reinforced outside the school. In other places like Hong Kong, a curriculum which introduces English gradually as a second language and then uses both languages equally as media of instruction seems warranted, so that first language competence can be supported and used in learning the second. Certainly in each type of setting, the value of beginning formal ESL education should not be considered as a separate policy issue from the learner's first language development.

The effects of social origin, ability level, learning difficulty and dialect

Colin Baker (1988) summarizes the scanty evidence available on the respective effects of high ability and level of family affluence on bilingual schooling. Children from low-income backgrounds and of average or below average ability may all be successful in bilingual schooling. This tentative conclusion also extends to children in schools that are sited in largely low-income communities and to children of below average reasoning ability. The evidence in favour of bilingual programmes for children who exhibit learning difficulties is less conclusive; but there are promising indications at least from studies based on majority language speakers in bilingual programmes, that second language immersion does no harm for special education pupils (Bruck, 1985).

For adolescent children in bilingual communities where the majority language is clearly the language of power, this imbalance significantly affects their motivation to use the minority language. Social pressures can pull adolescent students towards a use of the dominant language to the extent that they can use it, and these pressures may frustrate school attempts to use the minority language for instruction. For instance, Wald (1984) reports language preferences among early adolescent Hispanic children in the USA. In some cases, the preference for English exists even when the children have far greater conversational ability in Spanish. This is a complex issue for the sociology of language use; research-based knowledge in the area of age and language solidarity is only beginning to develop. A further complication is that different minority groups can have different achievement levels in becoming bilingual because of differing cultural values. Discussion in Chapter 3 suggests why this is the case. Different values and related discourse norms in a culture can support or interfere with the adoption of a new language and its discursive practices. For example, while Athabaskan children in sub-Arctic America may need to repress highly valued and influential cultural norms in order to embrace English, with its rather literate orientation, some groups of Asian children in the USA progress more rapidly in learning English than others because of general home-community pressures reinforcing high achievement in schools. Remarkably too, some new settler children do better academically than their peers who are born in the country.

All these matters are complicated by the interaction of social class, race, and language. For example, school achievement in the southwest and west of the United States is clearly stratified, with African Americans as a group at the bottom, Hispanics in the middle, and Anglo-Americans at the top. Yet while African Americans are native speakers of English and Hispanics have usually gone through a programme of subtractive bilingualism that might not augur well for their educational achievement relative to native speakers of English like the African Americans, it is the Hispanics who achieve better as a group in schools. In research in Australia's most cosmopolitan city (Corson, 1985), immigrant Italian, Portuguese, and Macedonian children, from low-income backgrounds who had learned their English in school as a second language, out-perform their Anglo-Australian classmates from similar low-income backgrounds on a battery of language instruments and in school examinations, even though the latter speak

English as their mother tongue *and* are matched in non-verbal reasoning ability with the former. In Canada across all socio-economic categories, groups of Canadian born children from immigrant Italian, Chinese, Ukrainian, and German backgrounds outperform groups of children whose mother tongue is English (Cummins, 1984). Clearly in all these cases, there are other aspects of cultural capital affecting the equation which may or may not have much to do with language. On the one hand, the Hispanics and the immigrant Australians and Canadians have rich experiences in two languages, a contact denied to their monolingual peers, and this may give real advantages as my earlier discussion suggests. On the other hand in parts of the United States, African Americans as a group are the victims of racial discrimination in almost every social context, not least in schools, and this could outweigh any language strengths that they may have relative to Hispanics. Teacher attitudes towards a particular group coupled with other forms of discrimination, may raise or depress academic achievement in ways that can modify many of the linguistic advantages or disadvantages that children possess. In Chapter 5 I return to this point.

Severe and often intractable problems exist in planning bilingual education for children whose mother tongue is a distant regional variety of a national language, as may be the case for Haitian Francophone or West Indian Anglophone new settlers in North America. Dialect-speaking Italian-born Australian or British children have been discussed in the literature (Tosi, 1984; Bettoni, 1985). But how can bilingual maintenance proceed in Italian and English for these children if neither English nor Italian is their true mother tongue? Policy responses in these cases vary depending on the context; finding just solutions needs careful investigation. Consulting the wishes of parents and knowledgeable community members in the matter is certainly basic to finding a just response in this as in other areas. As John Edwards and Joshua Fishman both observe, the one aspect of bilingual education less researched than student attitudes and interests is that of parental attitudes and interests. Edwards is amazed that programmes intended to bolster minority identity 'have not considered the existing parameters of that very phenomenon' (1985: 2). If the children's language variety is not too distant from the national language, as an Umbrian dialect of Italian may be for example, then minority immersion in the national language may be possible. If the children's variety is more remote from the national language, for example a Venetian or a Sicilian dialect, then mother tongue maintenance in that variety may be needed as a bridge to the national language and only then onto the majority language. In New Zealand, Raratongan (Cook Island) Maori is thought to be sufficiently removed from New Zealand Maori as to require separate language nests and separate bilingual units in some schools (Cazden, 1989; May,

1994). Elsewhere in New Zealand, some parents who speak a dialect of Samoan want nothing more than English for their children.

Social dialects of a language can pose problems of a similar order to regional dialects. In the USA many Hispanic students come from very low-income family backgrounds, live in segregated neighbourhoods, and consequently speak a form of vernacular Spanish which is far removed from the literary Spanish which bilingual teachers usually possess (Valdes *et al.*, 1981). Only research at single school level, coupled with access to outside consultants and the incorporation of decisions into a language policy, can offer solutions to problems that have this degree of specificity. Chapter 7 takes up this point.

Difficulties for minority students in transitional classrooms and maintenance classrooms

When transitional programmes address the curriculum through the medium of the majority language, even quite proficient bilingual students have difficulties. Tove Skutnabb-Kangas (1981) details these unusual stresses which may be little appreciated by policymakers who have never had to learn another language: listening to a foreign language is more tiring; it requires more intensive concentration; there are fewer redundant sections in discourse, so there are fewer opportunities to relax; and when speaking in the second language, there is constant pressure to think about the form of language used, allowing less attention to be paid to the content of utterances. Less proficient second language students attempting the doubly complex task of taking information from the lesson and learning the language at the same time, are under even greater stress of course. They receive less comprehensible input and less information in general than other students; the longer sequences of discourse may be unintelligible because key words are missed; opportunities to relax are fewer but they are more necessary; and the main defence against losing self-confidence may be to switch off from time to time and consciously opt out.

In contrast in a maintenance bilingual setting, the children can choose when to use the second language; they are motivated to use it whenever they wish, rather than expected to use it constantly; and they can resort to the first language whenever it is necessary for clarification, for elaboration, or simply just for a break. Talking about first (L1) and second (L2) languages, Skutnabb-Kangas anticipates conclusions reached by Cummins & Swain:

> All this means, then, that instruction through the medium of L2 during the risk period…does not give the minority child the same possibilities which the native child in the same class has to develop her cogni-

tive/academic language proficiency...and this seems to a certain extent to explain why even extensive exposure to L2 does not necessarily lead to a corresponding development of L2. If the child instead uses the L1 channel for cognitively demanding tasks until the L2 channel is well developed, the common underlying proficiency thus developed also benefits L2 later (1981: 120).

Hugo Baetens Beardsmore (1986) offers other reasons to support a maintenance approach that have a strong justice component: in maintenance bilingual programmes teachers are bilingual themselves, even though they may use only one language; and they act positively towards both cultures in the environment; in transitional programmes the teachers are usually monolingual and are often unwittingly hostile to the bilingual element in the children's make-up.

Policy Problems in Assessing Bilingual Children

Although deciding policies for bilingual assessment is made difficult by the complexities that arise when two languages come together in one person, any systematic attention to the problem is rare in educational systems. For example, minority first language children who are bilingual in the majority language, can sometimes carry an accent across into the latter. This is often the case if the majority language is learned much later than the mother tongue. As Courtney Cazden (1988) reports, an accent can seriously interfere with majority language assessment in schooling. In a study of Spanish-American children receiving bilingual education in California, the researchers conclude that the English reading teacher wrongly assessed the children's non-native pronunciation of the English in their reading texts, seeing the accent as incorrect decoding of the text. Cazden believes that the children's progress in English reading comprehension was undermined merely for want of lessons in the pronunciation of English as a second language. Such a small weakness can disguise genuine fluency. On the other hand, apparent fluency can disguise weaknesses. Baetens Beardsmore (1986) suggests that the flawless accent that young bilinguals are able to manage makes many observers neglect other aspects of their speech, especially in comparing it with the speech of older bilinguals who may carry a distinct accent from their first to their second language.

Jim Cummins (1984) discusses the over-representation of minority children in classes for the mentally retarded or in similar classes now classified as 'learning disabled'. Hispanics in the USA for example, can be over-represented by as much as 300% in these remedial classes. Cummins attributes this to the incorrect use of tests of psychological assessment with minority children. He offers recommendations: to ensure a just assessment, it is essential that one of the trained people testing minority children's language use is a fluent user of the child's mother tongue. Assessments made in the child's second language need to be used with care and should never be used as the sole basis for allocating the child to special education classes, even if the child is a long-term resident of the new country. This is because it is easy for teachers to be over-optimistic about minority children's language ability. Often the children can understand context-embedded and cognitively undemanding English in relaxed conversation, but their ability to use English in the instructional context may not live up to the high level of communicative competence required across all the levels that make up academic proficiency. Indeed when minority children come from a culture which is very different from the dominant one, their understanding of the surface forms of classroom interaction can disguise profound misunderstandings, similar to those discussed in Chapter 3. Related to this, Suzanne Romaine (1989) warns against an uncritical use of tests translated from the majority into the minority language, with little regard paid to differences in usage norms between the two languages in the children's new context.

The real cause of the plight of minority children placed in classes for slow learners is often overlooked. In one series of tests conducted in California, a mere shift from the English to the Spanish version of the Wechsler Intelligence Scale resulted in an average mean gain in IQ of more than thirteen points for pupils who had earlier been classified as 'educable mentally retarded' (Bolinger, 1980). A finding such as this must call into question the use of verbal IQ tests in any multilingual setting, since there are degrees of sociocultural difference that will affect the outcome of any test standardized by sampling processes that identify a mean and thereby downplay the probability of extremes of difference. Cummins (1984) also warns against tests that measure what counts as 'intelligent' within the dominant group, while excluding any culturally-specific ways that minority children have learned as 'intelligent'. He suggests that the intelligence test has no construct validity as a measure of previous learning, since the previous learning experiences of the minority children are not fully sampled.[5]

Again Cummins warns against testing children in the minority language if it is likely to have been affected by too little use and by recent and frequent exposure to the dominant language. The best form of assessment involves a difficult balancing act for teachers: it is best to be diffident about one's ability to judge a minority child's abilities, and to draw cautious conclusions in case harm results to the child by drawing wrong conclusions. Suzanne Moffatt (1991) explores the complexities of this problem, while studying the code choice of young Panjabi pupils in British schools. She finds that the overall language skills of the children in her study comprise mother tongue, second language English, their use of language mixing, and pragmatic skills. In Moffatt's view, to assess all these skills and to make a sound judgment about each child's linguistic competence requires a naturalistic non-test situation. This usually involves looking at language usage outside the school and using bilingual staff in a setting where peers are present. My preference for assessing bilingual students in either of their two languages, is to examine all-round communicative proficiency.

A policy for bilingual communicative proficiency assessment

This is an approach to direct observation testing which concentrates on the students' skill in using language for natural purposes in realistic situations. Communicative proficiency assessment examines the tasks language learners can carry out and how they carry them out: their total language behaviour and its productive capacity (Ingram, 1985). Michael Canale (1984) recommends five components for assessments of this kind. These provide benchmarks that school systems could set against their own procedures for assessing global language competence:

(1) tests of listening comprehension;
(2) tests of reading comprehension;
(3) tests of oral interaction;
(4) tests of written expression;
(5) a self-evaluation questionnaire.

In scoring the results of all the tests, assessors consider:

- the information communicated by students (i.e. its relevance, clarity, factual correctness and amount);
- the grammaticality of utterances used (i.e. vocabulary usage, word formation, sentence formation with attention to separating minor errors from major ones);
- the pronunciation or the spelling of responses;
- the appropriateness of the language used, depending on such contextual factors as topic, role of participants, setting, and purpose;
- the discourse cohesion, which involves the extent to which utterances function together to produce unity in the text and to suggest coherence of thought.

A minority assessment programme which included worthwhile tests of language covering each of the above five components, would provide an adequate baseline profile of student ability for placement and policy purposes. Once this information is gathered, naturalistic observation can be included as a check on the assessment of all students, especially those graduating from a bilingual programme into the English-only mainstream of the school's curriculum, or those who have already been judged as proficient but about whom there is some doubt. Carmen Simich-Dudgeon and Charlene Rivera (1983) offer 'an ethnographic approach to bilingual language proficiency assessment' which they have subjected to field testing. They call their approach a 'teacher observation system' (TOS) for use in answering the following questions (in Rivera, 1983: 117):

(1) What kind of functional language skills does the language minority student bring to school?
(2) In which language(s), contexts, and for what purposes does the student communicate best?
(3) In which language(s) does the student have the widest contextual range of communicative abilities?
(4) What kinds of communicative skills does the student need to master in order to participate appropriately as a member of the school speech community?

Assessing the language of learning disabled minority language pupils

This topic is too specialized for more than the briefest of outlines here. Yet, because special education candidates are now being placed in mainstream classes in many countries, the topic is very important in a discussion about language policy and social justice. Cummins (1984) provides a major reference in this area. The ethnographic approach outlined above, based on naturalistic observation, seems very relevant to Cummins's recommendations. I summarize some of his points below:

(1) For minority children already diagnosed as having language disorders, assessment and instruction should mainly concentrate on helping them to interact either with others or with a written text, rather than on the production of language forms; the task in assessment is for teachers to separate the effects of their language barrier from the effects of their language disorders and this can only come from attending to their practical competence in both the first and second languages.
(2) For minority children already diagnosed as hearing-impaired, descriptive assessment in both languages (including perhaps a sign language; see Branson & Miller, 1993) is of more value than normative assessment; the focus will be on what children have developed rather than on what they lack.
(3) For minority children who may be candidates for gifted and talented programmes, teacher observation must play a major role in identifying them; one piece of evidence may be the child's rapid progress in learning the majority tongue (assuming that 5 to 7 years is the average time needed for minority children to catch up in their use of the

language for academic work); a major factor in allowing these children to display their talent will be curricular and extra-curricular activities that encourage that display; *an important point for policy makers is that gifted and talented children will be no less represented among the minority children than among the majority.*

Local Decision Making and Social Justice

Some high immigrant regions and countries have severe difficulties in providing universal mother tongue maintenance schooling for their highly dispersed but often small groups who speak a diversity of minority languages. Fasold (1984) suggests some policy criteria to use in deciding on a second language of instruction in those settings where minority bilingual schooling is possible in at least some community languages:

(1) Where the language is used as a medium of wider communication, among sub-groups who do not share mother tongues, it should be preferred over languages that are not.
(2) Where the language has a large number of native speakers (at least 10% of the population) it should be preferred over small group languages.
(3) Where the language is equipped to serve as a school language, without extensive language engineering, standardization, specialist teacher training or creation of a literary tradition, it should be preferred over those languages that need a large development effort.
(4) Where minority group preference itself is against the use of their language for educational purposes then this is a strong factor against doing so.
(5) Where members of the minority are dropping out of school in larger numbers than the majority group, this is an important sign that the minority language needs support through its use as a medium of instruction.

Even these very reasonable suggestions from Fasold run into rather straightforward justice issues that cannot be resolved effectively at system level: Policy 2 discriminates against the children of small ethnolinguistic groups who may already be highly discriminated against because their languages are regarded as low in status; Policy 3 discriminates against those who may already be highly discriminated against because their culture and language is regarded as low in status; and the UNESCO committee (1953) proposes that ethnic groups like those mentioned in Policy 4 may need to be educated in the advantages that they are overlooking.

Clearly most decisions about minority languages in pluralist societies need to be made and implemented at the level of the school. Indeed, devolving decision making in this way in any act of social policy, seems a consistent use of the discourse ethic that Habermas has developed (see

Chapter 2). On his account, to apply the discourse ethic in policy action does not require a conception of what *the* just society would be. Rather it requires as many conceptions of justice as there are distinct possible conditions of society or subsets of society or culture. Every situation is a new setting for instigating the search for a contextually appropriate conception of justice through a use of the discourse ethic. This being so, it also follows from Habermas and Bhaskar that local minority communities should be involved in deciding the direction of their children's schools.

What is becoming clearer on the evidence from those countries where additive bilingual education for minority peoples is gaining respect, is that the community of minority tongue users themselves can begin to rise in esteem and in political influence at the same time as the rebirth or strengthening of their language. This is a complex phenomenon and there is no simple cause-and-effect relationship between on the one hand, increasing levels of bilingualism and on the other, an increased social standing for the minority language's users. But where the minority community itself becomes more in charge of the schooling process, the entire programme of schooling is directed towards elevating the status of the community and questioning the role of schooling in that process. Language questions become subsumed under much more important issues, among which language is only an all-pervading and sometimes distracting factor (Garcia & Otheguy, 1987). When minority language maintenance is initiated in a community, the minority members of that community become the experts: they are the advisers and real controllers of the bilingual education programme; their values shape the educational outcomes. Political mobilization with real purpose can begin to occur. Community attitudes are laid bare and discussed. Local people receive formal training as teachers. Parents participate in the activities of the school to a greater degree and they acquire skills that were previously not their own. All of these things and many more, contribute to the elevation of the minority group. Political consciousness awakens where perhaps previously there was none. And the language of the minority becomes available as a recognized political voice at the same time as their political will begins to assert itself.

It is likely that schools controlled and run by remote bureaucracies and staffed by teachers whose culture is not the culture of the local community, get in the way of all this. When majority culture educators look at minority children they tend to focus on what those children lack, and usually what they see is the absence of a high level proficiency in the majority language. This lack becomes the focus of the schooling that they offer those children. It is a commonplace for observers of educational reform to claim that policies of compensatory, multicultural, and anti-racist education imposed from afar, make little difference to educational inequality. These policies ignore the root causes of that inequality, which is very often linked to an absence of bilingual provision within the curriculum of specific schools. Sometimes that bilingual provision can be aimed at mother tongue maintenance, sometimes at enhancing the cultural esteem of minority groups, sometimes at some combination of these aims. Only a local community can really decide what is necessary. When communities themselves are in charge of education, when they themselves have the respect and the dignity that goes with deciding the future of their offspring, they come to see education in a much broader way. They begin to ask each other about the best way to educate their children and about what is wrong with the alternative processes of schooling that they are familiar with.[6]

Notes to Chapter 4

1. The suppression of the Maori began with the unlawful exercise of sovereign rule over these people by the British settlers (Hastings, 1988). The denial of Maori language rights in the nineteenth and early twentieth centuries, is well evidenced in attempts to stamp out their language through education, in ways which contravened and continue to contravene the Treaty of Waitangi signed in 1840 between representatives of the two parties.
2. While language is a central component in a person's cultural capital, other socially prestigious aspects of capital may be more powerful than purely linguistic factors in creating stereotypes by which people are judged and thereby influencing school achievement. Race, for example, is an aspect of capital that is fixed by historical and biological forces. Indeed purely linguistic factors, such as the possession of the dominant language or some variant of it, may be simply second or third order reflections of the social and cultural contexts of schooling (Troike, 1981). Stereotypes have a harmful effect in providing the content of social categories that people use in making judgments: they influence the way we process information; they create expectancies about others; and they create self-fulfilling prophecies (see Chapter 5: 108–10). Prejudices and racial stereotypes can affect the life chances of all groups when those groups are obviously different in some way from dominant groups. But separating discriminatory judgments about people from judgments that we feel we have good reasons for holding, is not always a straightforward matter, since discrimination varies not just between peoples but also across contexts. John Ogbu (1983) discusses the outcaste minority group in Japan, the buraku, who encounter disproportionate school failure in Japanese schools but who achieve on an equal footing with other Japanese descent students when translated into American schools. The burakumin are thoroughly Japanese but structural influences still deny many of them full admission to the culture in Japan (Okano, 1992). Again, Rudolph Troike offers the case of Finnish immigrants to Sweden who are viewed rather negatively as a group, since they are seen as the inhabitants of a former Swedish colony; but in Australia, Finnish immigrants have a relatively prestigious place among immigrants which comes about because they are perceived as Scandinavians, with all the positive attributes that that label connotes, and they can enjoy

their culture as well should they choose to do so. The important point to note from this is that in Swedish schools, the Finns do poorly as a group; in Australian schools, they do rather well. As Jim Cummins remarks: 'widespread school failure does not occur in minority groups that are positively oriented towards both their own and the dominant culture, that do not perceive themselves as inferior to the dominant group, and that are not alienated from their own cultural values' (1986: 22).

3. For example, see Britain's Swann Report (DES, 1985), Kingman Report (DES, 1988) and Jill Bourne and Deborah Cameron's discussion of both (1988). The Swann Report recommends policies for new settler minority language children which are almost the opposite of the policies that the research evidence suggests would be just and efficacious: i.e. the Report recommends rapid ESL provision for new entrant children, with the possible presentation of some minority languages but only as foreign languages in the curriculum of senior schooling.

4. But even the proclamation of an 'official language' can be contrary to justice.

Parler de *la* langue, sans autre précision, comme font les linguistes, c'est accepter tacitement la définition *officielle* de la language *officielle* d'une unité politique: cette langue est celle qui, dans les limites territoriales de cette unité, s'impose à tous les ressortissants come la seule légitime, et cela d'autant plus impérativement que la circonstance est plus officielle...Produite par des auteurs ayant autorité pour écrire, fixée et codifiée par les grammairiens et les professeurs, chargés aussi d'en inculquer la maîtrise, la langue est un *code*, au sens de chiffre permettant d'établir des équivalences entre des sons et des sens, mais aussi au sens de système de normes réglant les pratiques linguistiques (Bourdieu, 1981: 27).

Bourdieu laments the lack of precision of linguists when they speak of 'language' since they tacitly accept the official version of a language, which usually relates to a political unit and a linguistic norm that has been imposed as the only legitimate one. This recognition he claims, helps to reinforce the legitimacy of the official language and a minimum level of communication in the interests of economic and symbolic production. He instances the linguistic unification that accompanied the French Revolution: The bourgeois class won a *de facto* monopoly of the political apparatus while the speakers of local dialects 'collaborated in the destruction of their instruments of expression' (1981: 34). Again symbolic violence operates in this setting: those who are dominated apply the dominant criteria of evaluation to their own practices. Moreover, allotting single languages an official status by policy decree may create long-term problems when other languages come along with equal or better claims.

5. Minority children can come to school apparently knowing much the same world as other children do, but in very different ways; they can impose very different interpretative repertoires upon that world. When they confront assessment methods that teachers use based on the dominant culture, it is often the case that they are asked to display knowledge about 'x,y' when what they really know about is 'y,z'. Another problem for them can be that in conventional monocultural schools they are *never* asked to display their knowledge about 'y,z'; or if they are asked to do so, the question is not phrased in a way suggesting that 'y,z' might be the answer.

6. First published as 'Bilingual education policy and social justice.' *Journal of Education Policy* 7, 45–69 (1992).

5 Minority Social Groups: Non-Standard Varieties and Styles

'Speech is a mirror to the soul: As a people speak, so are they.' This harsh judgment, made by the Roman playwright Publilius Cyrus in the ancient world, did not die with that world. It is often the lot of the poor and other marginalized groups to be diminished by unfair judgments made about their linguistic capital. Chapters 3 and 4 examined social justice issues in the education of culturally different groups and minority language users. Many things in those chapters are also relevant to social groups who use a non-standard variety of a dominant language, rather than the minority language of a different culture. The non-standard language of socially marginalized people is still often used unjustly as 'a mirror' to their potential for achievement and to their worth as human beings. This occurs in any stratified society where many variations in vocabulary, syntax, accent and discourse style are socially marked, so that even a basic communicative exchange between individuals gives evidence of their place in the social structure. Accordingly, individuals with inappropriate linguistic capital for a given situation are poorly placed to exploit the system of differences that exists in that situation. Indeed relatively few language users are highly competent across a wide range of circumstances, since in general cultural profit or advantage accrues most from those modes of expression that are the least equally distributed. This chapter examines the roots of this common injustice and suggests policy directions that schools and school systems might take in softening the linguistic discrimination that affects minority social groups everywhere.

Standard and Non-Standard Varieties

In this chapter, I use the term 'language variety' to cover any non-standard form of a language whether a geographical or social dialect, a patois, a creole, or some other code of a language.[1] Although they are not always seen as self-contained or isolated language systems, varieties are socially or regionally recognizable. As a result, they are often distinguished by a name of their own. Although the number of features that all the varieties of a language share is always greater than the number they do not share, there are still good reasons for formally recognizing non-standard varieties since they are systematically and regularly different from the standard. Most speakers of a language use a variety which differs from the standard, and none of these varieties is in any sense inherently inferior to the standard in grammar or phonology.

Sociocultural and geographical variations within a language are signalling matters that are of great importance to those who use them. Varieties serve valuable group identity functions for their speakers; they express interests that are closely linked to matters of self-respect and other psychological attributes. It follows that language varieties deserve respect and recognition in education. This obligation raises an issue that has stimulated much educational debate: To what extent should the standard language be used as the language of education? Possible responses lie along a continuum that stretches from those who would have all of education conducted in the standard for whatever reason, to those who would have as much schooling as possible conducted in a suitable non-standard variety. The concept of 'standard language' itself is central in the debate.

Standard language and education

Imprecision in using the expression 'standard language' muddies the waters of debates about its use (Cameron & Bourne, 1988). We use the word 'standard' in two broadly different but related senses. One of these is as a synonym for 'uniform'; we talk about a standard measurement which is common to all, both invariant and normal. The other sense is more judgmental; it suggests 'something to aspire to', 'something excellent', 'the best there is', or 'the paradigm case'. The former sense of standard suggests only a convention: the 'standard' language is something agreed to as a medium of communication which is set in place in various ways, but subject to change if its users agree. The latter sense of 'standard' suggests evaluation and normativity. Here if we spoke of the 'standard' language, we would mean that it provided the most desirable code and as a result any non-standard variety would be an imperfect imitation of this norm. When 'standard' is applied to a language in this latter sense, it is an illogical usage; but it can still support severe injustices.

Pierre Bourdieu argues that school systems in general operate as though the latter sense of standard language obtained (Bourdieu & Passeron, 1977; Bourdieu, 1977; 1981). This observation seems particularly relevant to schools in his own country, where the Académie Française has directed its efforts over several centuries towards maintaining the 'purity' of the French standard. This has an unmistakable impact on French schooling. For example, Claudine Dannequin (1987) even writes of very young students who are non-standard speakers of French, as 'gagged children' ('les enfants bâillonnés') in their own classrooms. Through its practices, the Académie has lent institutional support in French education to what I am calling an 'ideology of correctness'. More indirectly perhaps similar practices are put in place by nation states almost everywhere, not just by France. As Bourdieu argues, these practices serve as a form of tacit language policy that legitimizes and sanctions the standard, creating a paradoxical situation for non-standard language users: they come to believe that non-possession of the standard is no excuse for not using it:

> La langue officielle a partie liée avec l'État. Et cela tant dans sa genèse que dans ses usages sociaux. C'est dans le processus de constitution de l'État que se créent les conditions de la constitution d'un marché linguistique unifié et dominé par la langue officielle: obligatoire dans les occasions officielles et dans les espaces officiels (école, administrations publiques, institutions politiques, etc.), cette langue d'État devient la norme théoretique à laquelle toutes les pratiques linguistiques sont objectivement mesurées. Nul n'est censé ignorer la loi linguistique qui a son corps de juristes, les grammairiens, et ses agents d'imposition et de contrôle, les maîtres de l'enseignement, investis du pouvoir de soumettre *universellement* à l'examen et à la sanction juridique du titre scolaire la performance linguistique des sujets parlants (1981: 27).

In the wider societies of the English-speaking world except in England itself, the ideology of correctness has been declining in recent decades, especially in those countries where non-standard varieties have never been stigmatized or socially marked to the degree that they are in Britain. Recent official documents for England and Wales have given renewed status in education to the standard, but on grounds deriving less from the class prejudices of the past and more from other arguments (DES, 1985; 1988; 1988).

Yet schools almost everywhere uncritically uphold the ideology of correctness. They accept the standard as a form of cultural capital whose possession elevates the academic status of the holder. Because some children start out in schools with more of this particular linguistic resource than others and are consistently rewarded for its possession, an injustice results for those many children who arrive in schools with less of the standard. For these children, the standard language valued in schools represents more than a mere convention. It is the model of excellence against which their own varieties are measured; it is correct, while their own varieties are less correct. As a result, non-standard language users often come to perceive their own varieties as things of lesser worth. This readiness of non-standard language users to stigmatize their own variety means that as children and later as adults, they often condemn themselves to silence in public settings for fear of offending norms that work against them in ways that they themselves sanction. Using Bourdieu's metaphor, there are many linguistic markets in which their speech is assigned a limited value. They are either silent within those 'markets' or they withdraw from them. In the middle and upper levels of education, both responses from children of low-income and marginalized backgrounds are common.

Many argue for a guaranteed central place for the standard language in education. Sometimes these advocates may be themselves native users of an elite standard variety. Often too they are native users of a non-standard variety to which they have added the standard later. The latter often appreciate the value of having both varieties, of being bidialectal. They urge use of the standard variety in schooling not out of self-interest or through ignorance of the place and value of other varieties, but because they feel that there are good reasons for recommending that the standard should have a central place, such as its suitability for use across a very wide range of contexts. They prefer it not because of its correctness, but because of its more general 'appropriateness'. Christopher Winch (1989) distinguishes criteria of appropriateness in language use from the criteria of correctness that firm rules provide.

Appropriateness and Correctness

We learn criteria of appropriateness when we acquire different language varieties. Each variety comes to us equipped with a set of implicit recommendations that are purpose related, and the use of these recommendations is context specific. In one setting when talking to certain people, it is better to use one variety rather than another if communicative efficiency is to be served. In another setting, the first variety may seem out of place. The level of formality or informality of the occasion is one factor that tends to influence the choice of variety that people make. It also affects the style of language that seems right for the context. For instance, it is hardly appropriate for sportspeople on a playing field to use a formal style with one another, unless they are serving some ironical purpose in doing so.

On the other hand, we learn criteria of correctness when we decide on firm language rules of syntax, semantics, and phonology that apply across all the varieties of a language. These criteria provide more than mere recommendations. They cannot be ignored if communicative effectiveness is to be preserved. When we ignore these rules of a language, we move outside it completely. So if we were to say that a standard variety for example, is distinguished from a non-standard variety because the one is more correct than the other, then we are implying that in that respect the other is outside the language entirely. This is nonsense.

In defending the use of the standard variety for teaching purposes, school policymakers have a case if they argue from the appropriateness of the standard across a wide range of contexts, rather than from its correctness. While an argument based on correctness would seem to fail on grounds of incoherence, the appropriateness argument has strong logical support, and in most contexts, as I argue, is supported by justice claims as well as on the following pragmatic grounds.

What makes a standard variety the standard in the first place is its practicality. A standard is hardly ever prescribed arbitrarily in nation states. Even if it is prescribed by administrative fiat, it never becomes the *de facto* standard until it possesses a good deal of practicality. Nor can an arbitrarily chosen variety ever be the standard on justice grounds. If the standard is only prescribed to serve the interests of an elite group such as the dominant members of the middle classes, then its nomination as 'the standard' for schooling would not serve society's interests at all, at least so far as those interests could be separated from the interests of the elite group. In this case 'the standard' would be no more than a prestigious class dialect, quite alien to those who did not possess it. Its enforcement through education would be an unjust use of power by the institution itself, seeking to give prestige to the linguistic capital of a privileged group. In contrast, a genuine standard variety of a language provides a more effective means of communication than non-standard varieties because it has appropriateness across a much greater range of contexts and people. It is far more acceptable from a practical viewpoint, in that it meets the acquired interests and expectations of many groups, rather than just the interests of its native speakers.

There are other clear practical advantages that Winch sees in using the standard. If that variety is both a national and an international language, access to it is empowering in all those contexts where it provides a medium of communication across national boundaries. If it is associated historically with the written language, access to it is empowering for individuals in the acquisition of literacy. If it has traditionally been the language of higher and technical education, access to it may give easier access to the technical registers of scientific and academic discourse. So more than vested interests are served when the standard variety is used as the language of schooling. Majority and minority group interests advance, because of the practical appropriateness of the standard to them. Indeed even if we were to think of dropping the standard from education, the impracticality of doing so would quickly frustrate that policy. There are daunting difficulties in trying to change even a tiny item of the standard such as the use of a single pronoun, as Mussolini found in his efforts to eliminate formal pronoun use from Italian.

Nevertheless a language policy decision in education becomes difficult in local contexts if there are very strong justice grounds for preferring some non-standard variety over the standard. The degree to which the standard variety meets the real interests of a community can vary considerably across contexts. For example in parts of Belfast, standard English conflicts with the interests of unified working class communities and so it is not valued as a code for interaction in those communities (Milroy & Milroy, 1978). Education carried out in the standard in such a setting can be alienating and fruitless. But if the standard variety of a language is a necessary acquisition for educated speakers of that language to make because its possession meets the objective interests of speakers as individuals and as a group, can we justify a form of schooling in most social contexts that is not conducted in the standard variety?

I believe that the difficulty can be minimized by adopting and elaborating on the language policy that the Bullock Report (DES, 1975) recommends: valuing the language variety that children bring with them to school to whatever degree is necessary on justice grounds, while adding to it, in every case, those other forms, functions, styles, and registers that are necessary acquisitions for educated people to make if they are going to use their language appropriately across a broad range of contexts. But I would add a necessary rider to the Bullock recommendation: for this 'valuing' to really count, it needs to be carried out in a genuinely *critical* context. In other words, children need to become really aware of the social and historical factors that have combined to make one variety of the language more appropriate in contexts resonant with power and prestige, while allotting non-standard varieties a status of appropriateness only in marginalized contexts (see Fairclough, 1992). In adopting this policy, we agree to provide critical awareness as an essential part of the fair treatment we extend to those children who come to school without the standard variety. What follows in this chapter and in Chapter 7 are suggestions about how this might be done. A good place to start is for professionals to become clearer about the dimensions of language pluralism that exist even in monolingual settings, and about the disparities of esteem that often result for non-standard speakers in schools.

Non-Standard Varieties

People living in monolingual societies sometimes find it difficult to appreciate that there are still regular, systematic, and wide variations in language use, in language attitudes, and in language behaviour among groups of people within their societies. These variations exist because of historical social divisions, different patterns of behaviour, differences in power, and differences in language experience. Because infants arrive in a language system that is already fully developed and functioning, there is a tendency for people to see the world of language as something stable and natural; as something which is not generated and controlled by social forces, by struggles, and by historical events. Because of this human tendency to take language for granted, it is easy for language communities to maintain an ideology of correctness in language, especially if it is in the interests of one dominant group or another to do so. Unlike the ideology mentioned in Chapter 4 that has allowed bilingual education to be marginalized for so long, this ideology has not needed reinforcing by a selective use of research findings.

The ideology of correctness is maintained by the commonsense prejudices of human beings themselves: the most difficult prejudices for education to overcome. Bourdieu describes a trait which is especially characteristic of the bourgeoisie: 'the tendency to hyper-correction, a vigilance which overshoots the mark for fear of falling short and pounces on linguistic incorrectness, in oneself and others' (1984: 331). He sees this tendency as a particular trait of the *petit-bourgeois*, the lower middle classes, as they seek to cement their status within the dominant classes of a society. Historically, responding to pressure from dominant groups, schools have supported this ideology of correctness; and as long as schools have legitimated this ideology, dominant and non-dominant communities of speakers have accepted it normatively.

The ideology of correctness creates frequent problems for the majority of speakers who do not always use the standard variety. In the company of their friends and associates, they may have to rationalize their use of the non-standard variety. They sometimes do this by ironicizing its features, in much the same way as they poke fun at the features of the standard variety in some contexts. In order to explain away major differences in language use, people sometimes pillory variations in the language use of others; they describe differences that exist as poor or sloppy speech, arising from the speaker's ignorance, laziness, lack of education, or even perversity. These prejudiced notions circulated in the discourse of language communities, reinforce the ideology of correctness and make the facts of the matter seem contrary to commonsense. But the facts are rather straightforward: we all make errors in our language use at some time or other especially when speaking informally, but the 'errors' that people often perceive in the language of others (who are usually from slightly different social groups) are not really errors at all; they are evidence for the existence of a different variety of the language, a variety which preserves its features as systematically and regularly as any language variety.

Linguistic stereotyping

The possession of a non-standard variety is something that few can ignore in others. More than this, non-standard speech provides 'evidence' for judgments in people's minds long before genuinely relevant evidence becomes available for or against those judgments. Non-standard language can create stereotypes connecting this use of linguistic capital with other social attributes. Even the subtlest difference in vowel sound can provide evidence for stereotypes. As mentioned in Chapter 1, for people in Philadelphia a change in one aspect of a single vowel in an utterance is enough to make a White speaker sound Black, and a Black speaker sound White (Fasold, 1990).

Like anyone else, teachers are prone to the influence of stereotypes. But because of the real power that teachers have over the life chances of children, they are in a unique position to put their stereotypes to work, sometimes with harmful effect. Stereotypes provide much of the content of the 'social categories' that we hold. Miles Hewstone and Howard Giles (1986) offer four descriptive statements about stereotypes:

- stereotyping stems from illusory correlations between people's group membership and their psychological attributes and traits;
- stereotypes influence the way information is processed about the members of groups (i.e. more favourable information is remembered about in-groups and more unfavourable information is remembered about out-groups);
- stereotypes create expectancies about other people and the holders of stereotypes often search for information and behaviours in others that will confirm those expectancies;
- stereotypes constrain their holders' patterns of communication and promote communication which confirms the stereotypes held (i.e. they create self-fulfilling prophecies).

As Chapter 1 argues, judgements of achievement in schools rarely depend on objective evidence alone. When teachers are influenced by the ideology of correctness and hold firm views about what correct language is, then the standard variety is usually elevated as an example. The standard ceases to be just a convention that has value because of its appropriateness across a great range of contexts. Instead, it becomes the paradigm case. At the same time, non-standard varieties become tacitly devalued; they become indicators of disadvantage, poverty, inferiority, or even shame. These evaluations can be used by teachers as inaccurate pointers to children's educational potential, especially if there are other indicators that reinforce teacher prejudices (such as children's dislike of schoolwork, lack of parental interest in the school, or evidence of disadvantage in the children's dress or appearance). Teachers' expectations can be adjusted accordingly and these can influence academic success, with children's true potential overlooked or reduced in effect.

The evidence of language itself is central in confirming stereotypes and activating prejudices: negative teacher attitudes towards the speech of culturally and socially different children undoubtedly affect teacher expectations, which in turn affect pupil performance (J. Edwards, 1989). In particular, a general and long-standing finding of research is that teachers' perceptions of children's non-standard speech produces negative expectations about the children's personalities, social backgrounds, and academic abilities (Giles et al., 1987). Recent studies suggest that although our awareness of this key injustice stretches back over a generation of research, in practice this has not lessened the injustice very much. For example in Britain in the 1990s, there remain grave doubts about teachers' ability to be objective when formally assessing oral language ability at senior school level. Findings there reveal that the standard variety is rated much more favourably than non-standard varieties, thus routinely discriminating against working class and minority group non-standard speakers (Sachdev, 1991). Moreover, it seems that teachers bring these stereotypes with them into the profession. Viv Edwards (1986) reports student-teacher evaluations of anonymous children's speech where both the academic and the interest level of speakers of minority and other non-standard language varieties was viewed less favourably. Remarkably, there is now much evidence that teacher attitudes to children's non-standard language use are more critical in judging the quality of language use than the children's language itself. There is even evidence to suggest that the stereotypes that beginning teachers from the majority culture hold about children from minority backgrounds causes them to 'hear' those children as non-standard in their language, regardless of how standard their speech actually is (Fasold, 1984).

This complex phenomenon raises vital social justice issues which may need legal or legislative action in certain settings. A celebrated court case took place in Ann Arbor, Michigan. As part of its judgment in favour of parents, the court required teachers of culturally different children to take a course of in-service training in sociolinguistics (Labov, 1982). In this case, the parents of African American children had brought an action against a school, alleging that their children were failing because they were wrongly labelled 'educationally disabled' on the basis of their use of an African American non-standard variety. It was found that the language variety used by the children in itself, was in no sense an obstacle to their success. Rather the expectations of pupil success that teachers held, based on their stereotypes about that variety, led the school as a whole to misperceive the children's real potential, thus causing them to fail. The children were deemed to be deficient in educational potential because their language variety was wrongly judged to be *deficient*.

Deficit and difference

Many words have been spent on the 'deficit versus difference debate' as it relates to children's language in education. I will be brief here since the debate is largely obsolete in theoretical discussions. The central issue was whether or not any single variety of a language is deficient or inferior in respect to the standard variety. As earlier sections in this chapter imply, a deficit view of language has no satisfactory logical basis since it requires one variety of a language to be the correct one. A deficit theory overlooks the obvious claim that some varieties are more appropriate within some contexts and that there is no way of firmly prescribing in advance what appropriateness might be for any given context, since participants might choose to use one variety over another for reasons of their own at the time. Because the deficit claim does not hold, a subsidiary claim about the impact of linguistic deficit on cognitive ability cannot be sustained either.

Although the deficit debate was a necessary clearing of the air in language questions, the terms of the debate itself were not very helpful. By balancing 'deficit' against 'difference' in so stark a way, the debate trivialized the range of positions that can be taken on these matters. The deficit position has long been cogently refuted, but it is also true that the difference position rather misses the point. When we talk about 'appropriateness', there is something more at issue than just difference. For example the language of a group of professors of English who are without computer training, will require many additions in vocabulary and many additional pragmatic references if they are to operate as effective computer scientists, or even pretend to do so. Similarly, children engaging in activities that are new to them extend their language in many functions, styles, and registers to meet those activities. As Chapter 1 argues, the special language demands that conventional schooling places on children from marginalized social groups and minorities unfairly requires them to show competence in what the school demands, while not equipping them with that competence or even justifying the demands. At the same time, the view that some children's language is in some sense deficient for the purposes for which they have developed it is plainly wrong. Language users develop the forms, styles and functions of language necessary to live the lives that they are living. They develop more when they need more, provided the conditions are right to do so. Ideally schools should be in the business of providing the right conditions, although for many children they are not.

Schools as places of alienation

Children whose home language is very close to the standard variety used in the school need to make fewer changes than others on entering schools. In this respect they have a decided advantage over those others. Indeed this advantage is similar in kind, if not in degree, to the classroom advantage that fluent bilinguals have over children who are still adding the dominant language to their minority tongue, but who must learn through that dominant language as their medium of instruction (see Chapter 4). But this is only one way in which schools are more alien for some than for others. Although schools exist almost everywhere in human societies, in many ways they are very artificial language environments that can often be out of place in the communities that they serve. One reason for this is that they require patterns of language use and systems of meaning, that are different from those that many children acquire or will ever encounter outside schools.

Perhaps in their conventional organizational form, few schools could ever resolve a problem that seems to have its roots in the nature of human language itself. Recent developments in the study of language seem to confirm that the reference or social meaning of utterances can rarely be decided away from the context of situation in which those utterances are used. In other words, the complete meaning of what people say cannot be grasped unless it is interpreted within its original situation of use and by someone very familiar with that context. Expanding this claim from single utterances to larger forms of discourse such as the message systems of schools, we may have to conclude that much of what goes on in schools has little meaning for all those participants who are not very familiar with the special context and the special culture of schools in general.

Like any culture, the micro-culture of a school has its in-groups and its out-groups. The out-groups of a school usually include the school's non-standard speakers. The significant out-groups in many schools in the USA are the African American vernacular speakers whose discourse structures receive so much attention in research. These speakers are marked as an out-group because of their racial background, as well as their non-standard speech. In line with William Labov's early studies, Frederick Erickson (1984) reports that the African American non-standard variety like other varieties discussed here is a fully developed, internally coherent, and entirely effective system of language for its in-group members. But in the same way as it is difficult for people who are not members of that minority in-group to follow or relate to conversations in the non-standard variety, it may also be difficult for members of that minority in-group to follow or relate to conversations in the other fully developed and internally coherent languages of schooling. As mentioned, all children coming to school need to develop new forms, styles, and registers of language to suit the unaccustomed demands that schooling places upon their language. While some children need to do more of this than others, many also need to acquire alien class values and orientations to the world. They are asked to learn these things through a class variety of language which may also be alienating.

So the injustice is less a matter of language than a matter of a broad class bias that reaches across the curriculum, pedagogy, and organizational arrangements of schooling. The case presented for using the standard variety as the language of schooling seems a strong one; but there seems no reason at all to maintain and extend the interests of one social group, whose middle class language variety is already privileged in the school, by basing everything else in the school uncritically on middle class values as well. John Edwards (1985) claims that any deficit view of language is saturated with a middle class bias, but this claim gets only part of the point. Schooling itself is saturated with a 'middle class bias'. Modern forms of schooling grew quite directly out of a tradition that valued the things valued by the upper middle classes; it proscribed things that were not. Schools are created and managed to serve values that have their historical roots in the upper middle classes of mid-nineteenth century Europe, whether those inherited values are benevolent, helpful, irrational, or malignant in the contemporary world. If middle class behaviour patterns are to provide the outcome criteria of schooling, one priority is to find ways to explore shortcomings in those patterns. In doing this there is much that falls outside this book's scope. But Chapter 7 attends to a number of matters that come into the domain of language policy. In particular it discusses approaches aimed at developing critical language awareness.

Pragmatic Matters: Accommodating Difference

Valuing non-standard varieties is not an easy thing for many people to do. For teachers, it may be contrary to a professional lifetime of tacit prejudice. Clearly the attitudes of teachers themselves are important variables here. Helping school staff members become clearer about the risks of stereotyping children is an early step which needs to be taken at whole school and system level, so that staff can support one another in making the necessary changes in attitude. The Ann Arbor experience offers a lead that policy makers at system level might consider: in-service education of practitioners in the sociolinguistics of schooling would certainly be helpful in identifying undesirable prejudices and eliminating the practices that result from them.

While valuing non-standard varieties in the first instance by not censuring their use, schools have a major obligation to provide sensitive opportunities and appropriate contexts where non-standard speakers can use the standard variety widely and well. Justice issues relating to this activity fall under several headings. In the next two sections, I begin by presenting the broad justice issues involved when asking non-standard speakers to engage in the practical activities of producing and receiving the standard variety. In later sections, discussion moves into more complex areas: assessing the language skills of non-standard speakers; and the relationship between minority discourse and literacy acquisition itself. Achieving academic literacy seems to involve complex interactions between cultural, social, cognitive, and linguistic forces.

Reading and listening to the standard variety

If viewed as simple linguistic decoding, receptive use of the standard variety creates few practical problems for non-standard speakers. For all of their lives, most modern children have constant exposure to the standard variety through daily contacts with the mass media. Evidence suggests that there are few practical difficulties for non-standard speakers in reading the standard. Joshua Fishman (1969) points to the high levels of literacy in the standard that non-standard speakers achieve in Japan, Germany, and Switzerland; and William Labov (1972) argues that the range of structures unique to Black English Vernacular would not account for the record of reading failure by these non-standard users in inner city schools. Efforts have been made in some places to present initial reading materials for new entrant children using non-standard texts, and there may be good reasons for doing so, especially if the variety that the children use is quite distant from the standard, as many Italian *dialetti* are.

No unusual threat to the interests of non-standard speakers results from the regular demand in schools that they engage in reading and listening to the standard variety. The standard is not likely to replace the non-standard variety, if the latter is valued in the school and is used freely for informal communication in the school and community. An analogy with additive bilingual education seems apt: no harm results from receptive exposure to a second variety of a language, provided that the first variety is maintained to a high level of proficiency at the same time.

Speaking and writing the standard variety

Productive use of the standard language in writing can create specific difficulties that may disadvantage non-standard users. This may occur even though non-standard varieties will typically have the standard variety, or something that is very close to it, as their written version. There are several documented ways in which the use of a non-standard variety can influence a student's competence in writing standard English. The evidence appears in studies of Black English Vernacular (BEV), in the USA (Reed, 1981; Whiteman, 1981) that have traced non-standard features in writing back to their use in speech by the writer. Instances of direct interference are limited, but a generation ago at least they seem to have been frequent.

More recent studies suggest that the above concerns are no longer as relevant. From her longitudinal surveys of the academic writing of large cohorts of students, Geneva Smitherman (1992) reaches two conclusions: the use of BEV in writing has significantly declined since the late 1960s; and the use of BEV does not presently affect scores received when assessors are rating specific writing tasks. She sees the latter as testimony to the various educational and social forces in the USA that have combined over the generation to sensitize teachers about non-standard varieties. Teachers now seem more willing to divorce assessment of success in mode of writing from attention to dialect related features of grammar. She believes that her second conclusion, that BEV use in student writing has declined, seems to be evidence that bi-dialectal African American students have now acquired greater facility in code-switching, and that this is perhaps due to their increased levels of literacy, schooling, and their media-exposure to the standard. At the same time, she points out that the oral repertoire of African American young people may still be diverging from the standard, and that it may even be thriving on that divergence. In his study of creole dialect interference in the writing of students in the West Indian island-nation of St Lucia, Christopher Winch (1993) reaches some conclusions that seem to support Smitherman. At the very least as Winch argues, the conventional wisdom that creole interference causes St Lucian children problems with their academic writing needs careful re-examination. The most common errors that could be attributed to non-standard interference by dialect-speaking young people in this former British colony, also appear in studies of students in Britain and may have rather different causes.

There may be a stronger case to show that a non-standard variety can interfere with students' ability to monitor and edit the appropriate use of verb forms, inflectional endings, spelling and punctuation. This seems to happen because usually a non-standard variety is the children's first language, so they cannot always depend on their knowledge of that variety to tell them whether a piece of text in the standard variety is appropriate or not. Carroll Reed terms this situation 'linguistic insecurity' and argues that it has a direct influence on the frequency of errors marked in students' written work. She gives several examples which appear systematically in student texts: exchanging plural and possessive '-s' markers; over-correcting in removing non-standard features, such as the invariant 'be' to the extent that standard uses of the 'be' are also removed from texts; and over-correcting by over-generalizing the application of the regular plural in standard English to produce forms such as 'mices' and 'sheeps'. I return to this editorial interference in a later section on language testing.

Insisting that students use the standard language in speech presents greater difficulties, both practical and ethical. Clearly attempts to force children to speak in the standard against their wishes, risk devaluing their varieties, along with all those attributes of identity that the varieties represent. It may be a tacit way of saying to children that their non-standard varieties are incorrect and should be replaced with the standard. Any question of penalties applying for failure to adapt to the standard or any duress in this area, is tantamount to efforts early this century to stamp out minority language use in schools, practices that seem disgraceful today but which were accepted as the right and proper course not many years ago.

Extension into the spoken standard variety, not replacement by it, does seem a fair practice to follow, since it is very much in the interests of individuals and groups of children in general to offer them this sort of competence for use across a range of discourse contexts. Whether this means promoting bidialectalism or not will depend on other factors: such as the linguistic distance between the children's non-standard variety and the standard. But if there is any risk of stigmatizing the non-standard varieties, then deliberately promoting bidialectalism in classroom speech seems hardly worth it. Over their many years of schooling, most non-standard speakers inevitably experience the standard in a diversity of contexts and this promotes a high degree of natural bidialectalism.[2] In settings where more is possible, there are sensitive approaches for changing classroom practices, in ways that will extend children's language repertoire and also develop their communicative and analytic competence more generally (Mehan, 1984; Young, 1992).[3]

The literacy dimension and minority social group discourse styles

Acquiring knowledge of grammar and lexicon and applying that knowledge to reading and writing in the standard variety, is only a small step on the road to academic literacy. In becoming literate, adults and children pass through a sequence of cognitive, linguistic, and social adjustments that are rather like those made in communicating across cultural boundaries. In particular, there is growing evidence to suggest that many speakers' oral styles are not readily translatable into the expository written mode demanded by the school (Gumperz, Kaltman & O'Connor, 1984; Michaels & Collins, 1984). In Chapter 3, I discussed the work of Heath and others in relation to culturally different children's discourse styles. In a similar way, children from minority social groups may be treated unjustly if their oral styles are not recognized in schooling. There may be important consequences for key matters of literacy acquisition and literacy development.

Debates about educational success and failure often centre on literacy development. People see high-level literacy as the minimum goal of every form of compulsory schooling. Clearly in schools, children start out unequally in the quest for literacy; but it is only in recent decades that the sociocultural nature of that inequality has been more fully explored (Scribner & Cole, 1981; Heath, 1983; 1986a; Wagner *et al.*, 1986; Hamilton *et al.*, 1993). In this range of studies which spans cultures and minorities, an important link is made between the mode and manner of literacy acquisition and sociocultural background: literacy is learned in specific settings and the methods for that learning vary across groups. As a result, there are broad variations in the critical purposes to which literacy is put across institutional and social networks. In particular, the purposes, effects and types of literacy for any single group, may be very different from those established and recognized in schools. Children's potential for achieving academic literacy may vary accordingly.

Shirley Heath (1982; 1986a) examines the ways of 'taking' from printed material that young children learn from their home setting. Sometimes these ways of taking are inconsistent with the patterns expected in schools. These patterns established in the home leave many children unconnected with the traditionally assigned rewards that come from literacy: job preparation, social mobility, intellectual creativity, and information access. As a result, the motivation for reading and writing is different and literacy has different meanings which correspond with variations in modes, functions, and uses. In particular, the academic usefulness of these skills is not enough to motivate their mastery. Heath (1983) develops two assumptions that are instructive here: firstly, each community's ways of taking from the printed word and ways of using this knowledge are interdependent with the ways children learn to talk through their interactions with parents and family; and secondly, there is little or no validity in regarding 'the literate tradition' as distinct from the 'oral tradition'. The one process merges into and creates the other.

Heath finds that mainstream, school-oriented children in their pre-school home setting, receive a form of enculturation which gives them three things: all the habits needed for asking and receiving 'what' explanations; experience of selectively attending to items of written text; and appropriate interaction styles for displaying a knowledge of their literate orientation to the environment in speech. She says that these acquisitions are finely tuned through recurrent exposure to activities of reinforcement in the home which routinely create knowledge that can be applied in school-acceptable ways.

In contrast are the children in Heath's studies who come from homes where there are no books, few reading activities of any kind, but explicit rewards for displays of language that show correspondence in function, style, configuration, and positioning between two different things or situations. These children are used to being asked for reason-explanations, not what-explanations. While they are not explicitly taught the names of attributes and events, they are familiar with group literacy events in which several people negotiate the meaning of a written text. When these children go to school they meet unfamiliar what-explanations. For instance, they are often asked to identify items by name which have only a flat, two-dimensional appearance on a printed page. Also when presented with conventional achievement tests, they score in the lower levels if there has been no prior adaptation in their behaviour. In short, they do not adopt the social interactional rules for school literacy events.

It seems that the printed word and the ways of taking meaning from it, have little place in the world enjoyed by Heath's second group of children, even though they do have diverging orientations to the world that can be highly desirable in formal educational settings. For instance, the sophisticated skills that they do possess to link two events or situations metaphorically, are never tapped in schools, and their display of these skills may mislead teachers into thinking that the children have difficulty thinking in straight lines. These lateral skills are not required of them until later stages of schooling and they are deemed too sophisticated for little children to possess. Chapter 3 records similar observations about the precocious skills displayed by Athabaskan children in Arctic America, such as the ability to make highly abstract presentations of narrative structure. In majority group children, these would be assessed as the product of a sophisticated level of thought and a lengthy period of formal education (Scollon &

Scollon, 1984). In both cases, by the time the skills are required in school curricula, the children have often missed the foundation literacy learning needed to support the presentation of their skills in school-acceptable ways.

Even children from families who strongly adhere to the dominant culture can constitute a minority social group in their orientation towards language and school learning. Caroline Zinsser (1986) examines children whose early life contacts with literacy and school discourse are largely through fundamentalist Bible school training, which on its own gives them a very limited orientation to the printed and spoken word. For these children the sacred text, and the catechistic forms of speech that focus on that text, provide a guide to daily behaviour and a means to personal salvation which is authoritative and absolute. Using categories developed by Basil Bernstein (1975), we might say that the pedagogy used in Sunday Schools is strongly classified and tightly framed: teachers and students have few options about what they are allowed to do with the Bible text; they cannot easily contrast it with other texts; they cannot select or reorder the material; they cannot ask 'what if' questions and fantasize about the outcome; and they cannot doubt and question the author's views. Zinsser argues that these early experiences of written texts give young children an orientation to literacy, to learning, and to discourse itself which is very different from what is valued in mainstream schools. If these children do not go to fundamentalist schools where similarly strong classifications and tight frames also occur, they may find that the forms of literacy and discourse valued in mainstream schools are very different from what they learned in their Sunday School setting. Similarly Heath (1986b) describes a third group of children from families who adopted fundamentalist practices in the home. These children were often criticized by mainstream teachers for their lack of imagination, their laconic answers, and for rarely asking questions or extending ideas with initiative and imagination. As Heath says, these children have different ways of 'taking' their literacy: they have not seen their parents incorporate information into their value systems from written materials, or use their literacy skills to aid their participation in institutions beyond their primary group. Instead, these children often possess well developed skills in labelling, learning under direction, and following the textbook. Like children from very different cultural minorities, many children like these whose parents would classify themselves as mainstream members of the dominant culture face incompatibilities and discontinuities between their socialization in the home community and the demands of schooling.

Summarizing her findings, Heath says that 'in each society, certain kinds of childhood participation in literacy events may precede others' and 'the ways of taking employed in the school may in turn build directly on the preschool development, may require substantial adaptation on the part of the children, or may even run directly counter to aspects of the community's pattern' (1982: 70). She draws two conclusions for language development from all this: firstly, 'a strict dichotomization between oral and literate traditions is a construct of researchers, not an accurate portrayal of reality across cultures' (1982: 73); and secondly 'a unilinear model of development in the acquisition of language structures and uses cannot adequately account for culturally diverse ways of acquiring knowledge or developing cognitive styles' (1982: 73). In Chapter 7, I present some of Heath's conclusions for making practical changes in school and classroom policies.

From all this, it is tempting to conclude that the poor school achievement of children from working class, low-income, or minority social group backgrounds is due entirely to discontinuities between the home and the school. Chandler *et al.* (1986) warn against applying this conclusion too firmly to literacy development. They argue that there are various minority social groups whose home experiences are not significantly different from the school's, at least in the areas relevant to literacy development. For example, many of the low-income and ethnically diverse parents observed in their studies seemed quite skilled in developing a school-like interactional setting in the home for their children. However, the researchers themselves admit that the reason for this continuity between home and school is that the families in their sample were in no sense isolated from the dominant culture: they had high educational and occupational aspirations for their children and few of them identified strongly with ethnic or religious subgroups. Again we see Bourdieu's argument illustrated: it is children's disposition (habitus) acquired in the home to be close to the dominant style (cultural capital) or to be distant from it, that determines the rewards that mainstream schooling offers them.

In the light of Heath's work, we can see that access to a literate discourse style is not equally easy for all children. Some children are clearly advantaged in bringing to the school a style of discoursing that is closer to the demands of the school and involves less learning on the part of the child. When the teacher's style contrasts with the child's, this hinders interaction and frequent interruptions are necessary for formal purposes. Misinterpretation becomes common, especially in the kinds of 'key situations' mentioned in Chapter 3.

Language testing

Ralph Fasold (1990) reviews work on the importance of the non-standard/standard issue in language testing procedures. For non-standard users there seem to be clear social justice issues at stake whenever screening tests for language development are being used, and where these tests assume the standard variety to be 'normal' language, as they usually do. Since test developers use standards of correctness in language rather than criteria of appropriateness as benchmarks when putting together their instruments, test norms based uncritically on the standard in this way will always disadvantage non-standard users. This seems to follow inevitably from the fact that non-standard varieties are systematically and regularly different from the standard.

As mentioned in an earlier section, even when non-standard speakers have wide access to the standard, their possession of two varieties can mean that they have to draw on an intricate and ambiguous web of suppositions in correcting their own written texts. Fasold argues that there are similar difficulties for non-standard users in answering a language test using the standard:

- non-standard speakers cannot rely on what 'sounds right', since what sounds right will sometimes be non-standard and therefore will be wrong in the context;
- non-standard speakers cannot always rely on a 'sounds right so it must be wrong' strategy, since in most cases this will be misleading too;
- while even standard speakers have instances of confusion between formal and informal uses of language (i.e. 'may' versus 'can'), non-standard speakers have many more instances of these differences to remember, and therefore many more of them to get wrong.

These ambiguities significantly affect scores recorded on language tests, but it is not just variations in forms and features of language that occur when there are social dialect variations. Aspects of Heath's work (1986b,c) draw attention to the array of patterns of socialization experiences that can create major differences in narrative style between standard and non-standard speakers of the same language. A difficulty in basing test formats on a limited range of narrative types is that the child from the mainstream home will be favoured over the child with a different form of socialization, and different narrative experiences. Heath recommends that test designers experiment and find ways to use a wide range of narrative types in assessment batteries.

Various assessment policy alternatives are possible in testing the language of non-standard speakers. The policy of having different test norms for standard and non-standard language users, which stigmatizes the latter whether test results are used critically or not, can be quickly ruled out on justice grounds. The policy of omitting socioculturally biased items which allows genuine weaknesses among all children to be overlooked, can be ruled out on grounds of test validity. One precaution that recommends itself is for test administrators always to use tests compiled by sociolinguistically competent designers. While this policy may already be widespread, it is more difficult to ensure that sociolinguistically competent people will use language tests in schools. Busy teachers often accept the results of language tests uncritically, especially when they are passed on secondhand from school to school or from grade to grade. Indeed perhaps the very practice of using pre-formatted and structured group language tests is an unjust policy to adopt and maintain. If weighty decisions about a child's interests and life chances are to be based on the results of a language test, then there seems every reason to make it an adequate and scrupulously fair assessment.

There are insights for those concerned with first language assessment in recent approaches recommended for assessing second language competence (see Chapter 4). Instead of measuring the more visible and highly recurring features of language, like pronunciation patterns, vocabulary use, and grammatical usages, other aspects of second language learning now attract more attention. Performing a thorough observation of 'language in use' is now a more favoured basis for assessment. When this form of 'communicative proficiency assessment' complements or replaces traditional language testing, the role of norms, statistics, and inflexible criteria of correctness is lessened. The 'norm' for all children becomes a measure of observed proficiency in communicating meaning, set against an individual assessment of their potential for development. Ethnographic methods are called for here, especially participant observation in naturalistic settings where the children's language use is not inhibited by them having unfavourable expectations about the interaction.

In Chapter 3, I examined the effect that cultural differences in interaction styles promote in the classroom, depending on the context for communication that is created. Expectation differences seem to promote difficulties for children from minority social groups too. William Labov's early work (1966; 1970) found that individual African American children in the USA revealed a high level of verbal productivity and creativity when the context was changed from a formal to an informal one that was more consistent with the interactional settings that the children themselves were most comfortable in. When using communicative proficiency assessment, we also reduce that other problem so familiar in sociolinguistic debate: the effect of the test and the tester on the language context itself, which can act as an inhibiting influence on the children being assessed. Perhaps teachers could more routinely question the privileged place of pre-formatted standardized tests in language assessment when the interests of non-standard speakers are at risk.

Language Matters Beyond Language

In this chapter I have ranged widely over issues in the debate about non-standard and standard varieties and styles in education. It is important to stress that language on its own is not the cause of educational failure: language itself has little power when it is divorced from powerful institutions and agents. The power of language comes from what it is used to do: the practices in which it is sited. Labov (1987) is categorical in claiming that the primary cause of educational failure for minorities is not language differences but institutional racism. Indeed the evidence suggests that the unjust use of power in maintaining minority stereotypes and class distance is the chief factor in educational failure, not language. Because of these exclusionary patterns that apply in stratified societies, even literacy itself can seem a vain achievement to those approaching it from a marginalized background. Bourdieu observes that individuals from some minority groups find that achieving 'success' in schooling involves a rejection of their social origins. David Smith (1986) echoes this view, recounting the routine social factors keeping minority children at a distance from literacy: they quickly come to believe that there is little truth in the claim that school success for them will lead to a better life; they recognize that there is a ceiling on their achievements held there by aspects of cultural capital that have little to do with being able to read and write; and they often conclude that to learn to read and write is to subordinate themselves to a game whose rules are set by a culture that they themselves are forever excluded from.[4]

Notes to Chapter 5

1. In monolingual communities, a range of language varieties are brought into the work of the school in one way or another: varieties used by closely knit social or ethnic groups. Coming from these backgrounds, the children may possess two or more 'codes' which they use in their everyday language, perhaps one code reserved for the home, another for the peer group, and a third for the school. This last code may be very close to the standard variety. The Patois used by many children in Britain of West Indian origin provides a continuum of codes which the children often range across, switching their code depending on the context (V. Edwards, 1986). Examples of code-switching of this kind are to be found to some extent in every community where modern schools operate. They offer a different dimension of language variation. For example, Hewitt (1989) identifies two kinds of 'creole' operating among Londoners of West Indian descent: the relatively stable community language of the older generations of West Indian immigrants into Britain; and the 'London-Jamaican' anti-language of the young. The former is a creatively developed community language, serving the normal range of everyday functions that community languages serve; the latter is a strategic and contextually variable use of Creole to mark race in the context of the daily anti-racist struggle that adolescents find themselves in. This form of

Creole is actually structured to heighten its contrast with other forms of language.

2. Jim Cummins advises that 'if the teacher consistently uses the standard form while accepting student utterances in the non-standard, then students will gradually shift to using the standard in the school context' (1981: 35). This advice is consistent with a general sociolinguistic principle that William Labov offers (1971): whenever speakers of a non-dominant language system are in contact with a more dominant one, those speakers will change their speech to accommodate the features of the more dominant system. This means that everyday interaction in the school context over an extended period will often be enough to give non-standard speakers productive control over the standard's features sufficient to operate effectively in the world of the standard. And all this may be achieved without risk of stigmatizing, provided the students concerned are motivated to identify with the school, rather than to resist its language and procedures.

3. The method for developing oral bidialectalism is the same as the method for developing oral language proficiency in general: we learn to speak by speaking, so that almost any oral language activities that occur in a motivated context will foster communicative profiency. Activities of role play, improvisation, simulation games and group discussion are widely available pedagogies for teachers at all levels of schooling (Corson, 1987). Using these methods, imaginative teachers can devise ingenious activities that will promote purposeful use of the standard in settings where pupil self-esteem is protected, and where the activities themselves can be doubly useful: for pursuing wider curriculum aims, and for developing proficiency in the standard. But none of this is really *educational* unless it is approached in a way that allows children to become critically aware about matters of correctness and appropriateness in language (see Chapter 7: 196–6).

4. Let me be categorical on this point. The acquisition of literacy is vital for everyone in the modern world. It would be disastrous if groups of minority children were reinforced in the view that literacy is not worth having, simply because the culture of many contemporary schools seems alien and irrelevant to them. There is no doubt that literacy is essential for adequate functioning on a daily basis in modern print societies, and for experiencing many of the most desirable personal rewards that are available in the modern world. However, I agree with Jonathon Kozol's conclusion (1986) that if literacy is not acquired along with those critical and analytical skills that good processes of schooling have always aimed to provide, then the function of literacy can be to domesticate and subordinate, rather than to empower and advance the interests of the newly literate.

6 Gender and Language Policy in Education

Cross-cultural studies of gender and language confirm that language plays a very diverse role in the social construction of gender. At the same time, studies of language socialization confirm that the effects of socialization through language appear very early in children's lives. Wherever cultural and social groups have been studied to date, the styles of interaction that caretakers adopt with very young boys contrast with the styles that they adopt with very young girls. Gleason (1987) argues that language used with young children is linked to gender with respect to the target and to the source of the message. It appears that girls and boys are spoken to differently in some ways by adults, and that adult men and women also speak to them differently in some ways (Berko-Gleason, 1975). Standing out among the variables identified so far are the levels of lexical precision and the politeness routines used with girls, as compared to those used with boys. Fathers also tend to interrupt children more than mothers, establishing this pattern very early in children's lives, and they interrupt girls more than boys, while male daycare teachers far exceed female teachers in their use of direct commands. Fathers also use many more direct commands than mothers, and they do this especially with boys. In their turn, by age four, boys use more direct commands than girls. On the evidence then, adults seem to be directly teaching their children social conventions for language use from their earliest years, and they use language to do this. In short, 'parents speak differently from each other; they speak differently to boys than to girls; and boys and girls speak differently' (Philips *et al.*, 1987: 1).

These early asymmetries in treatment and outcome intersect with the many other asymmetries already raised in respect to minority groups in Chapters 3 to 5, so it may seem that formal schooling arrives too late in children's lives to have much impact on the robust patterns of linguistic socialization that are already well established in infancy and early childhood. It might be concluded that even where there is willingness to attempt the purposeful reform of gendered discourse practices through education, such an attempt is unlikely to succeed because of the complex relationship between individual linguistic innovations and the long-standing discourse conventions that provide the more structured conditions for speaking.

In the discussion that follows I am using the notion of 'structure' to refer to the intractability of the social world: structures set limits to freedom often in tacit ways through a complex interplay of powers within diverse social institutions. In Chapter 3 for example, I present cultural values as structures that influence discourse norms; the very existence of the values is manifested in those discursive practices. On Bhaskar's account in Chapter 1, structures of power have no existence separate from the activities that they govern and from agents' reports [in language] of those activities. It is true that the discourse of individuals is heavily influenced by institutional practices: human agents are tightly constrained by discursive structures, and the effects of these constraints often show up in stereotyped and unjust oppositions that severely disadvantage females.[1] But it is also true that structures in their turn, are reconstructed and reinforced by acts of individual discourse. Indeed the very possibility of emancipation from oppressive ideologies and structures depends on this being so.

Since the mid-1970s studies of language and gender have been centrally concerned with social justice issues. One aim of these studies has been to identify the role that language plays in the location and maintenance of women and girls in a disadvantageous position in society. In locating my position within that debate, I am discounting the commonly expressed view that 'man-made language' inevitably keeps women in a subordinate position. I am doing so not simply because I have faith in the possibility of human freewill, but because the 'man-made language' doctrine seems to deny the possibility of human emancipation ever occurring. In a critique of theorists such as Dale Spender (1980), Elizabeth Frazer and Deborah Cameron (1989) debate the view that language is a key determinant of people's world view. Spender argues that men as the more powerful gender, have controlled language to the extent that women have had to internalize a male world view which is contrary to their interests and excludes an alternative encoding of a female world view. This set of arguments cannot succeed however, if power resides with people as it seems to, not in language itself. It is the way that language is traditionally used as an instrument of power, that excludes women from a foothold on power, not language itself.

Elsewhere too Deborah Cameron argues that Spender's version of 'Orwellian thought-control via malespeak' ignores the contextuality of meaning and its ultimate indeterminacy; no group can fix meaning or exercise power over it, whether this is done through 'passive inheritors' of the tradition or through 'an omnipresent conspiracy of men working to retain their semantic monopoly' (1984: 15). Spender points to the feelings that women sometimes have, that others do not understand them, or that their own experience cannot be put into words. In reply, Cameron says that this alienation from language 'is not just part of the feminine condition but an inescapable part of being human' (1984: 15). David Graddol and Joan Swann (1989) also disagree with Spender's position, though for slightly different reasons. They see the view that men are the sole-inventors and validators of words as an over-simplification which disregards the interaction of other forms of social inequality with gender. Middle class women or White women in many settings have considerable power compared with other groups, more perhaps than many working class males or more than men from minority cultures. Dominant classes of women have always influenced language in certain key directions. Cameron (1985) also points to the existence of powerful forces that on her account are essentially genderless: the mass media, the education system, publishing houses etc. To the extent that these reflect men's interests rather than women's, she suggests that we can expect them also to influence language towards 'male' meanings.

An alternative but related account discussed by Frazer & Cameron, comes from the French school of feminist theorists such as Julia Kristeva and Luce Irigaray (Moi, 1985). This account accepts the importance of language acquisition as the way that women internalize the patriarchal orderings of the world, but see it from a structuralist perspective that is removed from the more Whorfian views of Spender but which is like it in one respect: since language has been made to accord with the values of men, it operates in such a way as to put women 'outside' itself, so that when they use language as they must to operate as human beings, they alienate themselves from their own reality. Frazer & Cameron argue that neither Spender's account nor the French school's account manages to explain in any empirically satisfying way, how women are prevented from encoding an 'oppositional' world view in language, apart from in some limited areas of a culture's language practices. Beyond this, Frazer & Cameron contend as I do in Chapter 1, that we cannot give 'language' the power to determine social reality in the way that some writers would suggest. On the other hand, they see language as more than the mere epiphenomenon that positivists might see it as: i.e. reflecting social reality, yet independent of it. Rather, they see language as a social activity in which the construction of meanings and social realities largely takes place. As a result, they ask what the constraints and norms that affect speakers in social situations might be. For example, why are the discourse norms of a feminist discussion group with its emphasis on cooperation, listening skills, self-disclosure, and so on, disvalued, disused (at least by the privileged group of young women observed in their study) and even reviled in the world at large.[2]

This chapter looks at the role that education plays in creating unjust gender arrangements in society through its language policies and the discursive practices that it legitimates. In the next section, I begin by reviewing many of the differences that studies have found in the respective discourses of men and women. I then review the much smaller corpus of studies that describe differences in the discourse of school-age girls and boys. Finally, I review the language policies and discourse practices that schools often adopt which may help to create and reinforce disadvantages for girls and women.

The Discourse of Women and Men

Discourse practices across cultures

Fewer empirical differences in men's and women's language have been found than early theorists expected. Moreover, the methodological and theoretical imperfections in many empirical studies make firm conclusions impossible (Kramarae, 1981). In a summary of differences that appear in the literature (Klann-Delius, 1987), there is no suggestion that basically different 'languages of the sexes' exist. Her contention is supported elsewhere too. Reviewing the literature from anthropology and language, Susan Philips (1980) concludes that the fundamental features of men's and women's language in a society are unlikely to differ as much as social dialects differ, since speakers of different social dialects interact with one another irregularly, while men and women interact constantly. If there were major differences in the language of men and women, this would result in communication difficulties similar to those that occur between different social dialect speakers. Indeed, Philips goes on to cite work suggesting that a person's social status is more important than gender in determining the selection of certain language forms (see O'Barr & Atkins (1980) in Chapter 1): it is power as manifested in occupational status or in level of education, that seems to correlate more closely with the use of many discourse features such as various politeness forms, intensifiers, hedges, and hesitations. As perceived by observers, a speaker's use of these forms tends to convey an impression of powerlessness and lowly status, regardless of whether the speaker is male or female. Throughout the following discussion I return to this point about the centrality of power in the analysis of gendered discourse.

In some areas of language the evidence of gender difference is far from conclusive. Jan McPherson (1990) suggests that while research has challenged many stereotyped beliefs about women's language, it has also thrown up new stereotypes. For example, Lakoff (1975) claimed that women use more question tags than men (e.g. 'this is better, isn't it?'), and that this practice is evidence of the uncertainty and the hesitancy that characterizes women's speech. Later studies suggest that both women's and men's use of question tags varies considerably across contexts, and that question tags may have several different discursive functions: to include another speaker; to sustain interaction; to demand agreement. The use of tag questions between equals seems to correlate with conversational role rather than with gender itself; and where participants are not equal in status some tag questions are used more often by powerful than by powerless participants (Cameron *et al.*, 1988).

There are contradictory findings in other areas too (Philips, 1980): women talk less than men in some studies, but not in others; women's speech has fewer filled pauses in some studies, but not in others; and men interrupt women much more in some studies, while women interrupt either males or females in other studies. David Smith (1985) reports that female recipients of interruptions in one study contest male-initiated inter- ruptions at twice the rate of male recipients, making it difficult to attribute to female submissiveness or reticence the greater rate of interruptions by men that is found in some studies. He notes too that as conversational devices interruptions can support as well as control interaction: interrup- tions can be a positive use of discursive power as well as a negative one. For example, interruptions can signal enthusiastic agreement; they can elaborate on the theme of the speaker; and they often help keep a conver- sation going. On the other hand, as Jenny Cheshire and Nancy Jenkins (1991) argue, interruptions can provide evidence of poor listening skills, or signal a poor understanding of the cooperative nature of discussion. These several alternative interpretations suggest that studies of interruptions and other discourse events, in interaction between the sexes, need to be much more finely tuned.

Studies of gendered discourse conducted outside the dominant Western pattern of usage have also questioned some of the more enduring conclu- sions reached in earlier research. Certainly some differences do appear with regularity across cultures and social groups. For example, it does seem that women as a group use a wider range of pitch frequencies and more intonation in their speech than men do as a group (McConnell-Ginet *et al.*, 1980; Philips, 1980); and it also seems that women as a group talk less than men, at least in cross-gender interactions. However, a classic sociolinguistic 'pattern' portraying women and girls as choosing standard or 'correct' forms more often than males (Trudgill, 1974; Macaulay, 1977; Romaine, 1978; Pauwels, 1991), appears in other research to be an overgeneralization

(Coates & Cameron, 1988). Its identification as a pattern may derive in part from an inadequate sociological conception of the specific conditions of women's lives, and from the over-readiness of researchers to attribute particular psychological dispositions, such as conservativism and status seeking, to women as a group (Cameron & Coates, 1985). Indeed women from minority groups influenced by local conditions and contexts, seem to be more colloquial than their male peers.

It seems that sociolinguistic research has often drawn its explanations of gender differences in language from commonsense Western stereotypes about gender differences in general.[3] The Western pattern of usage mentioned above, in which women more often select standard rather than non-standard forms, now seems to have been only a feature of Western European societies or their former colonies (Philips *et al.*, 1987). Other research on the positive and negative evaluation of women's discourse, is a second area where no firm pattern exists, since variables other than gender now seem more important. Whether or not women make a greater use of non-standard forms than men, it seems that women's speech is not always evaluated negatively. Among Japanese, Mexicano, and Samoan men and women studied, there is interaction between gender, age, and status in the discursive practices adopted, and this interaction shows up in differences in language use and in its evaluation across contexts: men and women are not always different in their speech in the same way, at different ages, and in different settings marked by status (Philips *et al.*, 1987).

Across societies, power is the great variable that separates men and women from one another: routine female exclusion from public spheres of action also often excludes them from access to the creation, maintenance, and elaboration of dominant ideologies and the language used to express them. All the societies examined in Philips *et al.* (1987) display key political and public-speaking roles and speech genres in which women participate rarely, or not at all. Rarely are they direct participants in shaping the shared conceptual frameworks of dominant groups, which are applied in characterizing and evaluating actions, events, and other phenomena. But in the same societies, men are not notably excluded from the key activities that women dominate. In short, the men have more power and control than the women, and to that extent, greater command of the discourses of power; they are able to define the activities that attract status. From her studies in New Guinea, Bambi Schieffelin (1987) suggests that it is the activities engaged in by women compared with the activities engaged in by men, rather than gender itself, that associate with the linguistic choices that are made: men engaging in women's activities tend to use language in much the same way as the women would. Again the key variable in this is differential access to power. When men place themselves in relatively powerless situations identified by the activities that they are engaged in, their language tends to be indistinguishable from that of women in the same activities. If women themselves are under-valued in that society, then the activities that they engage in and the language used by them will be under-valued. The social solidarity of people doing these same activities, regardless of their gender, is expressed through the language that they use.

As the complexity of the domain of research into language and gender becomes more apparent, the role of power immanent in wider structural arrangements, should become even more important. Early research such as Lakoff's (1975), was based on explicit and straightforward linguistic features discovered in the speech of women that contrast with those of men. However as discussion so far suggests, these individual features are often artefacts of overall interactional differences in style between women and men that are reinforced by sociocultural practices and values quite removed from any obvious connection with language. For example, women and men usually belong to rather different subcultures which themselves have their own methods for empowering agents acting within wider social structures. The differences in language use that are often identified between men and women, are largely a product of different modes of socialization that arise within enduring sociocultural boundaries and structural constraints: men and women have internalized different norms for interaction within and between the genders, in much the same way as the members of different cultures, living in the same social space, have different norms for interaction and often misunderstand one another accordingly. But there is more than cultural difference in play here. In the same way as forced immersion in a majority culture can constrain the discursive practices of the members of a minority culture living in the same social space, structural arrangements reflecting the archaic values of dominant male social groups often constrain the discursive practices of contemporary women, even though they are far removed in time from those archaic values. In much the same way as a minority cultural group gets few opportunities to influence the discourse of the dominant group because of prevailing structures of power, women as a group also get relatively few opportunities to reform discursive practices that reach much beyond surface forms of language.[4]

Women in most cultural contexts are clearly an oppressed group when compared with men as a group. It follows that almost any gender differences in discourse are interpretable with respect to this clear difference in power between men and women. Such an explanation of differences in language as a result of dominance, is a necessary balance to add to a sociocultural explanation of difference, if only because subcultures of women are themselves plainly susceptible to wider power forces within cultures. At the same time of course, women usually have their own discourse norms that are not necessarily defined in reference to dominant male norms, or determined by historically dominant male values. For example in societies where there is a high level of formal education, models of language seen by many women as prestigious may be drawn from the class of educated women elites, whose own preferred norms may vary considerably from their male peers. So the context or setting of discourse, including the class, gender, and cultural interests of all the participants, heavily influences discourse practice.

Discourse practices in context

A developing aim of research into language and gender is to understand the differences that appear in discourse between men and women within particular contexts, especially in settings where unequal power relations traditionally prevail. A key example is in the setting of the home, where women have to work harder than men to maintain conversations, asking more questions, supporting and encouraging male responses (P. Fishman, 1983). Robin Lakoff observes a similar difference. In their turn, men in the home respond less frequently to women's attempts at interaction. Fishman concludes that men control the content and rhythm of conversation in this way; they establish their right to define what the interaction will be about; and they determine when and where interaction will occur. In the same research, the use of statements by men matches the use of questions by women. While men make twice as many statements, women ask more than twice as many questions to which the men often decline to respond, although the women almost always respond to male statements. Again even in this micro setting, it is the exercise of latent or explicit power that seems to support this pattern of differences: it is possible to explain the observed differences by reference to power relations that have been long established or legitimated as norms for interaction within the structures, the archaic values, the socialization practices and the discourse arrangements of societies.

The influence of unequal power relationships is also evident in the patterns of interruptions and silences that are recorded in male–female conversations. This second set of patterns suggests that men exercise rigorous topic control in conversations (Fasold, 1990): on the one hand, they often interrupt in such a way as to breach conventions about when to speak and when to remain silent; on the other hand, they decline to support the topics that women are developing. This marked tendency is consistent with the finding that it is women who initiate conversational topics, but it is men who control their development by their minimally responsive behaviour

(Klann-Delius, 1987). Again, these different patterns of interaction are much more than mere linguistic trends. Rather, they reflect the conventional levels of respect that dominant members of societies show for the thoughts, interests, views, activities, and rights of women. In response to the male patterns of interaction, women as non-dominant members of societies, seem to collaborate in their own discursive oppression. Parents pass on discursive patterns to boys and girls in early childhood, and as I indicate below, the same patterns are already well established in the discourse of school age children. They have become cultural interests that distinguish male from female discourse practices, so that from early childhood onwards most males and females seem to manifest and develop a broadly different understanding of the form and the purpose of conversational interactions.

In short, while girls and women see conversation essentially as a cooperative activity, men and boys see it more often as a competitive exchange. The quote below responds to a point made by Sally McConnell-Ginet. The authors discuss the asymmetrical relationship of dominance in male–female conversations, that seems related to the fact that women and men see conversation differently:

> Hence in any communication between a man and woman, the woman is unlikely to challenge the belief system that is needed to make sense of the man's discourse…When talking herself, however, the cooperative woman will adopt the man's world view in order to frame utterances. This is an asymmetrical relationship, McConnell-Ginet argues, since the man will never frame his talk in terms of the woman's value system. If there is a difference between the man's world view and experience and those of the woman, then it is the man's that directs the entire discourse. Eventually all instances of a word's use will reflect the man's value system rather than the woman's. This model does not actually imply that the woman changes her world view, however, only that the woman's experience and values never appear as assumptions in mixed sex discourse; that her world view is never the one in which the coherence of the discourse is grounded (Graddol & Swann, 1989: 170–1).

The authors expand their analysis to include the well attested tendency towards convergence in language behaviour that social psychologists identify: when people are conversing they tend to move their styles closer to one another. But when there is an unequal relationship as there often is between males and females, the more powerful model of conversing representing the male 'competitive exchange', wins out every time. Moreover when children continually witness a model of communication in which the male's world view consistently prevails, then they tend to reproduce that model themselves, especially if they are not encouraged to be critical of it. They come to regard it as naturalistically necessary: not just as the way things are, but as the way that things should be. So while research largely confirms the popular view that women and girls are good at interpersonal skills such as sympathetic listening, careful questioning, and sustaining flagging conversations (Cheshire & Jenkins, 1991), these skills may derive from imbalances of power in the social world that force women and girls to make a cooperative virtue out of an asymmetrical necessity.

So far, I have identified two sets of patterns that show up in male–female conversational contexts. Paula Treichler and Cheris Kramarae (1983) summarize other characteristically male practices that contrast with female practices: males interpret questions as requests for information; they often ignore the comments of previous speakers; they more frequently make declarations of fact and opinion; and they talk more often, and at greater length. Men also use taboo expressions in their speech much more often (Smith,1985). Separate research studies from Sweden, Brazil and the USA report that women use far less profanity and obscenity than men, a pattern that occurs in girls' and boys' speech as well. Other research also emphasizes the cooperative versus competitive dimension that appears in men's and women's interaction styles. While men shift topics rapidly, hearing other people's problems as requests for solutions, women use questions as part of conversational maintenance rather than as the requests for information that men use them for. Women also explicitly acknowledge any previous contributions that are made to the discussion. They interpret verbal aggression as personal, negative, and disruptive. For women, this competitive style of interacting prevents conversation from being used to show care and responsibility: to negotiate and express a relationship; to support and cooperate; and to establish a sharing, engaging, and communal exchange (Maltz & Borker, 1983).

Interpreting this evidence in a different way, Cameron (1985) questions whether women really are more cooperative in their talk than men. She wonders if their observed willingness to adopt a cooperative style might not be an artefact of feminist gatherings, where participants are urged not to interrupt, raise their voices, or show deviance from solidarity. Less attractive interactive functions can be served in this way: such as binding conversational partners to a specific attitude for political purposes and constraining genuine criticism. However, Diane Reay (1991) observes a similar consensual pattern among girls as young as seven years of age who also avoid strategies of questioning and challenging one anothers' ideas when working in a single sex group. Reay suggests that acting consensually in this way is not the same as being democratic, since democratic interaction always allows the possibility of conflict, which is something the girls in the single sex group in her study try to avoid in much the same way as adult women may do, on the evidence and on Cameron's account. This strategic use of 'cooperative' discourse by women then, seems far removed from an ideal speech situation, but it is certainly no more distant from it than are the competitive discourse practices often adopted by men.

On the evidence, there is not much to admire in the informal competitive talk of Western males in many contexts of interaction. Men's talk resembles a form of display, involving joke telling, boasting, ribbing, and verbal aggression. Men tend to take longer turns at talk and have a greater rate of controlling pauses filled with vocalizations, like 'um' and 'ah', while women smile more often and direct their gaze longer at their conversational partners. While women give many nods and responses such as 'yes' and 'mmm', to signal that they are listening attentively, men often give barely minimal responses to the talk of others, or none at all (Maltz & Borker, 1983).

These many contrasts in male–female discourse leave room for mis-understandings to arise in mixed gender conversations. This occurs especially when women are trying to manage affiliative goals, but have to do so within domains of interaction that are controlled by men whose attention is on the outcome of the interaction, not on its processes. This discursive quandary has a major impact in Western societies, where the process of winning access to positions of institutional power often depends on possessing the kinds of verbal skills needed to function successfully in roles created to meet the historical values and language norms of dominant Western males. When women take on these roles and values, conforming to these norms even if only temporarily, they risk being misperceived as pseudo-male. At the same time during their occupancy of the roles, they lose the personal satisfaction that comes from achieving their own affiliative goals in interaction through a use of their own preferred discourse styles. This is not to say however, that the preferred styles of women can be characterized as 'women's language'.

Lakoff's exploration of 'women's language' was critically extended by O'Barr & Atkins (1980), who also based their research on the observed frequency of different features of language. After examining more than 150 hours of courtroom testimony by women and men, they suggest that a better name for 'women's language' is 'powerless language'. They argue that the tendency of women to use 'powerless language' more often than men, is due to the greater tendency of women to occupy relatively power-less positions in certain social contexts. Thus social status and/or expertise in contexts is reflected in the discourse behaviour adopted by those interacting. Other research modifies this conclusion somewhat, since in situations where women possess the *de facto* power that comes from having genuine expertise, that power is not always enough to outweigh structural and historical differences in power that are based on gender. There is a diversity of examples: when female experts are in discussion with male non-experts (Smith, 1985), the expert females are perceived as less dominant and less in control even than the non-expert males. Valerie Walkerdine (1987) reports a study where even two four year old boys refuse to assume the role of powerless objects in their teacher's discourse, and instead with her consent recast her as the powerless 'woman as sex object' of their own discourse. Elsewhere speakers of either sex are more polite with male than they are with female ticket-sellers in a railway station (Brouwer,1982). Others find women using more 'women's language' across a range of contexts: in laboratory conversations, in interactions with police in a police station, and in requesting information (Crosby & Nyquist, 1977). Pointedly however, women and men in this study are both much more hesitant and indirect than are the police officials themselves in the police station setting; and in the railway station study 'all of the kinds of utterances that women are characteristically supposed to use more often than men — utterances indicating insecurity and politeness — were used more often by *both women and men* when speaking to the *male ticket seller*' (Brouwer *et al.*, 1979: 47 [italics in the original]).

It seems that where gender differences in speech do emerge they are strongly influenced by the particular discourse context, including the gender and perceived power of the addressee. But power is mediated through language; it does not derive from it: different inequalities that exist in power, dominance, expertise, and status intersect with gender, class and cultural differences and receive expression in different forms of discourse in different discourse settings. Nevertheless these expressions of power are rarely overwhelming influences. Free agents will always try to find ways to counter structural forms of determination. Indeed efforts to resist dominant discourse structures are often observed.[5]

The Discourse of Girls and Boys

Do differences in adult male–female language have a clear genesis in children's language? What can be said is that there are sufficient trends in the few studies to date to suggest that several sets of patterns observed among adult men and women, are already well established among groups of children who range in age from pre-school to older adolescence. While their respective language strengths and weaknesses seem to be converging, girls and boys do seem to have markedly different discursive interests and norms and these anticipate, reflect, and reproduce the different interests and norms of men and women. As I shall argue in a later section, schools give little recognition to these different interests and norms and often deliver unjust language policies to their students as a result.

Comparing girls and boys in general language ability

Exploring any differences in language ability that may be due to physiological differences between the sexes seems an important place to begin. If there were pronounced sex differences, they would probably show up to some extent at least in children's discursive practices. Indeed from the earliest decades of this century, many studies in psychology address this topic (Klann-Delius, 1987), but it is only in relatively superficial areas such as phonology, that girls as a group seem to have a significant qualitative advantage that might come from genetic differences between the sexes. At the level of the individual child, the incidence of language pathology stands out as a related and clear-cut area of difficulty which affects boys much more than girls (Tanz, 1987). This difference certainly transfers into differential school success rates comparing boys and girls as groups in certain aspects of literacy and in some other related areas of competence.

Apart from these few areas, there is disagreement about the extent of qualitative inherited differences in the language of boys and girls. Some reviews assert broad female superiority on various verbal tasks (cited in Tanz [1987] by Maccoby & Jacklin [1974] and by Harris [1977]). Others disagree (cited in Tanz by Fairweather [1976] and by Maccauley [1978]). What can be said is that any gaps between boys and girls do seem to be closing. For example in studies of child development, sex differences account for only 1% of the variance in children's verbal abilities (Plomin & Foch, 1981). Elsewhere too, clear-cut differences appear only in limited areas and it is more difficult to separate the influence of contextual factors during socialization from the effects of directly inherited characteristics.

When language competencies revealed in the school setting itself are examined, girls do have a measure of superiority over boys. In accounting for this it is difficult to say if it is girls' socialization or any inherited language competence as a group, or a combination of both factors that gives them this superiority. In British data gathered from Assessment of Performance Unit surveys from 1981 to 1983, and from International Association for the Evaluation of Educational Achievement studies of written composition, the girls' performance in writing, at all ages (11, 14, 15, 16+), is significantly in advance of boys' (White, 1990). The reviewer detects two patterns of performance in the data: more boys than girls are always in the low scoring groups, and correspondingly more girls than boys are in the higher scoring groups. Moreover girls seem to be superior in certain genres of writing: autobiographical and fictional narratives; argument; procedural plans; letters of request; data reviews and literary criticisms. In contrast, boys succeed more readily when using other genres: the use of semi-technical registers for explaining things; the use of descriptions of how things work; and the use of argument to support a strongly held point of view. Plainly the different cultural interests of boys and girls arising from different patterns of gender socialization, would account for much of this observed difference. Perhaps too the different cultural interests of boys and girls expressed in their performances in different genres, could also account for much of the differences in their performance in the global area of 'written composition' itself, if the above studies were further analyzed using the different genres preferred by boys and girls as critical variables.

Also based on national survey research samples, Herbert Marsh's studies in Australia examine sex differences in the manipulation of verbal and maths constructs. Arguing from his longitudinal data, Marsh (1989) suggests that sex differences favouring boys in mathematics and girls in verbal areas, are now diminishing. Clearly, the converging lifestyle and subject interests of boys and girls would again have much to do with any different language strengths that they develop. As these interests come closer together as Marsh believes they are doing in certain areas of the curriculum, such as mathematics and science, so too will the strengths and weaknesses of boys and girls converge. So it seems that fewer of the attributes that were once thought to separate boys from girls in language ability are now associated with biological differences between the sexes. Indeed, many factors in the early research into children's language differences might today be investigated not as 'qualitative' differences that have their roots in biology, but as differences in discourse orientation or language style. As discussion in the previous section suggests, males and females develop different language norms that reflect the different interests and values that they acquire through their gendered socialization. The same point can be re-applied to most of the differences that appear in the language of girls and boys: whether girls are verbally more cooperative, whether they show a more person-centred communicative orientation, or whether they are better in adjusting their communicative styles to varying communicative situations (Klann-Delius, 1987), all these attributes are more likely to be a result of differences in gender socialization than of any biologically determined provenance that 'makes' boys different from girls in language ability.

Comparing the discourse of girls and boys

Compared with studies of adult gender differences, studies of boys' and girls' language that are not predicated on assumed inherited differences are few, and most of them can be summarized briefly. Firstly, those studies that examine cooperation and competition in conversations between boys and girls have found the same patterns of male dominance even among children aged three to four years, as exist among adults (Esposito, 1979; Klann-Delius, 1987). For example in conversations between boy–girl pairs, the boys interrupt twice as often as the girls (Esposito, 1979). But this pattern of dominance through interruptions, does not appear when boys have conversations with older people; in that setting boys tend to give more listener responses than girls to adult speakers (Dittman, 1977). Once again structures of dominance seem influential in this pattern: the need to recognize and conform to power relationships, based on age in this instance, seems to influence the discourse of boys who in turn reflect the pattern by reversing it in their discourse with girls. Moreover, these patterns of dominance seem to correlate with the behaviour of parents and teachers when interacting with girls and boys (Klann-Delius, 1987): these significant adults make more listener responses and fewer interruptions when boys are talking than when girls are talking.

Among older children in oral English examinations, where mixed groups of adolescent boys and girls are called upon to show proficiency in collaborative discussion, significant gender differences appear (Jenkins & Cheshire, 1990; Cheshire & Jenkins, 1991). While boys and girls in these formal conversational activities, offer a similar number of minimal responses to other interactants such as 'yeah' or 'mmm', the responses serve very different purposes for the girls than they do for the boys. For girls the responses usually signal conversational support; for boys they are used to gain a foothold in the conversation. Also in this formal oral examination setting, boys seem to make many more inappropriate remarks that close down discussions than do girls. In respect to both these findings, it is hard to escape the conclusion that it is socialization into the norms for interaction in single sex male or female groups which influences the conversational behaviour of both boys and girls in this formal setting. Indeed there seems to be strong support for this inference in other studies looking at single sex group interaction.

Girls and boys do have very different modes and methods of interaction in their single sex groups (Thorne, 1986) and these are often reinforced in many social settings by careful segregation of the sexes. In their recreational activities girls tend to be less public than boys. They engage with one another in small groups or in friendship pairs, in locations where confidences can be exchanged in privacy. Girls' play also tends to be more cooperative and involves cooperative rather than competitive pastimes. The turn-taking that is a feature of their play is also a feature of their conversations with other girls. As a result, sticking to the rules of turntaking is treated more seriously by girls than by boys. When disagreements occur in girls' groups, speakers tend to express the disagreements indirectly by using fewer direct imperatives and more phrases that solicit engagement and promote a sense of groupness. Through their membership of single sex groups, boys and girls seem to acquire different rules for creating and interpreting discourse. In summary I think we can infer that these rules are themselves modelled on male or female adult roles. Children then proceed to re-apply their single sex group discourse rules in mixed contexts, often doing so dysfunctionally. The cycle of communication and miscommunication continues when the rules are reproduced in mixed and single sex adult interactions.

Research suggests that these informal but influential rules do in fact carry over into adulthood and inform the kinds of communication that single sex adult groups develop (Maltz & Borker, 1983). These differences that are preserved in the discourse conventions of the two sexes, often produce that significant degree of miscommunication between women and men in general that I have already noted. Typically the differences are also reproduced by very young boys and girls in their turn, modelling and learning the behaviour of adult males and females who were once small boys and girls themselves. Indeed the ideologies associated with these conventional rules become habitual when young children are encouraged to be acquiescent and uncritical of the world around them; they become socialized into reproducing these patterns themselves. While there may be obvious attempts at resistance, much of this process of reproduction has an automatic character to it, since the ideologies are far from explicit and go unrecognized at the time of their transfer. For much of the time they are transferred unconsciously by the modelling of adults who themselves take the rules for granted. So it would be wrong to say that schools are 'manipulating' the behaviour of boys and girls, or that children are 'indoctrinated' into acquiring male or female discourse conventions.

Language and Gender Injustice in Schools

Under several headings in this final section, I collate evidence about the common language policies and discourse practices of schools and their teachers. I argue that these practices and policies found in the objective discursive structures of schooling itself, help to create and reinforce disadvantages for girls and women. But since they fall within policy areas that schools themselves take responsibility for in most places, they represent areas where immediate policy changes can be negotiated, implemented, and evaluated. My presentation of the evidence about these key problem areas also implies its own solutions, which are taken up again in various ways in Chapter 7.

Textbooks, reading schemes, and their messages about gender

There is a tendency for modern literate adults to perceive books of almost any kind for children as an intrinsic educational good, and to believe that as long as children are reading it does not matter much what they are reading. But children can encounter widespread and early contact with gender bias and other types of discrimination in the textbooks used in schools, and these are often re-read by generations of children. School textbooks are powerful manifestations of taken-for-granted norms and practices. In particular, the representations of gender and race in beginning reader texts, and in graded reading schemes, help create models for later language use and for children's perceptions about how the world is. Early reading texts are highly influential sources because they are the earliest contact with books that many children receive, and they are presented within an institution regarded in the community as worthy of trust and carrying official authority. Even when schools are islands of alienation within communities, they are still regarded by the very young as highly significant places, and often as awesome social institutions where the need for obedience and conformity is never questioned. As the authoritative texts of the school, school books are always critical agents of socialization.

While strong evidence supports the view that non-sexist children's books do have a positive influence on achievement and also eliminate harmful stereotypes (Stones, 1983), schools as buyers in the textbook marketplace continue to support material containing gender stereotypes and sexist language. Even prize-winning children's books surveyed in the USA, are found to present adult women only in stereotypical roles: in addition to the roles of wives and mothers, they are limited to the roles of a fairy, a fairy godmother, and an underwater maiden. None of the women portrayed are in formal employment (Whyld, 1983). In a study of six reading schemes for early childhood classes (Lobban, 1987), the female world represented is found almost entirely to focus on domestic activity or childcare, while male adult characters do little in the home but always drive the car. The portrayal of girls in the stories is restricted to stereotype 'girl' activities like skipping and hopping, while boys are portrayed in a range of active roles and games. At the same time, the boys' toys and activities are remote from any caring behaviour; their activities anticipate future occupational roles, and they spend much of their time watching adult males doing jobs of work. The researcher comments that the world these texts portray is not only sexist, it is more sexist even than present reality where most children do have working mothers and witness the sharing of adult roles.

Early textbook research found that more than seven times as many men as women feature in school age books and more than twice as many boys as girls (Graham, 1975). This tradition of gender imbalance in texts has long reinforced the opposition between males as 'active' and females as 'passive'. The same study also notes that the pronoun 'he' usually has an implied or real male referent in school texts, rather than a generic use: 97% of the uses of 'he' refer specifically to male humans or animals. These imbalances remain prominent in some curriculum areas, where girls' motivation to participate and achieve could only be diminished by this minimal role representation. For example, a review of maths texts for the middle school years reports a clear tendency in the books to define mathematics as the province of males: adult women are largely absent and girls disappear from texts too by the end of the middle school age range. The researcher observes that the decline in girls' involvement in maths, from ages 7 to 16, matches their gradual disappearance from the pages of maths textbooks (Northam, 1987). While recent efforts to abolish the generic use of male pronouns in quality English materials, have probably reduced its widespread incidence in school texts,[6] the imbalance between female and male actors found in the early research continues. Females are still confined to a restricted range of roles (Stones, 1983; Cheshire, 1984; Smith, 1985). It is even claimed that the imbalance may have become more marked in recent years (Gupta & Lee, 1990). Again the stereotyping of roles in textbooks seems greater than in the societies that produce the books and publishing houses sometimes offer elaborate explanations for this mismatch. They suggest for instance, that while boys have a very strong preference for male oriented readers, girls seem quite willing to read about boys (Coates, 1986). However, Anthea Gupta and Ameline Lee suggest that an analysis of marketplace rationalizations of this kind, whether accurate or not, may miss the point, since textbook publishers in one of the countries examined in their study had not even given the matter of role stereotyping in their books any thought at all. In comparing textbooks produced in two different English-speaking countries, Gupta & Lee report portrayals of male and female roles that are strikingly similar cross-nationally: the incidence of male characters averages over 70% in both sets of texts; males tend to be principal actors; the numbers of male speakers in the texts rises significantly as the reading level increases; the mean length of utterances of males increases as the reading level increases; and males are portrayed in a far wider range of social roles than females, both in the written text and in the illustrations.

The semantic referents of texts convey other subtle messages which are more difficult to identify and counter. Rosemary Stones collates examples of sexism in children's books. Her pamphlet's title itself makes a strong point about how the discourse of children's books can communicate prejudiced views: 'Pour Out the Cocoa, Janet' is a sentence from an Enid Blyton book. While this sentence standing alone conveys no discriminatory message, if repeated and reinforced in a book it could leave young readers with the impression that females in certain settings are the servants of males. It does portray a taken-for-granted and sexist view of the world. But dealing with textual bias of this kind needs careful and concerted policy action, since there is often a fine line between critical textual analysis of this kind, and less liberal forms of censorship. In Chapter 7, I list some 'questions to ask about children's books', extending on a list that Stones recommends.

Gender differences in whole class teacher–pupil interactions

Although teacher–pupil discourse is regarded as a major area of gender injustice, much of the evidence assembled to date remains inconclusive. Jan McPherson (1990) provides a summary of the often contradictory evidence, citing other summary reviews (Brophy, 1985; Kelly, 1988). Clearly findings vary as the participants and context of the interaction vary: age, social class, ethnicity, level of schooling, subject matter, sex of the teacher, and level or formality of classroom activities all provide contextual variables that are theoretically of great influence. I outline some summary conclusions below, but firm policy planning needs much more research that introduces careful controls for these diverse variables.

In Alison Kelly's review of gender differences in teacher–pupil interaction (1988), there are strong general indications that female and male teachers tend to pay less attention to girls than to boys at all ages, in various socio-economic and ethnic groupings, and in all subjects. Also girls receive less behavioural criticism, fewer instructional contacts, fewer high-level questions and academic criticism, and slightly less praise than boys. While girls volunteer to answer questions as often as boys, they are less likely to call answers out. Finally it is well attested that these differences in interaction occur despite teachers' assertions that they do not treat nor wish to treat girls and boys differently (Sadker & Sadker, 1985) and teachers are often unaware of their differential treatment of girls and boys.

Some research on finer aspects of teacher–pupil discourse is appearing, looking for example at variations in the type of questions asked by teachers, and at the allocation of turns in interaction. There are reports that teachers direct more open-ended questions at boys in the early years of schooling, and more yes/no questions at girls (Fichtelius *et al.*, 1980). Consistent with other studies, this apparent expectation from teachers that boys 'might have more to say than girls' could in turn encourage some girls to think that they have less to say. Examining the different ways that turns at speaking are allocated by teachers, Graddol & Swann ask whether the quieter or the more talkative pupils receive a bigger share of classroom interaction. They argue that a 'competitive dynamic' underlies classroom transactions in which 'first in gets the floor' (1989: 60). It is the boys who tend to be 'first in' because the teachers' own non-verbal cues, particularly their gaze-attention, are important in systematically offering boys more opportunities for participation, thereby cuing them to answer earlier even when there seems to be an equal opportunity for boys and girls to contribute. Joan Swann (1988) suggests that boys are directly encouraged to contribute more to classroom talk by this gaze behaviour of teachers, who tend to look at boys at critical points more often, especially when an answer is needed. She also refers to studies where teachers have successfully created a gender balance in their whole class talk, by seeming to over-compensate in including more contributions from girls.

There is evidence in Michelle Stanworth's study (1983), that male and female British pupils in late adolescence experience the classroom as a place where boys are the focus of teacher–pupil interactions, while girls are on the margins. Even teachers describe themselves as more interested in the boys, and they are seen by their pupils as more concerned with the boys. They are also more aware of the identities of boys, and they are more willing to allow the boys to upstage the girls in interaction. In the same study, many of the girls who are not admired by their female classmates manifest interactional features that are more characteristic of boys, even though these are the very features that the same girls admire the boys for possessing. In other words, in their perceptions of one another the girls pillory the use of discourse practices that could allow them to compete with the boys, thereby collaborating in their own oppression.

It seems that by placing a lower communicative and prestige value on girls' contributions, teachers are reinforcing the cycle of injustice that begins long before schooling in the adult-to-child socialization practices of early childhood. The distinctive linguistic capital that older girls at least bring into mixed gender classrooms, is not often recognized as relevant to those settings. At the same time, the dispositions for viewing the world that many girls acquire in their own socialization discourages them from placing an adequately high value on a use of language norms that might allow them to compete equally. But again this communication of adult practical ideologies has an automatic character about it. Many studies do confirm that teachers are unaware of the fact that they treat boys differently from girls, and even disbelieve the evidence when confronted with it. Indeed, it is common for both male and female teachers to defend their actual practices with the sincere disclaimer that 'we treat them all the same, here' (Biggs & Edwards, 1991; Fennema & Peterson, 1985; Morse & Handley, 1985).

Variations in interaction according to context and participants

As earlier chapters confirm, structural arrangements often affect children from different sociocultural backgrounds very differently. Some girls and boys appear confident and at home in the setting of the school. They are supported by the cultural interests, values, and dispositions that they share with their teachers, and with those of their peers who come from similar backgrounds; they are empowered within the setting of the school by the orientation to the world that they bring from the home; and they are ready to convert the already valuable and similar cultural capital acquired in the home, into the high status cultural capital that the school offers. Others are not empowered in this way. They bring cultural interests, values, and dispositions to schooling that are inconsistent with the demands that teachers place upon them; and the cultural capital that is esteemed in their home communities is not readily convertible into the high status capital of the school. Already in Chapters 3 and 5, I describe the ways in which groups of socially or culturally different children are disempowered by the interactive norms that the school requires them to possess, even while it fails to provide them with an opportunity to acquire and use those norms. As the above section argues, gender can operate in a similar way when the acquired cultural interests of girls are not given recognition in schooling. Moreover, gender seems to interact with other variables to produce multiple disadvantages in classroom interaction. Grazyna Baran is an experienced secondary science teacher who talks about the problem as it affects many pupils in her London girls' school:

> Girls, particularly working class and immigrant girls, lack confidence in themselves and their abilities, especially in unfamiliar areas. Having spent a lot of time watching them, I have noticed that girls exert pressures on each other which reinforce this lack of confidence. There is pressure not to brag, 'show yourself up' or make a fuss; otherwise you may be labelled 'big-headed'. Discretion and modesty are valued, while outspokenness and self-assertion are suspect, if not 'punished' by the group (unless they express anti-authoritarianism).

Imagine a girl attempting to formulate a question in a science lesson under such pressures. She is likely to expose her vulnerability in two ways. First, she risks the censure of the whole group. Second, she almost certainly risks being dismissed and thus unintentionally ridiculed by the teacher for failing to pose the question in a sufficiently abstract frame of reference to be recognized by that teacher. In such a context, girls may readily reject scientific knowledge wholesale as being at odds with their own experiences (Baran, 1987: 91).

The pressure of peer group values that Baran describes here, is similar to the structural contradictions that minority cultural values create for some children. Moreover their impact on interaction in the conventional classroom is also similar: those affected are reluctant to play the school's game by revealing expertise, interest, or even self-doubt in their interactions with the teacher.

The compounding effect produced when sociocultural background interacts with gender in classroom discourse, receives only incidental attention in the research to date and mainly in studies addressing ethnic differences in interaction. Even so, there are clear indications of gender differences in studies already discussed more fully in Chapter 3. In Sarah Michaels's research (1981), young African American children use a 'topic-associating' style more often in 'sharing time' activities and it is especially the girls who do so. In replication studies, Michaels and Courtney Cazden (1986) confirm that the children's narratives which favour a topic-associating style are perceived more negatively and they find that African American girls use the episodic style more often.

Other patterns suggesting interactive incompatibility between teachers and minority children, appear in British and New Zealand research. For example, the kind of relationships that Afro-Caribbean children experience when interacting with their teachers in England is very similar for both boys and girls, but it is different from that experienced by majority culture children (Wright, 1987). Not only do all the minority children see themselves as being 'picked on' by teachers, but the proportion of the teachers' time that they enjoy is also very different from other student groups. Examining classroom interaction in a New Zealand girls' high school, Alison Jones (1987) reports that working class girls from immigrant Pacific Island families, receive only rare moments of teacher interaction, while middle class majority culture girls enjoy most of the teachers' attention. She sees at least two effects coming from this imbalance: the minority girls as a result, do not receive equal opportunities to learn school knowledge; and the same girls learn different things about the process of learning, becoming more passive receivers of knowledge and fitting the image that their teachers create for them. Finally, in their study of new entrant Panjabi children in Britain, Netta Biggs and Viv Edwards (1991) report only slight differences in the patterns of interaction that culturally different girls and boys initiate with their teachers. In contrast, the same study finds that teachers themselves initiate significantly fewer moments of interaction with the minority girls. The researchers argue that because different amounts of time and different kinds of teacher interaction are associated with different groups of children, then it must be the teachers themselves who are reluctant to interact with the minority girls.

By varying context of interaction, including the sociocultural background of participants, future research may reveal settings and practices that provide a more desirable basis for policy action. There are some indications in senior classrooms for example, that changes in the topic and the nature of the class activity can produce sharp differences in pupil-initiated contacts with teachers. In New Zealand, studies of girls and boys at work in six senior schools (Burns *et al.*, 1991; Burns & Bird, 1987) in mixed sex and mixed ability chemistry laboratories, suggest that different patterns of interaction can develop with teachers in this type of setting: more girls seek discussion with the teacher in dealing with their learning problems, while it is mainly the boys who admit that they are afraid of revealing any incompetence by approaching teachers. Perhaps pupil laboratory sessions of this type can promote marked contrasts in interactive patterns, since the large gender differences found in more formal activities where teachers control interaction, seem to disappear in less formal and practical sessions. Broadly consistent with the above studies, there is evidence that girls in early adolescence who are engaged in craft, design and technology courses, have more contacts with the teacher than boys, and they are also longer contacts. The girls interrupt more and they make more unsuccessful attempts to initiate contact. Indeed in these practical sessions, the usual ratio of teacher-to-pupil contacts found in formal classes, where teachers control interaction, is reversed (Randall, 1987). However the researcher makes a pertinent point about the school in her study: the teacher, the head teacher, and the local authority are all strongly committed to providing equal opportunities for girls. As a result, (woodworking) projects of equal interest to the sexes are available, and there is minimal gender stereotyping in the way that lessons are handled. It seems that in this positive context of female empowerment where teachers value the cultural interests of both girls and boys, girls are receiving a more just distribution of interactive opportunities and more control over the discourse.

Pupil–pupil interaction in mixed sex groups

Although oral language activities are under-used as pedagogies, there is no doubt that at all levels of schooling they are important for mastering the curriculum and for promoting cognitive development itself. Earlier discussion already indicates the tendency that young boys have to control mixed sex interactions, when adults are not directly involved. This pattern seems to translate to classroom pupil–pupil interaction. For example, while girls act cooperatively in single sex groups and competitively if they need to in mixed sex groups, boys are competitive regardless of the context (Whyte, 1983). At the same time, girls clearly have a greater preference for approaching their classwork through peer and group activities. In the New Zealand study of six senior schools (Burns *et al.*, 1991), many more girls than boys in mixed sex and ability chemistry classes want to consult other students about their work, and they do so when given the chance. While the girls enjoy discussing their work with friends and go out of their way to promote discussion even outside school hours, most of the boys in the same study say that they do not and would not consult other students under any circumstances.[7]

This gender difference in preferences about groupwork, among older students, is consistent with the very real differences in preferences and in interaction patterns that already begin to appear by seven years. But while the girls in her study enjoy groupwork much more than the boys, Diane Reay (1991) also reports that the girls are far more likely to go along with the suggestions of others in the group. She says that this is consistent with girls giving a higher priority to achieving consensus than boys. In contrast, boys tend to work at their group tasks using hierarchies of control, direct imperatives, and direct questions that challenge each others' ideas. Reay's finding that seven year old girls enjoy group sessions much more than the boys, is very important; but she may misinterpret its cause: she attributes this preference to the greater willingness of girls to please the teacher and to seek her approval; but if interpreted within the context of my discussion in this chapter, the girls' preference for groupwork in her study is early but consistent evidence that collaborative discursive interests and norms are more widely distributed among girls than boys. Indeed this conclusion is underlined by several other findings also reported in Reay's study: these seven year old girls already report a sense of oppression in mixed sex groups; they sense a devaluation of female experience; they are already aware of the different value systems that girls and boys have; and they believe that the boys' values are more highly regarded in the classroom. It is clear in this study of very young students, as in studies of older children, that male discursive norms and interests are very different from female.

These few studies offer only preliminary indications of patterns of interaction that may exist more generally. However when coupled with other evidence about adult discursive practices and about the norms for interaction that children in single sex groups adopt, there are adequate grounds here to suggest tentatively two developmental trends in discourse practices as girls and boys reach towards maturity.

Firstly in mixed group and whole class contexts throughout their school careers, girls as a group continue to use the cooperative interactional patterns that they are accustomed to using in their own groups; while boys as a group tend to shed these patterns as a result of the more competitive discursive norms met and acquired in their single sex interactions, which are ultimately modelled on adult single sex behaviour and increasingly influenced by it as boys mature. Secondly as a result of their own socialization within single sex groups whose interaction is also modelled on the adult pattern, girls as a group continue to develop competence and interest in a more conversational and cooperative approach to their classwork; while boys as a group thrive more on a competitive and individualist approach to the curriculum because they are increasingly socialized in ways compatible with that approach, and also because schooling itself at its more senior levels, does little to reward and reinforce the use of cooperative interactional patterns that would be more consistent with girls' acquired cultural interests.

My general point here is that girls may be systematically excluded from genuine participation in the kinds of intellectually developing activities in schools, that are appropriate to their acquired discursive interests, because of the interactional styles and the classroom techniques that schools traditionally use and which teachers adopt, often against their will. Yet, the observed willingness of girls to work cooperatively at senior school level offers an attractive opportunity for teachers. This finding not only licenses a greater use of oral language work with many girls, and probably with many boys too in the senior school; on grounds of social justice it also supports a recommendation that after consulting their preferences, girls *should* be allowed to approach the curriculum in this way if their culturally acquired interests are to be served. There are wider ramifications for other normative educational practices in this point too: for example the use of external and norm-referenced assessment encourages competition and individual performance (Burns & Bird, 1987), thus discouraging the very forms of cooperative learning that involve interaction with peers. Indeed many conventional forms of curriculum assessment may routinely disadvantage many girls in their learning, and undermine their motivation to succeed.

Policy Action

These conclusions assume that real injustices exist and need to be addressed through policy action. Two sets of language policy recommendations emerge from discussion in this chapter. Firstly as a result of their different socialization, girls and boys as groups clearly bring different norms of language behaviour to schooling, and for various reasons these group norms tend to diverge as children mature. Approaching the middle and senior years of schooling, children encounter pedagogies that are increasingly individualist and competitive, thus matching the discursive norms and cultural interests of boys and men in general rather than those of girls and women. Girls and young women find that the culturally acquired interests and values implicit in their norms of interaction with others, are not recognized or even much valued in education. This is especially the case at senior secondary or tertiary levels, which in their discursive practices largely remain the exclusive male domain that they were in former times. Girls and young women find that that distinctive part of their linguistic capital that they themselves place high value upon, attracts less status as they proceed through education. Following arguments in earlier chapters, this institutional misrecognition of a significant part of the cultural capital of girls and women seems an unjust use of power by the institution of education. This constitutes a form of oppression that schools would do well to reverse as soon as possible by shaping curriculum, pedagogy and evaluation practices to allow males and females who may already be socialized into a gendered use of language, to approach the same learning tasks in ways appropriate to their already acquired cultural interests. Following Bhaskar's conception of discovery, in introducing policies of this kind, educational institutions would need to place priority on consulting and confirming the interests of students' themselves, and then shaping institutional practices accordingly.

At the same time, it is clear that in various ways education is reinforcing the different discursive practices that girls and boys bring with them into schooling. The review of research on men's and women's language suggests that unjust uses of power are commonly exercised in and through the different norms of linguistic behaviour that males and females take for granted. My review of language policies currently operating in schools, indicates that those policies reinforce the unjust use of gendered power through discursive practices. I conclude that teachers and administrators in schools urgently need to reflect on the wisdom of continuing to reinforce those policy practices. Planned change seems essential if school graduates are to escape the cycle of school-reinforced socialization into interaction patterns that seem undesirable for men and women in general, and which many children plainly resist. For reasons of justice, change in some areas may need to be gradual to protect the educational interests of those children who have already been socialized into gendered patterns and norms of interaction and whose educational success may depend on those norms and patterns being recognized in pedagogies for the time being. Again, the task is to replace unwanted forms of policy determination with wanted policies: to replace a negative use of power with a positive one. The later sections of this chapter have tried to highlight some of these unwanted practices which schools could readily replace with more desirable policies that could well be emancipatory for both men and women. In Chapter 7 I take these policy recommendations much further.

Notes to Chapter 6

1. The presence in language of 'oppositions', based on gender, is an ideological exaggeration of contrasts between males and females which have their bases sometimes in biology itself, but more often in inappropriate socialization practices that are wrongly deemed to have their bases in biology. The misleading tendency for man/male/masculine to be associated with notions like 'reason' and 'action' in opposition to the misleading tendency for woman/female/feminine to be associated with notions like 'emotion' and 'passivity', is deeply embedded in Western cultural practices. Women are the objects rather than the subjects in almost all metaphorical discourse: they are the property, rather than the possessor, the moved, rather than the mover. There is a complex interplay between the ideological structures created by these common oppositions, and the activities of agents who are affected by them through choice or compulsion. As oppressive forms of determination, these crude oppositions are mediated and reinforced through language. As males and females seek out those who manifest the gender oppositions that are portrayed as appropriate in the discourse of the culture, the activities of the agents themselves reinforce those discursive oppositions. The oppositions become ever more powerful interpretative categories which provide compelling reasons and accounts, equipping other agents with taken-for-granted criteria for seeking out other desirably endowed agents.

2. On an optimistic note, Jenny Cheshire and Nancy Jenkins (1991) argue from their studies of oral examination processes among senior school children, that 'women's style' (not 'women's language'), rather than being a despised and powerless form of communication, is now recognized through official reports and oral language assessment policies in Britain at least, as an essential attribute of successful group discussion.

3. These stereotypes have also had their effect in creating and perpetuating disadvantages for non-Western women. In former colonial settings, the introduction of a newly dominant foreign language has often disadvantaged the women from dominated groups even more than their men. Wherever a colonial high-status language was imposed, indigenous peoples needed wide access to that language to win any participation in the dominant economic and political

system. Usually under those circumstances, it was men rather than women who first became bilingual, often because the colonizers themselves in line with their own cultural preferences, chose the men to be the representatives of the indigenous groups, whether they were better suited or not. In the case of Koori Australians, the men were not necessarily suitable representatives of the group as a whole, since often they had been imprisoned, chained, and beaten by a system of rule that diminished their self-respect and sometimes their very ability to speak on behalf of their people. Also in some parts of Mexico and Guatemala, this reproduction of the male authority structures by Western colonialists has kept women and girls away from the language of power and inhibited the development of widespread and functional bilingualism among Indian minorities.

4. The efforts of feminists and others to reduce the incidence of sexist language in written English provide compelling evidence about the possibilities for the emancipatory reform of discourse itself. Robert Cooper (1989) pronounces these efforts very successful in achieving their aim. Using a huge corpus of words drawn from American publications, he reports a dramatic decline in the rate of 'androcentric generics' in use over an eight year period. This change suggests that while the possibilities for language reform in such areas as gender usage may be heavily constrained by institutional structures, the more obvious features of discursive structures themselves can still be modified by the concerted action of individuals. But language is always responsive to this sort of pressure, since it is a set of conventions agreed by people over time; language is a key site for continuing struggle, and discourse practices can change provided the appropriate pressures are applied. Indeed, political success in deliberately changing language can even deflect attention from institutional structures that may be more resistant to change. There are wider and more subtle institutional forces that cannot be readily identified in patterns of language usage, and which accordingly provide no firm site for concerted action. For example, on the evidence of labour statistics, of high status occupational differences, and of salary differentials, the broader campaign for women's liberation has made much smaller gains. It is easier to change forms of language use than to change the institutional values, practices, and attitudes that subordinate women. As Cooper suggests, it is easier to write 'chairperson' than to pay a chairwoman as much as a chairman. Since the forms and structure of a language derive from the meanings and structures of society, success in the elimination of sexist language may only be temporary if wider structural reform does not accompany it.

5. Ralph Fasold (1990) notes the greater degree of 'style shifting' that occurs in the discourse of women speakers. This difference is usually accounted for in the literature as an attempt by women to achieve status in asymmetrical contexts by using favoured language forms. But Fasold would want to examine this trend from a different perspective. He argues that the way for researchers to look at this style-shifting by women is to ask why men use favoured variables so little; why do they engage in remarkably less style-shifting than women. Jenny Coates (1986) seems to recommend a similar change in perspective, which may be helpful in shifting the debate about gendered discourse so that theory based on

hierarchical opposition between the genders can be replaced by a more 'inclusive' set of categories of thought. The difficulties in moving the debate away from oppositional stereotypes and towards more inclusive categories, are clearly significant ones, since researchers themselves are subject in complex ways to the same oppositional categories discussed in Note 1. Furthermore, the differences perceived between male and female discourse seem to be reinforced by social class stereotypes of the most persistent kind, reaching across cultures. In Ireland for instance, listeners were asked to identify the gender of pre-adolescent children from tape-recorded speech. Where the listeners mis-identified the speaker's gender, there was a tendency for the boys who were mis-identified as girls to be from the middle class and for the girls who were mis-identified as boys to be from the working class. Masculine speech was perceived as 'working class'; feminine speech as 'middle class' (Fasold, 1990). Also, there is the long-standing convention in linguistic description for men and women to be hierarchically contrasted. For example, the grammarian Otto Jesperson in his seminal book *Language*, has a chapter entitled 'The Woman' but none 'The Man'. Women are the 'marked', the 'different' sex. Their language is described in reference to the male standard. However, on my account here it is the competitive discourse style favoured by many Western men that is the marked variety, since it tends to diverge from a norm that is preferred by most people, perhaps including most men.

6. Many studies examine the use of the invariant male pronoun and the generic 'man'. Clearly the use of sexist language forms has different effects on different people. Many women report that they see themselves excluded from groups that are referred to using the invariant male pronoun, or the generic 'man' (Martyna, 1978, 1983). But the impact of these sexist language forms, on the learning processes of young people in different contexts, seems to be clear-cut: college students presented with captions like 'social man' and 'urban man', choose pictures of men only, more often than they do if the generic 'man' is removed; school children of all ages interpret job descriptions that use the male pronoun or generic 'man', as directed at men applicants only; gender cues in job advertisements affect the choices that senior students make; and reading comprehension miscues lessen when non-generic pronouns are used (Frank & Treichler, 1989).

7. As well as being 'relational' in their topic-related interaction with their classmates, their teachers, and families, the girls as a group in this study are also much more relational in their understanding of chemistry itself than the boys. The girls are more likely to pay attention to relationships among concepts in their work, which is an attribute of students with a 'deep' approach to learning who are more task-involved and also more highly achieving (Burns & Bird, 1987).

7 School Action

Outside the School

The aim of this final chapter is to suggest how unwanted language policies in education can be replaced with wanted ones. Following the discourse ethic, presented in Chapter 2, the first task in an act of social policy making is to achieve consensus at system level by establishing any universalizable norms that could operate as principles across the system and that could increase the scope for meeting social justice goals. In language policy making, this clarification of principles means finding a realistic set of shared values that overarch all the various social and cultural groups that the political system contains (Smolicz, 1984). Although most of these values may come from the dominant group, they cease to be merely dominant values once they are found to be consistent with the just treatment of the interests of other groups. They then become the property of the political system as a whole.

At whole system level, whether national, provincial, or state, two principles guaranteeing key language rights seem essential (after Spolsky, 1986). These statements of shared values follow readily from discussion and conclusions reached in Chapters 4, 5 & 6. The first principle guarantees the right of children to be educated wherever possible in the same variety of language that is learned at home; or failing that, at least in a school that shows full respect for that variety's existence and for its role in preserving important ethnic, traditional, social, gender, or religious values and interests. The second principle guarantees the right of children to learn to the highest level of competence possible, the standard or official language(s) or the languages of wider communication adopted by the society as a whole.

Action in devolved local settings in line with the second stage in the discourse ethic, will follow from this action at system level. There are two clear reasons why the devolution of decision making down to local levels is essential in specific areas of language policymaking: firstly, devolution is needed to establish sub-norms for determining local compatibility between interest groups, whose views may not be well represented at whole system level because of the degree of pluralism that the political system itself contains. Secondly devolution is needed to agree on any necessary compromises, should genuine incompatibility exist. For example, incompatibility will arise when the values of cultural minorities support pluralist versions of the place of language in 'the good life' that are very different from the norm. A just form of policy action does not need a conception of what *the* just society would be. Rather, it requires as many conceptions of justice as there are distinct possible conditions of society or subsets of society or culture.

As a result, after the two overarching policy principles guaranteeing language rights have been agreed and elaborated at whole system level, the most important and difficult work will occur at the local level. This may be no larger than a single town, board, district, or school. Discussion in this final chapter attends to action at this local level. In conjunction with the family, including any relevant extended family or ancestral tribal group, the school is the principal site for implementing language planning. This chapter introduces three broad sets of recommendations for meeting the language policy problems that this book raises. The first section (I) addresses the need to create patterns and models of communication within schools, which free staff, students, and community participants to consider planned, rational, and consensual action in pursuit of their educational aims. The second section (II) examines some of the language policies that contemporary schools in many places are developing to meet the kinds of complex problems that this book outlines: language policies on gender, minority cultural groups, bilingualism, race, poverty, and disadvantage. The final section (III) argues that children need to acquire 'critical language awareness' through the curriculum and norms for discourse that the school provides. It includes recommendations for practice.

I. Social Justice through Communicative Action in Schools

Schools collaboratively managed through critical policies that are continually revised using the best available evidence about changing circumstances, are more likely to be places of staff and community commitment. This is because community and staff participation has to be deliberately sought in order to get at that evidence. But participation is both an end in itself and a device for producing other ends. When people come together to plan something, there is obvious value to them in the feedback, skill development, social interaction, and knowledge growth that they receive. More than this, participation usually fosters a commitment in people to the results or product of their participation, provided those results seem reasonable to them. In this way, critical policymaking can become a development activity that has rewards for a school at several levels. For example through their use of democratic and relational management, schools tend to escape the trap of having their procedures and styles of operation modelled only on dominant and outdated points of view, which are often filled with error and narrow in range. Clearly by implementing genuine collaborative management involving their own staff and community, schools limit the degree to which the wider system of education can constrain social action within them. In other words, collaborative management lessens the extent to which wider social formations, like the relationships that exist between schools, the economy, and the state, create the ideological framework that constrains discourses of reform and initiative within them. Those same constraining relationships can also be challenged by school policymakers, to advance the interests of the school and its community. When they are challenged in this way, unjust social formations themselves can be transformed and their undesirable impact elsewhere may also be lessened. At the same time by lending their approval and support, schools can reinforce the values in the wider social formations that seem worthwhile and desirable.

There is empirical evidence to support claims of this kind. For example, it has been found that active parent-involvement in decision-making can bring children from minority social or class groups closer to their teachers, who often come from the dominant class and culture; that the parents themselves grow in confidence and develop a sense of their own efficacy which impacts positively on student learning; and that the harmful stereotypes about pupils that teachers often develop, fall away as teachers begin to collaborate with parents (Comer, 1984; Cummins, 1986; Garcia & Otheguy, 1987; Greenberg, 1989; Haynes, Comer & Hamilton Lee, 1989; Rasinski & Fredericks, 1989). In the eyes of the public, autonomous schools are also more 'legitimate' places, a concern addressed by Jürgen Habermas who wants to remove the discursive randomness that typifies the management styles of organizations. In its place, he wants to install a discourse arrangement for resolving conflicts of interpretation as they develop, using a situation where asymmetrical relations of power do not prevail or even operate. For him a 'new' form of 'institutionalized discourse' is needed in public institutions if they are to recapture their legitimacy for people in general, their sense of direction, and the motivation of participants and adherents. In this section I look closely but selectively at this complex set of ideas from Habermas, which seems to have important applied value for policy action at the level of the school.[1]

Putting the discourse ethic to work in schools

In ideal and undistorted communication Habermas suggests, speakers can defend by word or deed all four of the validity claims: what is said is meaningful, true, justified and sincere (see Chapter 2). When all of the participants in a given speech context are able to do this, when all related evidence can be brought into play, and when nothing apart from logically reasoned argument is used in reaching consensus, then the circumstances provide an 'ideal speech situation'. A starting point in appreciating what Habermas is up to is to note that when he talks of an 'ideal' situation, he is not suggesting that any possible speech context has the characteristics of this 'ideal speech situation'. He admits that the conditions of actual speech are rarely if ever those of the 'ideal speech situation'. What he wants to show is that all exchanges of speech tacitly presume that near-ideal conditions apply. Indeed if communication is going to take place in speech situations and if rational consensus is an aim of the interaction, then these things on their own require us to presume that ideal conditions obtain. What conditions do people expect when they enter into purposeful discourse?

Firstly, most people expect that a speech situation that they enter will be one from which the true interests of the participants in the discussion can emerge:

- all participants must receive an equal distribution of opportunities to select and use speech acts;
- all participants must have an equal chance to initiate and maintain discourse;
- all participants must have an equal chance to advance their points of view, to question ideas, and to give reasons for and against claims made in language.

Secondly, people expect that argument and debate will proceed without undue external pressures:

- all participants must accept that accidental or systematic constraints on discussion will play no part in it;
- all participants must be assured of an equal chance to express feelings, attitudes, and intentions;
- all participants must be assured of an equal chance to oppose, permit, command, instruct, forbid, and any of the other things that any other participants are entitled to do.

Thirdly, people expect that the 'force of argument' will prevail; that the outcome of discussion will depend on the force of the better argument.

What remains after meeting all these conditions, is a democratic form of public discussion that provides a forum for an unforced flow of ideas and arguments: domination, manipulation, and control are banished. Again Habermas is recognizing an ideal that does not really exist; an ideal that is merely promised and expected in almost every activity of language. The existence of this ideal situation is inherent in the nature of communication itself. Humans expect that it operates every time they go to speak; in making an utterance people are holding out the possibility that a form of social life exists in which individuals can have free, open, and equal communication with one another.

From these ideas Habermas extracts a 'critical measure' of the 'quality of interaction' that takes place in social settings and in social institutions. Clearly certain things are often lacking in ordinary speech situations and their absence distorts communication. Usually too, other things will be present, like ideologies that distort communication in favour of the powerful (Corson, 1993b). Bureaucratic communication as often used in schools, especially larger ones, regularly falls short of the ideal, since its purpose is usually to command and to control; it always has some strategic purpose. This strategic use of discourse assumes the existence of roles, based on legal authority of some kind; it assumes that it is the role of some to receive impersonal messages, and to act upon them with little debate or question; and it assumes that the weight of tradition, of power, or of domination is more important in decision-making than the need for rational consensus. In all these respects, the normal bureaucratic communication of schools runs counter to the kind of collaborative and participative decision making that an ideal speech situation might allow. I want to reinterpret these ideas into the everyday practice of managing schools. The key to implementing this approach to management seems to lie in the way the concept of 'impartiality' is put into practice. Habermas shares this concept with John Rawls (see Chapter 2), and the latter may offer a little more guidance about its application in real world institutions.

Following Rawls's account, Brian Barry (1989) suggests fleshing out the idea of 'impartiality' in two different ways. The first approach is to ask the interested parties in any problem-centred discussion, what outcome they would favour if they did not know which position they were to occupy under a new policy. Doing this prevents powerful participants from abusing their superior bargaining power, since it denies them various kinds of knowledge, especially knowledge of their own identities in the hypothetical arrangements. This device creates a kind of game in which participants ask what result rational self-interested players would finish up with if they did their best in presenting to each other the greatest possible challenge in support of their case. But Barry's second approach is more like a debate than a game. Its method is to ask those involved to propose and defend principles for the distribution of benefits and burdens that they sincerely believe ought to be acceptable to everyone affected, and which no one could reasonably reject. The criterion for choosing these principles is that they should lead to an outcome in the situation that is both preferable to what would result if there were no agreement, and productive of as satisfactory an outcome as would obtain under conditions in which bargaining pressure is removed. In other words, this approach asks participants to argue not for what they would do if given a free hand in the matter, but for what they should do. In this second approach the objective is to convince opponents by making them see things as you see them, but in a two-way process. The debate is in good faith, in that participants must be prepared to be convinced, as well as to convince others. For some purposes this approach could enable participants to think of themselves as representatives of groups in the wider society, although not if this meant excluding the real representatives of minorities or other social groups.

These approaches suggest how the discourse ethic can be put to work. But there is a common objection to putting the ideal speech situation to work: if we are to achieve genuine balance in discourse, all participants need to have similar knowledge about the subject matter of the policy discussion. As well as having particular details relevant to the policy issue itself, Iris Young (1981) concludes that all participants approaching social policy issues need to have broad and specific knowledge of the particular society that they are considering: they need to know the basic, natural constraints of their location, the climate, topography, the character and general amount of land, and material resources to which they have access etc.; they need to have basic demographic knowledge, such as how much space they have per person, what resources can be produced relative to the population; they need to know the sort of problems their technology can solve, and the level of productive capacity at their disposal; they need therefore to have a good grounding in the culture and traditions of their society; they need to appreciate the tastes of their artistic and decorative tradition; they need to have a set of shared symbols and stories; and they need to know their language, the games that they play, their educational practices etc. In short for participants to engage in free, open, and equal communication with one another, on matters of policy complexity and managing an institution collaboratively, they need to be well educated to begin with.

If participants are in possession of this knowledge, and if there is genuine goodwill in the administrative setting, the ideologies of special interest groups should have fewer distorting effects. Indeed, given continual practice and the incentive that comes from having genuine policy purposes and decision making power, the influence of the three principal distorting functions that ideology itself is said to serve (Giddens, 1979) may lessen or disappear:

(1) the representation of sectional interests as universal: i.e. by defining interests specific to a particular group so that those interests are perceived as universally valid;
(2) the denial or transmutation of contradictions: i.e. by reformulating fundamental system contradictions as more superficial issues of social conduct;
(3) the naturalization of the present through reification: i.e. by defining present organizational realities as 'the way things are' and objective, so that alternatives seem unworkable or unrealistic.

Public policymaking regularly incorporates these functions of ideology into its decision-making practices. In doing so, it marginalizes the interests of less powerful stake-holders, and forestalls change. In some places, though, the interests of minority and other disempowered groups are being deliberately consulted, and school policy makers are responding to the results of that consultation.

School action in three specific contexts

In this section, I give particular attention to schooling for ancestral minorities. But the ideas discussed have direct relevance to sociocultural minorities of all kinds. In curriculum policy making in the Northwest Territories of Canada, a form of multicultural curriculum development has taken local ethnic diversity into account, and curriculum planners in schools try to build upon the various interpretative frameworks that exist within communities (Connors, 1984). This means that free-flowing and wideranging dialogue is initiated between the cultural groups that make up each community, and this forms the basis for curriculum planning and for decision making, responding to the reasons and the accounts that minority people themselves offer as expressions of the cultural structures that they value. In this setting, compromises are made if there are cultural incompatibilities, and the resulting curriculum is valued as something co-produced by local cultural groups. It has a meaning in local situations and incorporates all necessary linguistic and cultural characteristics. In outline, this seems a version of the discourse ethic at work.

Rock Point is a rural Navajo community school in the USA, which returned to parental involvement and community control (Holm & Holm, 1990). At Rock Point, the local language and culture is the basis of the curriculum. The School Board is drawn from the community itself; it tries to represent the interests of the community as a whole, even when the immediate effects of longer term goals seem unrewarding or threatening to important sectional interests. The authors report on the kind of communicative action that has empowered four key groups within the school: its Board, its staff, the parents, and its students. From the outset, each group needed to overcome the relative disempowerment that they felt in relation to outside powers and to one another. Firstly, dating from its earliest meetings, the Board insisted on high financial and ethical standards in order to give legitimacy to its management, especially in the eyes of the government's funding authorities who they feared might find a pretext for re-assuming control over the school. As a result, outside agencies were impressed with their management and found it difficult to believe that the Board itself was really running the school. Secondly, the staff themselves were empowered by two things: by their sense of success when it became clear from the stream of visitors attracted that they were seen as competent; and by their sense of expertise when the quality of the vision that they themselves had of what good Navajo language education should be like, was obviously respected in the eyes of outsiders. Thirdly, the parents were empowered too because their own first language became the language of the school, giving them genuine access to the instructional and governance process. The parents had open access to Board meetings; a Parent Evaluation Committee studied the school's operations three or four times a year, and reported to the Board and the staff on its findings; parents were the first resource for curriculum content and the school regularly hired them as instructors; and Parent Conferences were held twice yearly for each class. For these meetings, parents observed classes in the mornings and met with teachers in the afternoon, usually with their own children present. This last practice resulted in a very high level of parental participation in the parent–teacher conferences. In the early 1980s it reached more than 85%. Lastly, the students themselves were empowered through their social and academic success, their own sense of progressive mastery of the curriculum, and the value that Rock Point placed on their Navajo-ness.

Australia offers another example of successful communicative action at work in a minority school: in this case a community school in the north-west of Western Australia that is founded on traditional community structures, controlled by an all-Aboriginal council, and whose classes are conducted inside the settlement itself, and under the close watch of the local community (Bullivant, 1984). Literacy activities in this school focus on elements of everyday tribal life, and they use texts prepared on the settlement. Numeracy work concentrates on hunting themes and on the gathering of pearls. The only role for non-Aboriginal teachers is in literacy and numeracy teaching. Tribal elders or Aboriginal teachers handle other aspects, all within the traditions set by the culture itself. In this, and in the earlier examples, the influence of unwanted forms of cultural determination coming from wider social formations, has been removed. In its place, the various participants are reshaping their institutions; they are also contributing a good deal to the transformation of those wider social formations by way of their own example. On the evidence offered by these and other preliminary essays into self-managed, minority schooling, it is readily apparent that once minority people are allowed to assume fuller responsibility for what they are doing, and if their institutions are equitably funded, a fascinating dialectic develops between the schools and wider agencies.

Modifying or replacing majority culture schools?

New Zealand offers different approaches to modifying majority culture schools. In 1989, a radical reform of educational administration enabled the devolution of much educational decision-making away from national level and down to new Boards of Trustees that are elected for every school in the country. Mandatory requirements for each school, are that it insert into its formal charter a strong expression of commitment to non-sexist and anti-racist values, and guaranteed support for the educational rights of the ancestral Maori people, especially a commitment to the Maori language. This is because legal interpretations of historic treaty arrangements in New Zealand give all Maori people the right to an education in Maori, should they demand it (Hastings, 1988). Beyond this entitlement, the requirement that schools operate according to a charter drafted in consultation with community groups, aims to give minority people considerably more scope to exercise a fair measure of influence over their children's education (Department of Education, 1988). This development allows and encourages the modification of existing schools, to take more account of minority presence within them. In section (a) below I describe a school where modifications occurred that anticipated the reforms and provided a model for later developments elsewhere in the country.

(a) Modifying Majority Schools: Effective Bilingual Schooling

Courtney Cazden (1989) and Steven May (1994) both offer rich descriptions of this inner-city primary school. Richmond Road School has a well functioning, pluralist curriculum and organizational structure. In 1990 the school's student profile was 20% Samoan, 20% European New Zealanders, 18% Maori, 35% other Polynesian, and 7% were Indian and others. To bring about reform over a lengthy period, the school's principal, himself Maori, had purposefully communicated a vision to his staff, based on his insights into cultural questions. But even after his death, the school continues to demonstrate its capacity to be a 'self-sustaining system', using continual communicative action to take on the task of reform and improvement that is necessary to keep a worthwhile system operating. Cazden describes how Richmond Road is different:

> In contrast to the isolation of teachers in single-cell classroom schools, Richmond Road teachers work in a setting of intense collectivity. Children and staff interact in complex organizational 'systems', as they are always referred to: vertical/family groupings of children; non-hierarchical relationships among the staff; curriculum materials that are created by teacher teams at the school and rotate around the school for use by all; and monitoring systems for continuous updating of information on children's progress (1989: 150).

For his vertical grouping system, the principal borrowed the example offered by non-graded country schools. Six *ropu* (vertical groups) operate in shared or separate spaces, one of them including a Samoan bilingual group, another a Maori bilingual group, a third a Cook Island Maori bilingual group, and a fourth the ESL language unit for non-English speaking newcomers to New Zealand. The fifth and the sixth *ropu* are English-speaking only. Each *ropu* includes children from the entire age range, from five year old new entrants to eleven year olds. Children stay in the same *ropu* for their entire primary schooling, working with one home-group teacher in frequently changing vertical home groups of 16–20 pupils. Also attached to the school are Maori, Samoan, and Cook Island immersion culture/language pre-schools ('language nests'). The three dual immersion bilingual units, operating in three of the primary school *ropu*, receive the graduates from these pre-school language nests, provided parents agree. During half of each morning and every other afternoon, the teachers in these units speak only Maori, Samoan, or Cook Island Maori, and the children are encouraged to do likewise.

Paired teaching and reciprocal instruction is common in this school. The provisional authority possessed by the late principal, remains a model for all the school community members: 'whoever has knowledge teaches'. As a result the official hierarchy of ascribed statuses has much less meaning. For example, although the school's language leaders/assistants have no formal professional training, they function as full teachers in virtue of their undoubted expertise and on-the-job training. Again, the school's caretaker (janitor) is involved in the educational work of the school as a valued colleague, supporting children and staff, respected by parents, and a friend to all the children. Parents too contribute their special knowledge and 'the front door is always open'. The school is organic to its community.

In this institution, the obvious stress on communal activity for the students is extended in other directions too: relations are developed at various levels. The vertical grouping of the *ropu* makes cooperative curriculum and resource development by teachers possible. Organized into five curriculum groups that deliberately cut across the *ropu* teaching teams, teachers collaborate in making 'focus resources' for school-wide topics that follow a multi-year plan, so that all minority groups are assured of exposure to each topic. Each team makes materials at ten reading levels for use in four learning modes. Each teacher is responsible for making a number of different items. When ready, materials are presented to colleagues during staff meetings, and they are then rotated throughout the school, staying in each *ropu* for fixed periods. Clearly as well as discursive collaboration, there is efficiency and effectiveness here. Like the school itself, curriculum materials are matched to the community that the school serves, and they target the needs of the students.

Richmond Road is also a learning community for adults: they learn about teaching, about other cultures, and about themselves. By laying stress on workshops and conferences, on contact with up-to-date theory, and on worthwhile staff meeting discussions, staff share and explore their own and each other's cultural and class backgrounds, which are as diverse as the childrens'. By working together themselves, teachers learn about collaborative techniques for learning, and this offers a sound model for the students. Cazden quotes one staff member: 'I think that's why the children work together here, because they can *see* us working together' (1989: 150). It is plain that the overtly competitive nature of regular schooling is missing from this collectivist environment. It is also plain that the school shows high regard for a range of minority culture discourse norms, like those discussed in Chapter 3, and for the values that support those norms. The self-esteem of the pupils including their growing sense of pride, their sense of who he or she is, and their sense of involvement in a worthwhile community, is put ahead of their academic performance. Yet the environment for academic development does not seem to suffer as a result. Cazden sets Richmond Road against a United States report on 'effective schools' (Bryk & Driscoll, 1988); she finds that that report's essential features are matched 'amazingly well' at Richmond Road:

- shared values, especially about the purpose of the institution, what students should learn, and how teachers and students should behave;
- a common agenda of activities that provide opportunities for interaction and link students, faculty and administration to the school's traditions;
- a distinctive pattern of social relationships that embody an ethos of caring (from Cazden, 1989: 143).

At Richmond Road, the instructional leader was able to communicate to the staff and community his vision of what a multi-ethnic school for children and teachers should be. According to May (1994), the principal's success came from his ability to cultivate an enthusiasm in others for his restructuring, and from his willingness to give people all the time that they needed for change. May also confirms that his plans for change were gradual and carefully managed, and that he brought about structural changes over a period of 8–9 years. Coming from a minority background himself, the principal knew that traditional forms of schooling often perpetuate inequalities for minority children. As a result, he pursued policies of reform that blocked and countered pressures on the children to conform to the dominant culture. May's critical ethnography of the school which was critiqued itself in the drafting stage by the school's staff, details the principal's policymaking strategy. I incorporate some of that detail below to illustrate similarities between the forms of communicative action recommended here, and the actual practices followed in Richmond Road's development.

May observes that the principal himself in all the major stages of the reform process, was the catalyst for change. But in promoting change he always showed willingness to incorporate the knowledge of others and to build it into his own thinking. In critically considering the school's problem context the staff were empowered by him to look for issues, to raise problems, and to take the lead in discussing them in formal meetings. He asked staff always to look for alternatives, especially to break away from the constraints of monocultural ways of doing things. While he promoted a strong sense of ownership over the curriculum by teachers, he did this in a context where everything was decided according to what was best for the children. This became the overriding normative principle for the school. To build a climate for change, he recruited staff sympathetic to his vision for the school. He also encouraged those who were unsympathetic to his vision to leave, and he waited for this to happen before pushing forward with radical changes.

Richmond Road raises expert knowledge to a level of priority that is rare in schools. In order to achieve genuine balance in policy discourse, as Iris Young advises, all participants need to have similar knowledge about the subject matter of the policy discussion. In promoting this level of staff expertise the principal used staff development as the key strategy, encouraging teachers to see the school's problems from many different theoretical perspectives. The staff library has numerous subscriptions to high quality, cross-disciplinary journals, which are read by all the staff and often used as the starting point for the professional development programme that has been built into the structure and timetable of the school. Participation in this programme is a professional duty; full attendance is expected; and meetings often last as long as three to four hours. Once a problem is identified the development meetings target the field of the problem through a stimulus paper by one or more staff members, or through the distribution of a collection of readings on the topic. In-depth discussion is often followed by a week's break for wider reading by all staff, for stimulating ideas, and for interest group discussions. Finally in another full meeting, policy action is proposed and implementation proceeds. Through this process as May points out, the staff have become used to adopting a theorized approach to their practice, developing expertise at the same time, and working always to keep communication lines open between themselves.

Priority has also been given to opening and maintaining communication lines with other people who have an interest in the school's policy and structural development. Early in the history of the reforms the staff created an open door policy for its community. They deliberately worked to reduce the conventional gap that stands between parents and teachers by giving parents a sense of their own status and efficacy, and by extending a welcome to them to enter the school and to say what they like. To initiate a sense of involvement, the school regularly holds community events to celebrate the opening of new developments; it incorporates the ceremonies and customs of the minority peoples themselves into these events. The school also holds regular cultural ceremonies, which community members attend in great numbers. As a result, May discovered that at the school parents feel drawn to contribute to policymaking, to teaching, and to other activities that occur within the different cultural teaching units. They feel free to observe or participate in class activities at any time. In their interaction with community members, staff strive to develop inclusive and reciprocal relations with all parents, but especially with minority people. In their behaviour, disposition, and speech they try to display intense respect for human difference and for cultural difference. Such an atmosphere has allowed community consultation and involvement in the development of school policy to grow naturally. For example the separate creation and organization of each of the three pre-schools on the premises, was community driven, and the current development of a fourth pre-school similarly responds to community suggestion and advocacy. In these pre-schools the buildings are controlled by the school's Board of Trustees, but the parents control their own finances and sort out their own rules. Consonant with the principal's original aim which was to elevate those with little power, these practices empower the parents to do it all themselves.

For more than a decade as May records, the school has involved significant and influential members of the minority community in matters of formal governance, and given them real power to direct the school in the community's interests. As a matter of policy the school encourages these leaders to mediate and to resolve difficulties that occur for minority group children, or even among minority community members. This policy includes appointing professional and ancillary staff drawn from the minority communities, giving them status in the school, and involving them directly in school governance. With these community structures in place, the task of consulting the interests of parents and community members, and setting these interests alongside the interests of teachers, pupils and other staff, is made more simple. In doing all of this, the principal built commitment to the changes through dialogue, through helping people to see that conflict and criticism are inevitable and productive, and through fostering a sense of self-worth among staff which encouraged them to withstand the inevitable pressures created even by gradually introduced radical reforms. At the heart of this commitment building was the principal's policy of having staff, pupils, and parents choose to be in the school, after learning of its differences when compared with conventional schools. This policy of frank disclosure also extends to choices about enrolling in units within the school. For example, parents are always fully counselled on the role and purpose of bilingual units, and then given the choice of enrolling children there or in the English-only units. This choice extends to the children as well, who also have the option of using either of their two languages at any given time in bilingual classroom programmes.

Throughout its policy development, the school has manifested a critical realist approach to power relations within the wider system. In furthering the interests of the school, this has meant being knowledgeable and sceptical as a staff, about those power relations. It has involved resistance and contestation where necessary, provoking and anticipating change. But most fruitfully, it has meant taking strategic advantage of rule-changes in the wider system to solve school problems and to further the process of reconstruction. For example, May records that the school introduced the first inner-city Maori bilingual unit, as soon as a change in the rules allowed it. Also in handling its internal power arrangements and decision making, the school has tacitly followed the course that Habermas recommends. The policy makers integrated conflict in a constructive way into their problem identification, compromising where necessary by agreeing to solve each group's incompatible problems as best they could. For example, although the Samoan community was the largest and the first community group to request its own pre-school and bilingual unit, the Board of Trustees under the chairmanship of a Samoan parent, acknowledged the right of the Maori community who are from the ancestral people of the country, to have the first pre-school and bilingual unit. But then with that development firmly in place, support for the Samoan developments followed quickly and received unanimous endorsement.

In implementing reform as May points out, the principal developed a policy of frank disclosure about the developments, but moved in careful stages to address his more complex problems. Even after broadcasting his plans to the staff and the community and after involving them in the initial decision-making process, he still made only small changes and did so gradually with constant consultation. While underlining the fact that there are no short answers to complex policy problems, he took pains to convince the community that the school was engaging in genuine reform. He achieved this by demonstrating to the community the success of each stage in his reconstruction and then by consulting them again, modifying the process, and moving on to the next stage. In addressing the more professional aspects of the reforms the school is also organized on a consultative basis, so that formal curriculum teams consider curriculum problems. In this process, individual teachers are released from class time, on different mornings, to participate in these cyclical policymaking sessions, where problems are identified and tested against the knowledge and interests of teachers. In these cycles of communicative action, the problem terrain is continually traversed and the theories of participants are continually tested against the evidence available, including that most important form of evidence: the views and wishes of participants themselves.

In the long and complex history of reform that May reviews, the school has developed a tradition of using trial applications of its policies and evaluating the critical responses of people to the trials. For example, willing senior teachers over several years trialled and then modelled for others the new family grouping structure, using the features of the ideal family as a model for inclusive and extended relations. The principal gave these senior colleagues complete discretion in trialling, adopting, and discarding different arrangements, while promoting open communication with the parents of involved students. When the school identified a successful model, the policymakers gradually encouraged interest among other staff and then established other similar units. While working from the model preferred by the trial group within individual units, the school still allowed teacher discretion over structural details such as timetabling, teacher turn-around in responsibility, etc. This whole process took 5–6 years. As a long-term outcome of the reforms, the school has allowed the structural changes to flow through into pedagogical changes, elevating the status of all participants in the learning process. May sees Richmond Road as a 'relational school' (Skilbeck, 1984): it manifests a democratic decision-making framework among staff, an established consultation process with the local community, and it does all this in an environment that builds on and strengthens its pupils' contacts with their own cultures.

(b) 'Monocultural' Minority Schooling

Richmond Road is not unique in providing this consistently multi-ethnic and multilingual environment, although it is a rare New Zealand school that has progressed very far in this direction. Even so, mere modification of existing schools is clearly not enough for some minority communities and the recent policy reforms do allow communities to go much further. The response to minority rights in New Zealand is no longer limited to the creation of multi-ethnic schools that incorporate the values of minority cultures into dominant culture educational values. If Maori or other socio-cultural groups, are unable to exercise a 'fair measure' of influence over the school's direction because of 'undue pressure' from the dominant community, the new arrangements allow the establishment of separate state-funded schools, consistent with national objectives. Below, I examine the early development of minority culture and language primary schools, which are similar in aim and scope to the Australian and North American schools discussed a little earlier, but also different in that they are becoming an integral part of the national pattern of schooling and spreading rapidly across New Zealand wherever Maori communities exist.

To understand the development of the innovation, it is helpful to know that it was preceded by an earlier Maori educational innovation. The *kohanga reo* or 'language nests' movement is a remarkable development which has occurred with virtually no government sponsorship. Anyone from any culture is welcome to send their pre-school children to *kohanga reo*. Many children begin in early infancy, and continue until they start school. The *kohanga reo* aims to recreate the atmosphere of a traditional Maori home; it has no formal structures except opening prayers, regular meal breaks, and occasional ceremonies to greet guests. While the *kohanga* has no structured curriculum and little equipment, there is plenty of singing and movement. The children create their own games but are able to stay close to adults if they choose to, because there are always lots of adults taking part in activities, interacting with the children, and providing models in language and behaviour. Beginning only in the mid-1980s, the hundreds of *kohanga reo* are now sending thousands of their graduates into state primary schools. Many of the children are well on the way to active bilingualism and biculturalism, since they inevitably acquire English and the majority culture outside the language nests where that culture's dominance is unchallenged.

With the *kohanga reo* initiative so successful, ordinary state primary schools are now often ill-equipped to maintain the Maori culture and language development of these pre-school language nests. As a result, Maori communities across the country have begun to establish *kura kaupapa Maori* ('Maori philosophy primary schools': see Chapter 3). The national reforms in educational administration have lent impetus to this movement by allowing small groups of people to establish their own state-funded schools, provided that a minimum number of children can be guaranteed and provided that certain government requirements relating to the charter and the Board of Trustees are met. In the early 1990s many of these schools are operating, or are approved and planned.

It would be wrong to create the impression that it is the simple need to provide a suitable school destination for the graduates of the 'language nests' that motivates the creation of these Maori culture and language primary schools. Of equal importance, the *kura* respond to a passionately felt belief among many Maori that the European-style school system that has been their sole avenue to formal education for over a century within the state provided system, is not appropriate organizationally or pedagogically to the sustenance and the development of a Polynesian culture. These new schools give due respect to Maori communicative action; they try to restore *mana* (power and respect) to the Maori learner in a meaningful way by creating an environment where Maori culture is the taken-for-granted background against which everything else is set. For the pupils, being Maori in these schools is the norm; the school and classroom environment connects with the Maori home; cultural and language values are central; Maori parents make decisions for their children unimpeded by majority culture gatekeeping devices; and the *whanau* ('extended family group') assumes responsibility for the education of their children along with control and direction of the school itself. At the same time, these schools are concerned to teach a modern, up-to-date and relevant curriculum following national guidelines set by the state, whose outcome will be the production of fully bilingual and bicultural graduates (Hingangaroa Smith, 1990).

Moreover, this cultural autonomy does not necessarily mean cultural separatism. Instead it means having the resources and the wherewithal to run a parallel system, exposing children fully to the necessary heritage of human civilization, but on Maori terms where like the conventional system *anyone* will be able to enrol. This last point deserves stressing:

> Being Maori will not be a prerequisite for entrance but the language of communication as it will be of instruction, will be Maori. Organisational structures, content of the curriculum, forms of evaluation and pedagogical styles will also reflect the ethos of a basic Maori structure (Penetito, 1986: 12).

No doubt similarly patterned secondary schools will follow. One long-term aim for Maori communicative action, is the development of a Maori language and culture university on an equal footing with other universities in the country. What is certain about future developments in New Zealand schooling is that the Maori people will continue to use wide processes of professional and community participation and consultation, since these reflect enduring values in the culture.

The discourse ethic in the classroom

Promoting community and staff participation in structural and curriculum reform is not an easy thing for teachers in schools to do. Yet it may still be less difficult than promoting participation and discursive fairness in their classroom work with students. If the discourse ethic is a true reflection of the ideal context of interaction for human beings, then classrooms everywhere are much in need of this kind of reform. The discourse ethic is said to prevail when all contributions to human interaction in a setting are meaningful, true, justified, and sincere. For most of the time, teachers assume that they are communicating meaningful content, in a context where that communication is a legitimate or justified activity. But truth and sincerity themselves are often missing from contemporary classrooms; this may occur because of the pressures of externally imposed curricula, with their emphasis on 'outcomes'; or because of the strategic professional purposes of teachers themselves, which can receive priority ahead of the interests of students. When classroom events do take place in an environment where trust and sincerity are missing, those same events tend to lose their meaning and their legitimacy for pupils; and all four validity conditions required by the discourse ethic disappear from classrooms. But it is not just fairness that suffers under these conditions. There is clear evidence to confirm that if there is no trusting context of interaction in classrooms, student learning itself is severely affected.

Extensive studies of classrooms in a variety of school systems report that where trusting relations exist, students spend most of their time and energy on learning. But where they do not exist, teachers spend excessive amounts of their time on marginal activities: organizing and negotiating relationships; establishing rewards and punishments to make reluctant children perform tasks; and disciplining and censuring children who are not working, or who are disrupting the teacher's activities. Trusting relations develop when teachers and students perceive one another as involved and at work on the project of learning (McDermott, 1977). In a study of many American secondary classrooms, this kind of trust-developing environment seemed to be missing from classes at all ability levels. Instead, children were seen as passive receivers of humdrum tasks: listening to the teacher; writing answers to the teacher's question; taking tests. They had only limited opportunities to answer open-ended questions, to work in cooperative learning groups, or otherwise to control the classroom's discursive activity. Moreover when the study focused on students in lower ability classes there were even greater restrictions on students, since the content of the learning seemed to be watered down for the weaker ones: 'high-track students got Shakespeare; low-track students got reading kits. High-track students got mathematical concepts; low-track students got computational exercises. Why?' (Oakes, 1985: 192).

A look at the history of modern schooling helps explain some of the limitations of conventional schools and classrooms. The concentration on control and passive student activities in classrooms reflects the ethos of control that is still an outstanding feature of conventional school organizations. In this respect, modern schools have not changed very much in their general aim since their inception, in the middle of the nineteenth century. The political architects of modern universal schooling, beginning in English-speaking countries in the decades around the Taunton Report in Britain (1864–1868), were acting in direct response to fears about what many children would otherwise become if an attempt were not made to change them by controlling their socialization through compulsory schooling. These architects had before them the recent memories of the democratic revolutions across Europe and America in 1848 and earlier, and they were mindful of the bitter and costly contemporary uprisings of subject peoples in defence of their cultural rights. They were anxious to avoid any extension of similar experiences, and they saw schooling for the masses as a way of initiating their own lower orders into the technologies and values of the mainstream culture, and as a way of assimilating and taming the culturally different. These architects saw schooling as a way of making children 'better', as a way of 'civilizing' them in line with the canons for 'civilized Man' that the architects themselves or people very like them, had established.

Structurally schools remain very much in this mould. Often in spite of teachers' best efforts, classrooms tend to reflect the structures of the wider institution. Moving more in the direction of the discourse ethic would change all this by structuring classroom activities to promote cooperative, active, interactive, and purposeful learning, where the control function of the setting and of the teacher becomes an instrument of last resort, not first. The simple act of the teacher withdrawing from centre stage and abdicating the 'absolute rights' suggested in a later section under 'gender' (p. 187), removes the key cause of communicative distortion in classrooms and allows cooperative discourse practices some room to develop. Using more formal cooperative learning approaches is known to result in increased academic achievement, more positive attitudes, and better relationships (Slavin, 1983). But less formal oral language activities, especially group work in its various forms and approaches, also provide a ready vehicle for this (Corson, 1987). Jeannie Oakes (1985) sees three advantages in the cooperative strategy: firstly it offers an incentive for students to interact with each other, as learning resources; secondly it offers a way of accommodating learner differences; and thirdly it offers a way of softening the effects that initial differences in student ability have on assigning rewards for learning. Cooperative group work expresses the cultural values of a greater number of girls and boys in our classrooms than do pedagogies based on the individualization of instruction and on direct teaching. Jim Cummins (1988: 144) contrasts the major characteristics of this kind of interactional model with the transmission model of teaching. For him the interactional model offers:

- genuine dialogue between student and teacher in both oral and written modalities;
- guidance and facilitation, rather than control of student learning by the teacher;
- encouragement of student–student talk, in a collaborative learning context;
- encouragement of meaningful language use by students, rather than correctness of surface forms;
- conscious integration of language use and development, with all curricular content rather than teaching language and other content as isolated subjects;
- a focus on developing higher level cognitive skills, rather than on factual recall;
- task presentation that generates intrinsic rather than extrinsic motivation.

It is easy to see the connection between these approaches and the central ideas of 'language across the curriculum'. This approach to the language curriculum has received renewed and vigorous expression among the significant movement of language theorists and practitioners who see point and purpose in the development of 'language policies across the curriculum'.

II. Social Justice through School Language Policies

School language policies are viewed by many in education as an integral and necessary part of the administration and the curriculum practice of modern schools. A language policy is a document compiled by the staff of a school often assisted by other members of the school community, to which the staff give their assent and commitment. It identifies areas in the school's scope of operations and programme where language problems exist that need the commonly agreed approach that is offered by a policy. This policy sets out what the school intends to do about these areas of concern; it is an action statement (Corson, 1990a).[2] This section examines issues of education raised in this book that deserve careful attention in language policy: minority social group issues; cultural minority issues; and gender issues. The section concludes by discussing the importance of community education in a cohesive school language policy.

Minority social groups and language policy action

Chapter 5 surveyed Shirley Heath's studies of children from different home backgrounds and their approaches to literacy in schools. Her research illustrates the diversity of social differences that schools often have to respond to. In almost every school community there are many minority social groups who bring their own ways of knowing about language to schools, only to find that the school demands something different from those ways, something which they do not have and which the school does not provide. Heath's recommendations for the early years of schooling, suggest modest but creative ways for treating differences in socialization that are rarely as great as the differences between children from different cultures, but which may go unrecognized for just that reason (1982: 72–73). I offer her ideas for reforming early literacy practices and for the treatment of narrative repertoires, as brief insights that may stimulate thinking about other areas of language examined in Chapter 5. For example, what special arrangements *could* individual schools make to accommodate non-standard users of the majority language, especially arrangements for valuing different discourse norms themselves in classrooms?

Firstly, Heath considers children who have had contacts with books, but rarely in a decontextualized setting like the school which encourages them to see the books set against other experiences and activities. Compared with mainstream children, they have had less generalizing exposure to the content of books and to the various ways of learning from them. Heath argues that these children in their early schooling may not need more presentation of labels, or the names of things and events; nor do they need a slowing in the sequence of introducing the kind of 'what-explanations' that are linked to bookreading. Rather, they need these activities to be extended into other domains; they need models that reveal distinctions in discourse strategies and structures; they need to be re-introduced to an active participant frame of reference to a book and to become active information-givers, mediating in their search for knowledge between the content of books and other aspects of their environment. I see these not just as suggestions for the early years, since this relational approach to literaćy is often missing from the middle years of schooling too; it appears even less in the senior years, where books often become divorced from meaningful contexts and practical activities.

Secondly, Heath considers those children who have little or no exposure to taking meaning from written texts but who have developed a sophisticated competence in analogical reasoning: in seeing a resemblance between one experience and another through metaphor, playful fictionalization, and a re-creation of scenes that suspends reality. She stresses that this high level skill must be maintained through to later stages of education where its use is most desirable and valued, but that the same children need the foundation skills of composition and comprehension: things like learning to recount factual events in a straightforward way, and to recognize appropriate occasions for using reason explanations and affective expressions. In contrast to the first group of children, these children may need to learn to label, to list features, and to give 'what-explanations'. They may also need to learn the stylization which is characteristic of books, and especially their decontextualization: their capacity to represent, in the present, something which is absent.

Thirdly, Heath suggests that mainstream children whose preschool experiences prepare them well for entry to school, could benefit from exposure to a use of the analogical skills in storytelling and explanation-giving that the second group of children bring naturally with them into school: that range of skills that majority culture teachers seem to have difficulty in valuing. Often skill in using different narrative genres is linked more to some social groups than others. In addressing the issues raised here, school-based research into local patterns of language socialization may uncover wide variations in children's access to different narrative genres. Again, Heath gives examples of what is possible here: alerting children to different narrative types, by asking them to bring in tape recordings or to simulate interactions with adults in the wider community; using videotapes of different narrative types, used in service situations; and using role modelling in the classroom, to compare and discuss how narrative types are used (1986c: 93). Heath identifies four universal types of narrative: recounts, eventcasts, accounts, and stories. Although these four narrative types are universal across cultures, not all children arrive in school fluent in all of them. Even when children are fluent, variations in the use of these forms across groups can lead to discontinuity, within each type, between what the school requires and what the child brings. Other areas of discontinuity between the home and the school may be more context specific. Pupils can reveal these discontinuities at different ages, in different school subjects, in different learning situations, and in the company of different people. A school language policy or a school department's language policy may need to support different students at different times, and in different settings, with recommendations directed at specific areas of their expressive, transactional, and affective uses of oral and written language.

Finally, this section needs to address the difficult issue of valuing non-standard varieties in the classroom. Most recommendations offered in this area are either statements about what not to do or that side-step the issue entirely. For example, the Kingman Report into the Teaching of English (DES, 1988) in Britain where non-standard varieties of English are greater in number than anywhere else, places a proper stress on 'historical and geographical variation' but curiously ignores social and cultural variation, perhaps in the vain hope that these latter varieties of English will disappear if they are ignored. One ingenious response to valuing non-standard varieties is suggested in the work of the 'Survey of British Dialect Grammar' (Cheshire, Edwards & Whittle, 1988). This project begins with the view that there is very little information on dialect grammar for teachers to consult that could be brought into the classroom setting. The project's aim is to establish a network of teachers and their pupils who might help in collecting this information by taking part in collaborative classroom projects. The method of data collection is a questionnaire, but the project minimizes problems of sensitivity by asking teachers to recognise the children themselves as the experts in matters of local language variation. So the approach both empowers non-standard speakers and elevates their status in the eyes of their classmates. Any teacher taking part agrees to undertake work with children on issues such as standard and non-standard English, language variation, and language change, drawing on lesson suggestions and resources provided by the project. In all discussions the teacher takes the role of the non-expert. In this way, all the children's awareness about language issues is raised and gradually information can be gathered to the benefit of all concerned. This project offers a strong clue about the kinds of pedagogical approaches that can be introduced in communities where non-standard variation exists. Because this is a controversial area that affects different schools in very different ways, there is more reason for schools to have a sensitive and agreed policy that deals with it in imaginative ways appropriate to the local context. Later in this chapter, one theme addressed in a critical language awareness curriculum is 'promoting critical awareness of variety'; this would be a very helpful vehicle for making staff and students in a school more relaxed about non-standard language and more ready to value it.

Cultural minorities and language policy action

As mentioned in the Foreword, throughout this book I have distinguished informally between minority social groups and cultural minority groups, because the language injustices that these two sets of groups encounter are of a different order. But since it is possible for any single minority social group to be less like the dominant group culturally than any single cultural group, much of what follows is relevant to the education of social *and* cultural minorities. The recommendations about bilingual schooling presented throughout Chapter 4, should be seen as a supplement to the recommendations made here about school action for cultural minorities.

(a) Changes in School Structures

Following her studies of cultural minority pupils in schools, Susan Philips (1983) wonders who will carry out innovations in teaching methodology used in classrooms inhabited by cultural minority children. She acknowledges that teachers are too busy and too powerless as individuals to make much impact. School administrators have an important role of instructional leadership to offer here: by working towards reform in classroom practices and using language policies designed to create schools more responsive to the needs of minority children. These policies need to be structurally linked to the minority communities themselves whose children are affected by the policies; there are many policy alternatives for doing this (Corson, 1990a). These language policies need to respond directly to the range of acquired cultural interests identified in the final paragraphs of Chapter 2.

Wherever different cultures intermingle successfully in schooling, a dynamic interplay occurs between structural change and modifications in values and attitudes. This dynamic depends on communicative action to decide areas of cultural compatibility, and to negotiate areas of incompatibility where some compromise may be necessary. Through negotiation and community education over many years at Richmond Road, the principal reorganized the school's grouping system, edging it from a horizontal to a vertical arrangement, from heterogeneous to homogeneous language and culture home groups, and from a hierarchical to a flat and more egalitarian management system. Efforts to lessen undesirable structural constraints such as those that prevent minority staff from being hired or minority community members from having a voice in governance, go hand in hand with changing people's beliefs about the worth of those practices. When this occurs culturally diverse staff begin to model relations of equal status; racist words and phrases disappear from the language of the school; the languages and varieties used by the children become more valued; and the ideology of 'treating children all the same' can be seen as a racist value, rather than an expression of justice.

Cultural minority children are better served by teachers who share the same cultural background (Osborne, 1991). This is because the children will more likely identify with culturally similar teachers and heed them. Yet even this accommodation may not be enough if the structures of the organization still encourage all staff to conform uncritically to dominant professional values. Sometimes attempts by minority teachers to promote culturally sensitive interactions are frustrated by a preference among others for 'doing things the school's way' in order to fit into wider promotion and seniority structures. This pressure to accommodate to the dominant culture's institutional structures can often lead minority teachers to become intransigent in their own values. Sometimes too they can become overhard on minority children, trying to make them successful to an unreasonable degree in both cultures. So changing the culture of some of the teachers on its own is not enough. The very organizational structures of schools themselves including the values that once were accepted without criticism, may need to be changed to allow genuine cultural alternatives to have an effect in practice. The principal at Richmond Road found that some teachers needed to leave the school, and everyone needed time if reform was to happen. Once this kind of change occurs, changes in classroom practices can be trialled and evaluated by setting them against the discourse norms and cultural values that the children bring to the school, and by carefully introducing new norms and values so that the children feel more 'at home' in both the dominant and the minority culture.

(b) Changes in Classroom Practices

Susan Philips also mentions the 'total irrelevance of the curriculum content' to the lives of the Indian children in her Warm Springs study (1983: 132). She discovered that the children were unresponsive to materials that presupposed a cultural background that was different from the background that they themselves had actually acquired. The situation was made no better by the fact that Indian teachers were not available to make the alien materials relevant and to elaborate upon them. If minority children are to succeed in schools, it is important that they feel comfortable about the classroom context itself. When anxiety is present in any situation, little learning is possible. Having a culturally similar teacher to work with is very helpful in reducing the sense of alienation that children feel in schools. More than this though, as Chapter 3 indicates, there are styles of control and interaction which some teachers use that are more suited to making culturally different children feel comfortable. Cazden (1988) distinguishes between two styles which she calls 'personalization' and 'privatization'.

'Privatization' names a strategy for minimizing 'face threatening situations' by not calling on children for public and competitive displays of what they do not know, but correcting them individually where necessary and in private. Many have argued the relevance of this teacher style to Native American children. Based on the values and emphases presented in Chapter 3, privatization also seems a good pedagogic practice for use with minority children elsewhere. Perhaps the education of children everywhere would benefit if privatization were more widely used, since the practice of correcting children in public in order to make a teaching point to the rest of the class often strikes at their dignity and self-esteem, no matter how carefully teachers handle it. In contrast, Cazden's other style 'personalization', links up with the *cariño* value mentioned in Chapter 3. As a strategy, personalization is less concerned with eliminating 'face threatening situations'; rather it reduces their negative effect on children by the use of simple courtesies: affectionate forms of address; diminutives; and phrases showing clear respect for the rights and dignity of the children. When used well, this personalized style can also reveal the teacher's informal awareness of the world of the children, their families and homes; it can also incorporate whatever non-verbal expressions of *cariño* are welcome in the culture.

Also at classroom level, Cazden believes that more effective change occurs when the focus is on classroom situations, rather than directly on cultural differences. For example, skilled teachers of young children are often very competent in providing individualization of instruction in the new entrant classroom. In this approach, the teacher moves from one child to another rapidly dealing with learning problems. But often among culturally different children this approach can promote an undesirable degree of differential treatment, if the children are unaccustomed to a one-to-one interaction with adults outside the home and are threatened by it. Young Polynesian children for example, are used to interacting with adults informally, but they are more relaxed with adults when working in a collective rather than an individual setting. Cazden (1990) recommends a use of small group learning contexts, where the teacher can still personalize teaching while extending conversations using the resources of several interlocutors. She also recommends the use of 'wait-time': when teachers wait for three seconds or more before responding to a student utterance, students speak longer and in more detail, allowing teachers to respond in turn. In choosing a topic for talk, Cazden suggests three types: topics specific to the local culture; topics specific to individual children; and topics that are familiar to the teacher and the child. Indeed, shared experiences provide the best basis for interaction with children of any age and culture.

Working with minority children is often more than a skill; it is an act of cultural fairness. Kathryn Au and Jane Mason argue that 'teachers success-ful with minority students may be those who achieve a balance of rights by trading control over participation structure dimensions', and that 'less effective teachers may be those who attempt to maintain conventional classroom participation structures, only to pay a price in student disaffec-tion and loss of control over lesson content' (1983: 165). Philips also draws similar conclusions for teaching methods more generally. Although the approaches described below may not work in all minority classrooms, they do suggest a process of thinking that can be valuable in changing classroom learning environments, to make them more compatible with the cultural backgrounds of minority children. In fact, the participant structures favoured by the Indian students in Philips' studies are better represented in some pedagogies than in others. For instance, as mentioned, Ronald and Suzanne Scollon (1981) believe that the critical thing for Athabaskan child-ren is the extent to which parties to an interaction assume a mutual right to make their own sense of the interaction. They say that this unfocused form of interaction demands freedom from pressures of time, participant crowding, and impersonal media. More than this, it requires an agreement among participants that they will not try to focus the situation unilaterally. This suggests a very different role for teachers; it is one in which few conventionally trained teachers would feel relaxed.

Warm Springs Indian children also seem to feel more comfortable when they have more control themselves over their own interaction. The group project format seems very suitable, and Philips suggests that this pedagogy may be used for a greater range of purposes, and at younger ages with Indian children. She also reports that the Indian students have greater competence in maintaining interaction over longer periods with larger groups of children. This occurs without the teacher's supervision both in formal project group work and in informal playground interaction, and this competence reflects the great deal of practice that they receive in their own communities in interacting without the help or direction of a dominant individual. Philips also recommends greater use of one-to-one contact by children with teachers and teacher-aides, as a way of overcoming the reluctance of the Indian minority children to demonstrate individual profi-ciency while working with a group. Perhaps there is a tension between this recommendation and the difficulties that Cazden reports for the individ-ualization of minority instruction in New Zealand, since the act of revealing proficiency on a one-to-one basis to relatively unfamiliar adults, can be quite contrary to cultural values, whether it is sought in group or in individual settings. One way to lessen the apparent contradiction in Philips and Cazden's two points, is to recommend that where individualization is necessary for culturally different children, the teachers and their aides should possess the status of respected and trusted friends in the lives of the children themselves. On the other hand, perhaps it is the very ideology of 'assessing and evaluating' personal strengths and weaknesses that is contrary to the values of some minority cultures?

Perhaps schools could critically examine the ideology that lies behind the search that Western teachers constantly make for evidence of student performance. Perhaps schools could modify their practices a little. Minority peoples often see this preoccupation with assessment and evaluation as a strange interest at best; and as a culturally offensive obsession at worst. There are alternative ways to evaluate pupil performance that have the merits of subtlety and cultural sensitivity. The ethnographic approach to bilingual assessment discussed in Chapter 4, clearly has wider uses across the curriculum. Also peer tutoring followed by peer feedback in the presence of the teacher recommends itself as a method that would better suit the orientation to learning of many minority children. Yet the need remains to extend children's performances into new areas. As minority children mature, Philips suggests, they can be eased into patterns of interaction that are new to them. For example, teachers can introduce activities developing leadership skills by encouraging children to speak on a matter of concern to all the children, or to take an individual role in furthering a group goal as in a team debate. As long as personal conceit and self-aggrandizement are not evident outcomes of an activity, then children from many minorities that are collectivist in their orientation to the world may participate eagerly.

The stress on literacy as the main point of schooling can be a decided disincentive for children from many cultural groups who do not value literacy in the taken-for-granted way that Westerners often do. Formerly in Europe, the use of literacy was an oral and even a collective activity. Now the uses of literacy to which most Westerners are accustomed have grown away from these older uses that literacy once had. But the same uses persevere in many other cultures and these cultures are certainly literate, but they value literacy in a different way (Hamilton et al., 1993). As a result, the Western inclination to confine most literacy events to the private and often silent domains of libraries and conventional classrooms sets literacy apart from the values and world views of many minority people. While the latter value literacy, they often feel uncomfortable with the behaviours that the school sees as necessary for its acquisition. Chapter 5 argues that the ways that literacy is acquired, viewed, and used vary across cultures and across social groups. These 'ways of taking' literacy are often different from those recognized and valued in traditional forms of schooling. Heath (1986b) suggests three highly undesirable ways in which members of minority groups can accommodate to the formal literacy requirement in schools:

(1) they may learn to read and write only with excessive effort;
(2) they may come to see written uses of language as unrelated to oral uses and consequently give literacy a marginal cultural position;
(3) they may reject literacy as having no relevance to the ways in which one makes sense of the world.

For many minority groups, school forms of literacy can simply get in the way of the things that they have learned to value and appreciate most about their own culture: things like oral interaction, sharing, community, ligatures, collective action, and collaboration. Philips gets part of the answer when she suggests that the minority people in her Warm Springs study are reluctant to share what they know in written form with non-Indians, because of the loss of control over that knowledge that might result. This is certainly a common fear among people whose cultural secrets are private to the group, but there seems a wider and more compelling explanation for this common reluctance to embrace literacy as wholeheartedly as Westerners do. There seem to be pronounced differences in cultural values between societies that are historically literate and those that are not. Literacy activities that schools promote are often an intrusion which threatens to replace other things that are more valuable in the lives of minority peoples, notably the ligatures that keep the culture together. Accordingly if minority children are to take literacy up successfully, the way that schools introduce and develop it needs to complement rather than threaten to eliminate the lifestyles that rightly have high cultural value.

The main point that comes from the research to date is that if education is going to empower culturally different children, there needs to be a measure of compatibility between their home culture and the pedagogical styles selected for use in classrooms. Except in those minority schools like the *kura* which are monocultural in aim and scope, increasing cultural compatibility may never mean totally replacing the majority with the minority's values. Commenting on the Kamehameha programme in Hawaii, Cathie Jordan says that achieving a comfortable minority environment means translating ethnographic information into improved classroom practice, in order to produce cultural compatibility, not cultural isomorphism or specificity (1985: 112). Reproducing the home culture in the school is not the aim, since that would disadvantage children from other cultures present in the same class. The aim is to translate relevant values across, by adopting teaching methods that accommodate the values. She suggests three sets of principles for this translation process:

(1) a principle of 'least change', which means selecting from the array of conventional practices rather than inventing new pedagogies;
(2) using several translation strategies for selecting pedagogies, depending on ethnographic data and academic goals consistent with the target population of children;
(3) ensuring that the translation process is non-linear, weaving back and forth between current practices, the culture of the children, and trialling new practices in a collaborative pattern, using experts in pedagogy and in the culture.

In Jordan's view there are two key dimensions to the task: to discover and describe features of the naturally occurring contexts either in the community or at the school, that are conducive to desirable forms of child behaviour; and then to re-arrange classroom practices accordingly.

Gender

Chapter 6 ends with policy conclusions about gender and schooling. On the evidence assembled there, school language policies do create, reinforce, and perpetuate powerful forms of gender discrimination. Two sets of recommendations follow in this section: the first suggests a range of organizational changes that conventional schools can achieve with minimal institutional disruption. The second looks at two complementary ways of modifying discursive practices and norms in schools: through a negotiated and agreed school policy on gender and language; and through professional development activities examining evidence from studies such as those collated in Chapter 6, followed by classroom change.

(a) Changes in School Structures

If schools are to create a working environment where the discursive interests of both males and females are valued, then the organizational climate or culture of the school as a whole needs careful attention. I believe that the best way to attend to this problem is through a whole-school language policy that encourages non-discriminatory discourse practices to flourish. Achieving this is not as difficult a policy task as it may appear, since many of the changes to school administrative practices that feminists have been advocating are the same as those that many educational administration theorists already recommend (Shakeshaft, 1987; Stockard & Johnson, 1981; Yeakey, Johnston & Adkison, 1986). On the account of educational administration that I am advocating here, effective solutions to the problems of organizations are found in discovering the intentions and interests of participants, and in trying either to change some of those intentions or to work in harmony with them. An interactive, relational, and collaborative use of power outweighs the exercise of power through authority and hierarchy.

Through policies eliminating undesirable discursive practices in the school's administration and management, schools can adopt many language practices that may be welcomed by males and females alike (after Starratt, 1991; Lees, 1987):

- reducing the use of impersonal or bureaucratic language in official communications;
- softening formal messages with more humour, less pomposity, less condescension and a use of vivid metaphors linked to the real world of the organization;
- sending messages to staff and students which personalize the recipient;
- using the first person as subject and only the occasional passive verb;
- introducing a language of institutional symbols and mottos that expresses collaboration rather than competition, cooperation for shared rewards rather than winning for personal glory;
- taking positive policy action to end the denigration of girls by boys in the school and its grounds;
- taking positive policy action to challenge the pervasiveness of verbal sexual abuse;
- fostering an environment where laughter is common, where frequent greetings are given using people's names, where real achievements are recognized through public expressions of congratulation;
- creating a school ambience filled with displays of students' work, and where participants are relaxed about giving and taking criticism, without fear or offence.

Where the cultural values or interests of women and girls are viewed as inferior, no amount of structural re-arrangement will make women and girls feel at home. For values of justice to really count, they need to be inserted into the discourse of the place; they need to be articulated sincerely by significant figures in the organization so that they become part of the taken-for-grantedness of the place. Women prefer to see certain values in themselves as administrators, and in men too: they have a preference for taking a genuine role of instructional leadership in the school; they prefer it when the practice of administration is not separated from teaching itself; they also prefer not to overspecialize in function, especially in a managerial function; they dislike extremes of hierarchy, where power is delegated impersonally, and where freedom of action is constrained. In exercising power themselves, women prefer to act in a way that transforms the notion of power, seeing it less as 'power over others' and more as 'power for' and 'power through' others.

Drawing on the evidence available about female work behaviour in schools, Charol Shakeshaft offers four broad descriptions that are helpful here: firstly, relationships with others are central to all the actions of women as administrators; secondly, teaching and learning are the major focuses of women administrators; thirdly, building community is an essential part of a woman administrator's style; and fourthly, the line separating the public world from the private is less well defined for women (1987: 197–8). I believe that this last point highlights a significant need that women (and men) rarely find satisfied in formal organizations: to work in an environment similar to one in which they would choose to live. In short, women prefer to share themselves with others, in the same way as they have learned to share themselves while growing up and in their childhood socialization, although often men do not learn to share themselves in this way. But this means that as teachers and administrators women prefer an interactive and collaborative environment in organizations that allows their acquired cultural interests and discourse norms free expression. It follows of course, that the discursive interests of female students will be similar.

As a result of different patterns of socialization from their earliest years, girls and boys as groups bring different norms of language behaviour to schooling, even though males and females on the evidence may well be converging in their actual language strengths and weaknesses. On the other hand as children mature, male and female group norms for using language, as distinct from group language abilities, tend to diverge even further; girls find that that aspect of their linguistic capital which was perhaps used and valued much more in the relatively interactive and child-centred environment of their primary and middle schooling, attracts less status as they proceed through their schooling. As argued in Chapter 6, this decline in the use and the evaluation of discourse norms preferred by girls and young women is a discriminatory use of power by the institution of education that needs urgent addressing. Policy makers could soften the effects of this in several ways. Below I suggest three possible policy directions for post-primary (post-junior) levels of schooling. Each of these policy options has a single aim: to arrange curriculum, pedagogy, and evaluation practices so as to allow students who may already be socialized into quite different norms of language use to approach the same curriculum in ways consistent with their acquired cultural interests:

(a) Plan school timetables and classes so that students have a real opportunity to express their preferences about the contrasting pedagogical styles of teachers in central curriculum areas, and so that they have a good chance of having their personal preferences recognized and met in their various class placements.

(b) Plan school timetables and classes so that males and females pursue selected curriculum areas in single-sex groups.

(c) Structure the school itself so that males and females receive their schooling in single-sex mini-schools sharing an overarching administrative structure and coming together as a single school and in mixed classes as often as possible.

The strength of policy (a) is that it allows those many students who do not share the dominant discourse norms of their own single-sex groups to opt for a pedagogical arrangement consistent with their own preferences. Indeed my major objection to (b) and (c) is that they do not allow this possibility. This can also be a serious weakness of single-sex schools wherever they operate: exclusively single-sex arrangements tend to reinforce and sharpen male or female discursive practices, whether those practices are desirable or not. A further strength of (a) is that it would allow students greater opportunities to tailor their courses to suit personal strengths and weaknesses. Many girls for instance may prefer single-sex groups for science and maths classes, while opting for language and social science groups that are mixed. A weakness of (a) is that its success depends on the school's ability to recruit sets of teachers who can offer genuinely complementary approaches in pedagogical style, while still maintaining consistently high levels of student success.

The strength of policy (c) is that suitable staff may be attracted to one or other of the two mini-schools by the opportunity they offer for teachers to follow their own preferences in pedagogical style within an institution that is structured to be supportive of that arrangement. For example, teachers oriented to a collaborative, interactive, and less didactic engagement with the subject matter of their specialisms may prefer the guaranteed clientele and climate that the single-sex girls' mini-school in (c) would offer. Another strength of (c), but only when compared with exclusively single-sex schools, is that the sexes would only be partly separated: in (c) careful planning could allow regular and extended opportunities for males and females to meet and mix. A serious weakness of (c) and of single-sex schools in general, is that they continue to disadvantage the many males or females whose discourse preferences are markedly different from the norm for their sex. A modification of the arrangement allowing willing members of the opposite sex to cross over institutional boundaries would probably stigmatize those students in the eyes of both males and females.

Policy (b) has all the weaknesses of (a) and (c). In spite of this, its structural simplicity would probably make it the most popular with school administrators. A strength of (b) is that it may promote staff professional development if the same teachers are asked to work at different times with male and female groups. Teachers may discover and develop alternative pedagogical styles and discourse possibilities that they could not easily use with mixed sex classes.

Because of the need to give priority to consulting and confirming the individual interests of students themselves and then to shaping institutional practices accordingly, policy (a) seems the best option to follow. However in particular contexts none of these policies may be possible, especially if a school is small and cannot offer more than one class for most curriculum subjects. In this case if justice is to be served, there seems little alternative for instructional leaders but to put professional development policies in place so that teachers are encouraged to provide alternative group arrangements within their single classes. The next sub-section and the third major section of this chapter deal directly with this matter.

(b) Changes in Classroom Practices

It is clear that in various ways common discourse practices in classrooms reinforce the different discursive practices that girls and boys bring with them into schooling. Teachers and policy makers in schools urgently need to reflect on the wisdom of continuing to support those classroom practices. In these brief recommendations for school policy action, I follow the topics and themes of Chapter 6.

The process of selecting reading texts for classroom use needs concerted policy attention to provide agreed guidelines for those managing the process. The third major section of this chapter ('critical language awareness') offers some 'questions to ask about children's books'. But these are more than good discussion points for developing language awareness, since they were written for actual use by people responsible for choosing books for young children. In choosing books for older children, it is important that the books avoid painting a falsely rosy picture of prevailing language injustices in society. Some recommend selecting books that provide a non-sexist context, even if that context contains language which in the interests of social realism is not gender neutral. Some suggest another approach: selecting books that highlight injustices in the way that language itself is used, but which encourage readers to reflect on the book itself as an example of the point that it makes. Whatever the preferred course, it is important that professional users of books communicate their needs to publishing houses. Teachers and schools in some places make a point of communicating to publishers and their agents any strong satisfaction or dissatisfaction felt for particular books. Informed and constructive professional criticism of this kind is a powerful force in the literary marketplace.

Because most teaching in most places still depends on the didactic discourse of the teacher, recommendations about eliminating unjust practices in whole class teacher–pupil interactions should provide a centrepiece in a language policy. Since teachers in general are very resistant to the evidence of discrimination in this area, a process of information sharing followed by professional development activities seems a good way to go. As a starting point, there is certainly a place for collaborative action research projects conducted by willing teachers with one another and then shared more widely, using observation studies or audio-visual media to examine each other's taken-for-granted whole class practices. In beginning to grapple with this policy item, teachers are embarking on a school language research task that could provide a development target for a whole year of in-service work.

Many suggestions made in an earlier section about teacher interaction styles with culturally different children, also apply to interactions with girls and young women in general. As Chapter 6 concludes, female discursive norms are often different from male norms. Because females tend to place high value on strengthening affiliative links between people, their discursive norms seem to be different in broadly the same collectivist directions as are the discursive interests of many ancestral minority peoples. Indeed it would seem that dominant male norms of interaction are really the 'marked' variety in spite of their dominance; they constitute a norm which most people would not prefer if allowed the choice. Perhaps the real interests of boys and men would also be served by changes in teacher–pupil interaction practices to eliminate imbalances in the use of power such as the following: the unrestrained use of the imperative; the use of the (absolute) right to speak last; the use of the (absolute) right to contradict; the use of the (absolute) right to define the world for others; the use of the (absolute) right to interrupt or to censure; the use of the (absolute) right to praise or blame in public. These negative things are deeply ingrained habits that many teachers consider to be part of the very stuff of teaching. I believe that this is a teacher ideology that would not withstand critical inspection and challenge.

There are positive steps that can be taken too. Michelle Stanworth (1983) recommends that teachers give higher priority to reshaping the sexual distribution of interaction in classrooms: by singling girls out for more recognition; by remembering their names, and using them; by creating a comfortable and non-threatening environment for interaction (by sitting down in a child's desk to address the class, for example; or relaxing the posture). Other changes can express an ethic of care; they involve making the discourse practices of classrooms courteous, respectful, and caring. An earlier section on 'the discourse ethic in the classroom' suggests other talk reforms, including paying serious attention to the key validity claims of the discourse ethic itself. Indeed like many of the suggestions above, developing a speech situation in classrooms that maximizes sincerity, meaningfulness, truth, and legitimate communication would clearly be for the general good.

The role of community education in minority language policy

In spite of the school's best efforts, a language policy that stops at the school gate is unlikely to have much impact in areas that really matter. In particular, as earlier examples from Canada, the USA, Australia, and New Zealand confirm, policies of genuine reform intricately involve the school's community in its work. In encouraging this community involvement, it may be necessary to reduce the influence that agencies from outside the local community have over the school's operations, since community involvement can be frustrated when people find that all the major decisions are taken by remote officials who do not share the culture of the place.

Joshua Fishman (1990) lays stress on good neighbourhood organization in reversing language shift and in promoting minority language interests more generally. Social support for families can come from a range of activities instigated by the school or through its specialist services: providing home visits by minority language speaking social workers; the organization of parent groups and bilingual language exchange centres, which often become self-sufficient in place of formal support systems; provision to teach parents not just the art of parenting, but the place of that art within their own culture; and close links between the activities of the school and the activities of the family, especially in relation to childcare or playgroup arrangements that offer contact with adult specialists in tutoring, computers, dance, drama, writing, library research, athletics, and after-school jobs. All of these activities in Fishman's view, have usurped the traditional role of the family as the major partner with the school; they are also intense arenas for language use, for the communication of language attitudes, and the promotion of language competency. As earlier sections have argued, the empowerment of local minorities can come about when these school extension activities also draw the community into the running and support of the school itself. Given time and careful nurturing by staff and the school executive, the local community may assume a role that supplements and largely displaces the professionals from areas that are properly the responsibility of those with the same cultural interests as the children.

When a school's neighbourhood includes minority social groups drawn from low-income and otherwise marginalized communities, there are major problems to overcome in implementing policies for local control of education through community participation. Cathie Jordan (1988) highlights the frequent lack of experience and involvement of the poor in educational policy making and planning. The urgency of any devolution of decision making down to the level of the local school and its community can mean action at a greater pace than local communities can possibly absorb. The sudden devolutionary reforms in New Zealand came up against this problem in many places and it was not easily resolved, since in retrospect it was clear that a careful programme of 'community education' about the changes needed to precede the reforms themselves. Local people often need community education to manage new responsibilities and it is unlikely that any two communities will be the same in their need for expertise. In line with the devolution approach implicit in the discourse ethic, any agreed over-arching policy will need to be fragmented and given different directions at local levels to match different social histories, different community contexts, different leadership styles, and different local cultures. All these things combine to create different conceptions of minority social group identity that may be more subtle than the different national attributes of minority cultures, but more intransigent because of that subtlety. Moreover, formulating and implementing policy at local level in a relatively unsophisticated community is demanding of the time and energy of those few people who have expertise and who are offered leadership. For instance, a Maori language policymaker friend of mine was regularly involved with more than a dozen committees at the level of extended family, family group, tribe, and nation, and few of these were specifically related to education. A commitment of this kind is needed from many expert individuals on behalf of the group, if local control is to do more than manage a dominant curriculum, reflecting dominant organizational and pedagogical styles.

Modern schools seeking to reduce the social distance between themselves and the communities from which their students are drawn are trying to extend participation in policy making to parents and others as well. Although in modern democracies parents and community members are increasingly better placed to influence a school's programme, even among the affluent there is often very strong reluctance to participate very much in school governance. In advanced industrial societies parents willingly concede authority to professionals (Murphy, 1980). It takes persistence on the school's part to overcome this reluctance to participate. At the same time it takes strength of purpose not to cater simply for the needs and interests of the politically active in preference to the apathetic (Pascal, 1987), of the rich in preference to the poor, or of the culturally similar in preference to the culturally different (Fargher & Ziersch, 1981). The implementation of a language policy will need careful communicating to parents and to those critics of a school who tend to demand product rather than process from its curriculum. This will pose a serious difficulty in those communities where parents perceive schools as existing expressly to reproduce a particular cultural bias or to maintain a social status quo. A wise policy about policy making will mention ingenious but practical ways in which parents can be involved in the design of policies or at least be kept informed about the stages in policy development. If this is to be more than tokenism, the goals and organizational reality of the school will need to be communicated over a long period to the community, as at Richmond Road, beginning in small ways but extending deliberately and purposefully until regular two-way communication becomes commonplace and natural. An imaginative policy may be needed for just this task alone, providing a bridge to other developments.

III. Social Justice and Empowerment through Critical Language Awareness

'Critical language awareness' denies the possibility that humans can be fully objective in making judgments about complex language matters. In this and other respects it is very different from the rather descriptive approach to knowledge about language known as 'language awareness'. Most language awareness activities accept the descriptive account of language as a given; they assume that the norms for language behaviour established in conventions of use over time are rather unproblematic and uncontested. But critical language awareness goes beyond these assumptions; in its statements about the place of discourse in the social world, it seems very consistent with the critical realist ideas outlined in Chapter 1. As it has developed to date (Clark *et al.*, 1990; 1991), critical language awareness works from the ten claims summarized below:

(1) critical language study tries to explain and not just describe the discourse of a society;
(2) socially dominant forces have the power to shape the conventions that underlie discourse, just as much as any other social practices;
(3) conventions of language and discourse tend to be 'naturalized'; they are accepted as unproblematic givens;
(4) conventions of language, such as rules of use, receive their value according to the positions of their users in systems of power relations;
(5) different conventions embody different ideologies;

(6) critical language study needs an historical orientation, to link it with the past events which structure language and which determine its forms and the future effects that its present structures might have;

(7) discourse is determined by its conventions, but it is also a voluntary and creative activity that allows its users to critique the same conventions;

(8) discourse is both socially determined and creative;

(9) discourse itself is a site and practice of struggle;

(10) critical language study is a resource for developing the consciousness and self-consciousness of dominated people.

Earlier sections of this chapter discuss the possibilities and some of the constraints in using communicative action as a model for the reform of school management practices. In this final section, I am discussing a critical activity for use with students themselves. By reducing the ten theoretical claims to manageable curriculum themes, the approach to critical language awareness identifies three major categories of issues (Clark *et al.*, 1990). These provide some direction for a curriculum, and I use these categories as sub-headings or themes for the rest of this section.

Promoting social awareness of discourse

The intention in this theme area is to encourage students to approach meanings more critically, rather than take them for granted. A sophisticated understanding of discourse as a site of human struggle is not a prerequisite, since acquiring that understanding seems to be one of the goals of study in this theme. Working within the theme, students examine why access to certain types of discourse is restricted, and how imbalances in access affect individuals and groups. For example, students might examine the routine imbalances in communication that occur between teacher and student, doctor and patient, or judge and witness. If handled skilfully, scepticism about legitimate power relationships need not result. On the contrary, students may come to see how power that derives from justified authority, from knowledge, or from expertise often results inevitably in an unequal distribution of access to discourse. At the same time because of the critical component in such a study, students would become more alert to those occasions when an unequal use of discourse in special contexts is used unjustly.

In setting out a formal programme of work under this theme, the following questions could be asked about the meanings of controversial expressions and passages of discourse (after Treichler, 1989):

(1) Where do meanings come from?

(2) What does 'a meaning' formally consist of?

(3) What is its language history?
(4) In what and whose texts does it figure?
(5) Whose texts does it circumvent or undermine?
(6) Does a meaning exist, if no dictionary affirms it?
(7) How do the lexical entries of an individual relate to those of the culture?
(8) What strategies come into play when meanings and counter-meanings clash?
(9) Who may intervene to resolve disputes?
(10) How does the weight of prior discourse constrain the production of future meaning?
(11) How does meaning constrain usage?
(12) When we consciously produce meaning, where do our data come from?
(13) What role do the following have in determining the meanings that people develop and use: introspection, eternal verities, lived experience, empirical research, cultural productions, theories of how the world works, dreams, other speakers, other texts?
(14) What authorizes a given usage at a given moment?
(15) Whose interests do particular meanings and usages serve?
(16) Who may authorize meanings?
(17) Who may interpret them?
(18) Whose interpretations are authorized?
(19) What are the consequences — economic, symbolic, legal, medical, social, professional — of given meanings?
(20) What are the consequences if meanings are not fixed?
(21) Does any given meaning construct, or entail, the potential existence of its opposite?
(22) Can one circumvent such binary oppositions?
(23) What claim can 'new' meanings establish, within a system of social arrangements and material conditions that privileges 'old' meanings?
(24) On what grounds can these questions be addressed?

Clearly there is material here for both a student curriculum and a programme in staff professional development. These questions are so basic to education that an attempt to exemplify their application in the school curriculum risks trivializing their point. I will take that risk and mention some simple examples of language use that everyone encounters, at one time or another.

The curious place of swear-words, obscene expressions, and curses in language can make a fascinating study for young adolescents if they find their interest in the subject awakened by sophisticated and trusted teachers. For instance, students can consider the historical fact that most of the swear-words in English that refer to natural bodily functions and bodily organs were once ordinary and useful expressions that rank among the oldest words in the language. Children are interested to learn and to speculate about how bourgeois or puritanical Victorian concepts of order and cleanliness produced a fear of being offended by the very mention of such 'untidy' functions and organs. This zest for order and tidiness in public practices tended to stigmatize the words themselves and outlawed them from future polite use. Although this historical taboo appeared in many languages, not just English, the legacy of the taboo seems to linger longer in English-speaking countries where people still feel constrained to whisper when requesting the lavatory, or hurry to change the subject when certain words or meanings are used. Because of that legacy even today, when people are much less inhibited in such matters and regularly laugh at taboo usages on television and at the theatre which they would never adopt themselves, people still have to find euphemisms to refer to functions and organs on a daily basis that are fundamental to ordinary living. While this is only a minor problem when set against the greater problems of life, it has become so widespread a problem for users of English that there is little consensus about what substitute words should be used to refer to mundane things that can no longer be easily named as they once were.

Children can draw many liberating ideas about language and ideology from such a study. There is also much humour in the subject and it seems harmless humour. Apart from the possibility of offending some people who may not be as critically aware of language, there are no great power issues involved since few human interests are at stake when people use words to describe bodily functions and organs that everyone shares, after a fashion. However, taboo language also has more sinister and oppressive attributes and a critical study of a different corpus of swear-words and curses can yield powerful moral insights. After considering the harmless side of the topic, older children may be interested to go further into the use of taboo language by exploring how various social stigmas and cruel imbalances of power attaching to things like illegitimacy, gender exploitation, and sexual orientation became translated into words which are still in use as terms of abuse.

Another example which also links with discussion in the next subsection is in the way that the following higher and lower status language activities are often linked to people who differ on one or more of the dimensions of power discussed in this book:

Lower Status	Higher Status
gossip	cross examine
make appointments	interview

Lower Status	*Higher Status*
tell jokes	give a sermon
offer invitations	make a speech
give recounts of events	lecture
write personal letters	debate
use a recipe	write a report
use an instruction manual	write a book

Which social, cultural, or gender groups are more likely to engage in these activities? Under what circumstances if any, would the activities lose or gain status if the setting and the language users were varied?

Promoting critical awareness of variety

Working within this theme, students can examine why some languages and varieties are different in status from others; why they are valued differently in different settings; what historical events have produced different valuations of language varieties; and what are the effects that devaluing a language variety has upon its users. There are as many possibilities for pursuing this theme as the school's social context allows, since every local community contains examples of variety. They may be the relatively subtle markers of status that distinguish groups in monolingual societies; or they may be significant boundaries that keep cultural and sub-cultural groups isolated or alienated from one another, even while sharing the same social space.

Note 1 in Chapter 5 describes two West Indian creoles in use in one area of London. While one is a genuine community variety used by people of all ages, the other is a language of resistance that is used and shaped by the young to provide a deliberate sub-cultural contrast with other varieties closer to the standard. Two varieties like these co-existing in the same social space could require different kinds of treatment in a language awareness syllabus. The place to treat the community creole of the older generation could be within a more descriptive language awareness section of the curriculum, where value is placed on this variety as a necessary and esteemed local supplement to the standard language and as one that emerges from historical events and circumstances. But it would be unrealistic for teachers to try to use the adolescent 'language of resistance' as a descriptive item in the classroom. Clearly by definition that variety would be out of place there, since its structures are determined by the contrasts it offers to other languages of conformity and these are deemed by anti-conformist adolescents to include the language of schooling. The place to treat this creole of resistance is not so much in language awareness lessons, as in social and political education that extends into critical language awareness.

For younger children, the use of slang can make a fascinating study of an ever-changing variety that children already know and contribute to themselves. Children's slang is often rich and dynamic, but it is also ephemeral. Indeed for most of the time slang is short-lived. If slang words 'stick around' for long enough in a speech community, they tend to become respectable and accepted into its language, since they are doing a necessary job by carving out a meaning that has enduring relevance in the lives of some of the language's speakers. Lars-Gunnar Andersson and Peter Trudgill (1990) define slang as 'language use below the neutral stylistic level'. This may not seem a very helpful definition, but it does emphasize the judgmental character of slang. When we describe language as 'slang', this is a relative and evaluative use of the word not a descriptive one, since one person's slang can be another person's everyday language in a different time and place. For example, the standard French word *tête* (head) derives from a slang use of the Latin word *testa*, whose original meaning was 'pot' or 'bowl'. At some stage in the history of Latin/French, the word became a respectable descriptive term for a part of the body which now is often referred to by using other slang expressions that are similar in meaning to the original meaning of *testa*. Describing language as slang is an exercise of power by the person so describing it; the use of slang is also a small search for power by the person using it. So a classroom discussion of slang can be most useful in examining the link between language and power. For Bourdieu (1981), the use of slang is one way of pursuing distinction in a dominated market: people poorly endowed with cultural capital in a given setting, like children disempowered in an adult context like the school, try to distinguish themselves in that setting by their use of slang.

Approaching the subject of correctness versus appropriateness in language with children can be difficult, but it is the central topic to explore within this theme. The process can be helped by the range of prejudices about language that children inevitably acquire in their socialization, which can provide the subject matter for a programme. Even among children from different social backgrounds within the same speech community, there is likely to be broad agreement about what counts as prestigious language and what does not. As Chapter 5 suggests, this happens because even children from non-elite backgrounds are still likely to agree that aspects of their own language are not prestigious. Under this topic of 'correctness versus appropriateness', there are two apparently contradictory aims that need exploring.

On the one hand, students need to realize that their use of less prestigious forms and expressions will be judged unfavourably in many social contexts and may cause them to be disadvantaged as individuals in those contexts. Again, a discussion of slang or taboo words can provide a way into this point. On the other hand in the interests of their own critical language awareness, children need to know that language used regularly and systematically by people for their own purposes is not incorrect. Perhaps children can be helped to grasp this difficult social paradox by some examples of language forms that are widely judged to be 'incorrect', but whose use is more frequent among language users even than the so-called correct versions. Andersson & Trudgill (1990) cite the form 'I done it' which is usually regarded as a mistaken form of 'I did it'. This happens in spite of the fact that 'I did it' is normally used by no more than 30% of native speakers of English. The more common form 'I done it' is regarded as mistaken usually because of the social background of those who use it: its users are rarely those with wealth, status, power, prestige, and education; and their language is unfairly stigmatized by those in possession of high status capital including the power to ordain whose language is right, and whose is wrong.

There are other examples of 'incorrect' variations that are commonly used across English-speaking countries, often by the majority of speakers: 'a man what I know'; 'she ain't got it'; 'we never done nothing'; and 'back in them days'. Andersson & Trudgill make a valuable point that has great application as an instructional principle in this area: *while discrimination may result in many contexts from a use of forms like the above, which is reason enough to urge students to be aware of the stigma that may attach to them, students also need to be aware that by avoiding their use they are doing so for social reasons, and not for reasons of linguistic correctness.* Restating the point from Chapter 5, children need to become aware of the social and historical factors that make one variety of the language more appropriate in prestigious contexts, and others only in contexts at the margins of polite discourse.

Second language varieties need separate treatment in a syllabus for critical language awareness. Usually people are not asked to be critical of the biases that they hold about other languages and extreme prejudice is not uncommon. For example, people in monolingual societies are sometimes irritated when they hear a non-dominant language used in public. At times, this is because they are unable to understand what is being said. But at other times, people seem to be quite threatened by the use of a language that they do not know. If students are to make a start in overcoming the problem of 'other language prejudice', non-dominant languages have to be brought into the classroom in some regular way, in a context where they are used by respected individuals to serve some useful purpose or some familiar courtesy. This practice can also give an enhanced status to the languages of minority groups, but even this can be misunderstood.

The use of minority language phrases and expressions by people who do not speak the language well and who are not from the minority is often seen as pretentious or tokenistic. Perhaps English speakers are influenced by stereotypes derived from their experiences with French speakers in France who are sometimes portrayed as resenting their language being used poorly by non-native speakers. English speakers may even use this to rationalize their reluctance to learn and use the everyday expressions of other languages. But this stereotype is not at all true of the French as a whole, and it may not be true at all of other language speakers. For example, serious attempts by non-Polynesians to use endangered Polynesian languages are regarded quite differently by Polynesian people themselves. When an outsider has taken the trouble to learn how to greet, to thank, and to refer to culturally specific things in appropriate language, Polynesian people regard this as a mark of respect felt for the culture and for its language. Rangi Nicholson, a Maori linguist, remarked to me: 'it may be tokenism, but we are glad to have such tokens'. Nor is this welcoming attitude confined to native speakers of endangered languages. Suzanne Romaine (1989) refers to Muslim women in Britain, who suggest that English-speaking professionals in social service fields might ease tension and remove barriers in cross-cultural communication by learning and using a few essential phrases and greetings in other languages. So to get 'critical second language awareness' moving in the classroom, students need to know that language can serve many empowering purposes which are often of greater importance than just the communication of some content or other.

Promoting consciousness of and practice for change

Mere critique of the status quo is not enough for critical language awareness. The critical study of language tries to encourage students to contribute to improving wider practices. Activities suggested in the previous sub-sections are also ways of exploring this theme. Any language awareness activity will be useful here if it stresses the dynamic nature of language and the reciprocal role that every individual's discourse has in creating and being created by social structures. For example, adolescents will take some pleasure in discovering new and reasonable ways in which the conventions of standard language appropriateness can be subverted, perhaps following tactics not unlike those followed by the reformers of sexist language forms and functions in recent decades. Working within this theme, students can examine how social struggles and changes in power relations can change language; what potential for language change and what constraints on change exist in contemporary societies; and how improvements can be brought about. In designing a programme for this theme, many topics are possible. Here I list only a sample of activities. They fall under headings that may overlap. For instance, several of the topics try to develop practice related to the process of 'wording' the world.

Labelling

The labels commonly used to characterize various minority groups in a given community provide topics for debate and analysis. Sometimes these labels are specific to a local area or region. The first group of questions below queries the neutrality of the labels that are often applied rather uncritically when referring to people with disabilities:

(1) Should people with abnormal hearing, vision and speech competencies be referred to using words like 'blind', 'deaf' and 'mute'?
(2) Why has 'dumb' almost disappeared as a label of disability?
(3) Would it be fairer to avoid common metaphors or simile expressions that are negative, like 'deaf as a post', 'blind as a bat'?
(4) To what extent is 'disability' a social construct that has meaning over and above any single physical or medical basis that it might have?
(5) Are the more 'politically correct' substitute phrases such as 'differently abled' for 'crippled' helpful or unhelpful?
(6) What causes phrases to become fashionable and then less acceptable from time to time?

People also use labels to refer to human behaviour itself in ways that vary depending on the background of the speaker and the context of the utterance. Murray Edelman discusses distinctions that can arise:

> Class or status differences may also entail wide differences in the labellings of identical behaviours. The teacher's underachiever may be the epitome of the 'cool' student who refuses to 'brownnose'. The middle class's criminal or thief may be a 'political prisoner' to the black poor. Such labels with contrasting connotations occur when a deprived population sees the system as unresponsive to its needs and organised rebellion as impossible. In these circumstances only individual non-conformity remains as a way to maintain self-respect. To the deprived the non-conformity is a political act. To the beneficiaries of the system it is individual pathology. Each labels it accordingly (1984: 52–53).

Other labels prescribe broader differences between people. To what extent do biological criteria justify a use of the following as objective expressions of 'difference' between human beings?

(1) Gender and its associated expressions.

(2) Race and its associated expressions.
(3) Culture and its associated expressions.

Gender

The following list of theories about men and women would appeal to older students as discussion or debating topics (Kramarae, 1981: 3–4):

(1) women are more likely than men to have difficulty expressing themselves fluently in dominant (public) modes;
(2) men are more likely than women to have difficulty understanding what members of the other gender mean;
(3) women are more likely to find ways to express themselves outside dominant public modes of expression;
(4) women are more likely to state dissatisfaction with dominant public modes of expression;
(5) women who consciously and verbally resist the ideas of the dominant group will change dominant public modes of expression;
(6) women are less likely to coin words that become familiar and widely used;
(7) women's sense of humour differs from men's.

In compiling the above list, Cheris Kramarae based her ideas on assumptions that are also worthy of classroom discussion:

- women and men see the world differently because of their different experiences and activities;
- men's political dominance makes their perceptions dominant;
- men's dominance hinders the free expression of women's alternative models of the world;
- women are forced to restructure their own models to fit the received male system of expression if they are to participate in society.

Sexist Language

In spite of the many successes in reforming sexist language, children will continue to meet texts that contains the following discriminatory usages:

(1) generic 'he', 'him' and 'his', used to refer to an undefined male or female;
(2) 'man' used alone, or in compounds like 'manpower', 'chairman', 'man-made', to refer to an undefined female or male agent or qualifier;
(3) gender marking, especially through the use of feminine suffixes added to words like 'poet', 'author' etc.;
(4) names and titles of address like 'Mrs John Smith';
(5) syntactic constructions that render males active and females passive.

By seizing the moment and discussing these anachronisms whenever they come up in children's reading activities, teachers can create opportunities for addressing wider issues of language change and control. Other sexist usages are more difficult to remove from language. Sometimes the words themselves have a double role: they subtly discriminate between the genders, but also fill important ordinary language functions that cannot be easily dropped from everyday usage. They perpetuate gender discrimination, even when their users may not intend anything of the kind. Eliminating their negative influence depends on speakers becoming more critical and sensitive to the nuances:

king	queen
governor	governess
lord	lady
mister	mistress
patron	matron
sir	madam
bachelor	spinster

David Smith (1985) sees these two lists of words as really not synonymous at all when used within certain dimensions of meaning. Action, power, and authority are suggested by the list on the left; other secondary sexual connotations attach to the list on the right. Older children could benefit from a discussion of these sets of words, especially if it leads into questions like the following:

(1) Why is it that when a word becomes associated with women it often acquires semantic characteristics that are stereotyped?

(2) Are there other gender specific words and expressions in common use that are acquiring similar 'semantic degeneration'?

(3) Are there words and expressions that refer to oppressed or minority group members that have picked up unfavourable connotations?

Other terms are often associated with sexist stereotypes. The National Union of Journalists in Britain cautions against relying on stereotypes in describing women and men: 'there is no reason why girls and women should be generally characterized as emotional, sentimental, dependent, vulnerable, passive, alluring, mysterious, fickle, weak, inferior, neurotic, gentle, muddled, vain, intuitive'; and there is no reason 'why boys and men should be assumed to be dominant, strong, aggressive, sensible, superior, randy, decisive, courageous, ambitious, unemotional, logical, independent, ruthless' (NUJ, 1982: 6). Children in the middle years of schooling would enjoy debating the relevance of these lists, especially since changing social and language conditions now throw many of these stereotypes into sharp relief.

In an effort to explode the myths that lie behind more subtle gendered usages, David Graddol and Joan Swann (1989) examine pairs of everyday words to see how they differ in spite of their apparent complementarity:

She mothered the children in the village for several years.
He fathered the children in the village for several years.

Anne really did mother those kittens.
Brian really did father those kittens.

There are two language awareness questions here: What is different about these meanings; and do the differences carry over from these verbs into the meanings of their cognate nouns? Other pairs of words from an earlier list in this section such as 'governor' and 'governess' and 'master' and 'mistress' could be put into sentences or used as a basis for dictionary exercises to explore their change from near synonymy to the debasing of the female term. Again, exercises could examine changes in the meanings of words like 'hussy' (originally = 'housewife') and 'wench' (='girl') and compare these with changes in the meaning of words associated with social rank or status: 'churl'; 'knave'; 'villain', and the once common practice in some places of referring to men from minority groups as 'boy'.

Graddol & Swann identify other common practices, such as the neutral words 'woman', 'lady' and 'girl' placed in a derogatory context (e.g. 'a rather hysterical lady'; 'a silly old woman'; 'my girl on the typewriter will help you'). They also criticize the way that non-parallel terms are used for women and men: as in 'three university students — two girls and a man — were abducted'; or where a woman's appearance is given emphasis; or where women are described more often in terms of their relation to someone else. The Australian author, Gwen Wessons made an early contribution to feminist thought in a book whose ironic title was 'Brian's Wife, Jenny's Mum'.

Discursive Bias

This is a very large language awareness topic that is central to any curriculum for political education, social education, or as an introduction to citizenship and life skills. Exercising political freedom wisely, involves sophisticated powers of analysis. The most basic of these is the ability to decide whether someone is speaking sense or nonsense: 'crap detection'. A basic part of this skill is knowing whether or not a speaker is reporting accurately on events. Mikhail Bakhtin observes that 'sly and ill-disposed' polemicists know very well which ironic backdrop should be brought to bear on the accurately quoted words of their opponents, in order to distort their sense (1981 [1975]: 340). But systematic bias of this kind is not confined to politics and advertising. Dwight Bolinger (1980: 71) points out that bias is so pervasive that hardly a sentence in normal speech lacks it, while many utterances contain nothing else but bias. He uses the question 'Why did you have to go and let yourself be talked into that?' as a specimen sentence which floods the hearer with almost unanswerable accusations. For example: 'have to' implies compulsion, but in the circumstances of the utterance there need not have been any; 'go and' implies a wilful act, when in fact the logic of reasonable persuasion might have brought about the actor's change in heart; 'let yourself' implies that the actor was out of control; and 'being talked into' implies passivity, when the discussion the sentence refers to might have been a genuine exchange of views. Clearly, the constructions used in Bolinger's sentence put the hearer on the defensive, without saying frankly what he or she is accused of. At the same time, the opening 'why' pretends that an explanation is required for a string of insinuations that are presented as factual and cannot be answered.

Sometimes speakers are unaware of the force that their choice of verbs carries for listeners. Others are only too aware. Some verbs actually entail acceptance of the speakers' biased view of the truth or falsity of what they are saying. These are called 'implicative verbs' (Bolinger, 1980: 80–2); they entail the truth of the proposition in which they appear and a speaker does not use them unless the claim is believed to be true. For example, the sentence 'He thought it was too late' has no such entailment; but the sentence 'He realised that it was too late' entails truth. Other verbs entail the speaker's denial. For example, the sentence 'She said that I had lied to her' has no such entailment; while the sentence 'She pretended that I had lied to her' means the speaker is actually denying that she did lie. Other verbs can entail the speaker's scepticism. For example, compare 'They said that they were present at that time' with 'They claimed that they were present at that time'. Elsewhere too, implicative verbs can draw listeners unwillingly into a conspiracy. The following sentence appeared in the discourse of a formal meeting: 'They even had the cheek to ask for it at half price' (Corson, 1993b).

Propaganda is a form of discursive bias that needs careful planning. When propaganda is transparent, it tends to backfire on the propagandists. Being able to spot the hidden messages of political propaganda is a key competency for education to pass on, since citizens in a democracy who lack this critical ability are a danger to everyone. Propaganda puts to work those functions of ideology that were presented early in this chapter (p. 159), and it does so with deliberate intent. Like ideology in general, it is easier to identify propaganda when it is used by those with whom we disagree or by enemies, than when it is used by friends or allies. But people in general are becoming more aware of the euphemistic phrases that their own politicians and the military adopt to disguise their actions:

making someone redundant	= sacking or firing them;
down-sizing expenditure	= cutting spending;
neutralizing the enemy	= killing them;
denying the enemy the population resources	= forcibly resettling [Vietnamese] villagers and/or murdering them;
a surgical strike	= annihilation of life within a fixed area.
collateral damage	= death or injury to non-combatants or allies

Some of the most ruthless and effective propaganda was used by the British in the First World War (Brekle, 1989). To achieve their political and military ends, the British propaganda specialists used eight basic approaches. These could provide syllabus items in a course of propaganda studies:

(1) The use of stereotypes ('bull-necked Prussian officer').
(2) The use of names with negative connotations ('huns').
(3) The use and suppression of facts (retreats designated as 'strategic withdrawals').
(4) The use of exaggerated reports of cruelty ('Belgian nuns violated'; 'children's hands cut off').
(5) The use of slogans ('a war to end all wars'; 'God is on our side').
(6) The use of one-sided reporting (small victories exaggerated; large defeats glossed over).
(7) The use of unmistakably negative characterizations of the enemy ('German militarists').
(8) The use of the 'bandwagon effect' ('where were you when your nation needed you?').

So effective was this British propaganda programme in the First World War that the Nazis used it as a model to be learned from for their own pro-gramme in the 1930s. According to Herbert Brekle, Hitler rebuked the Germans for not understanding the value of propaganda as a psychological weapon. Hitler ordered that all statements issued by his government and the press must be one-sided on all questions; they must appeal to the primitive feelings of the masses; and they must repeat the same points without end.

Is there really a difference between 'advertising' and 'propaganda'? Both are acts of persuasion but the one tries to 'convince' people and the other tries to 'seduce' them (Sornig, 1989). Propaganda often exploits the apparent trustworthiness of the persuader in order to manipulate the relationship that exists between speaker and listeners. The power that advertising has largely comes from its ability to constitute taken-for-granted meanings by broadcasting them widely and often. Examples of discursive bias in advertising abound in modern societies. Bolinger mentions the following euphemistic terms often used by advertisers: 'crafted' for 'manufactured'; 'fun size' for 'small'; 'standard' for 'average'; 'rinse' for 'dye' (1980: 116). He recommends four approaches to challenging biased messages in the media, asking that information passing through one-way media channels should meet these testable propositions:

(1) the messages are clear;
(2) the messages identify themselves with what they say rather than with who says it;
(3) the messages are free of snares and biases, such as presuppositions, entailments, concealed agents, existentials, deletions, hidden sentences, question-begging epithets and the running commentary of intonation and gesture;
(4) there are no sanctuaries, no sacred precincts guarded by taboos or traditional courtesies, such as soap operas filled with personal problems but ignoring social ones.

To put these propositions to work, Bolinger suggests a single course of action: to make language serve the flow of messages as it should, people must be free to talk about language itself. In other words, people need to feel free and competent in using language to *expose* distorted language.

Prejudice in Language

Chapter 1 mentioned the distorting power of the narratives of National Socialism (p. 3). These established and legitimated a prejudiced world view within which anything was possible because contrary narratives were proscribed. There are many other examples of prejudiced narratives that create unjust structural constraints and these can be found in the history of every society. For example, even after the abolition of slavery in the USA as Bolinger observes, the narratives that White children heard all around them taught them to despise their former slaves as surely as parades and band music taught them to respect the flag. Also, I might add, the narratives of America's cinema and television westerns have taught generations of the world's children insensitivity to the rights of aboriginal peoples. Supported by the narratives of other genres of film and television, they have given a fatally distorted value to the use, status, and possession of firearms and weapons of destruction.

Part of the power of prejudiced language comes from the use of 'dysphemistic terms': words that do the opposite job to euphemisms. These have a special role in politics but they are used wherever people try to dehumanize others. Hitler's characterizing the Jews as 'creatures' aroused little concern at first, but it began the deadly process of depersonalizing the victims and became highly effective because there existed no institutionalized rejection of it. After Hitler had ordained that 'creatures' must be treated like the parasites and vermin that exist everywhere but cannot be seen, then separation, suppression, and eventually 'extermination' became possible. But today when educated people try to use words or jokes to stereotype racial or social groups, this tends to stigmatize the speakers rather than their targets. Pressure groups like the National Union of Journalists in Britain have issued guidelines on race reporting that caution journalists about their usages: 'Don't say 'black', 'Asian', 'of West Indian origin' or 'immigrant' unless 100% essential to the story' (Macshane, 1978: 20). Although new prejudices and stereotypes are appearing all the time, a widely adopted curriculum of critical language awareness can make it more difficult for the prejudiced to create and popularize new dysphemisms of oppression. While use of the vocabularies of prejudice seems to be on the wane at least among educated people, the syntax of a language always remains the most powerful vehicle for expressing prejudice and for shaping distorted perceptions of the world. The art of rhetoric makes skilful use of this sophisticated tool of power.

Rhetorical Language

Rhetoric was once taught as an essential part of the curriculum of an 'educated' person. To be judged as 'educated', a young person had to have rich encounters with the speeches and the rhetorical techniques of Demosthenes, Cicero, and their heirs. While rhetoric has fallen into disuse as a formal school subject, it has sharp relevance for critical language awareness. But rather than teaching rhetoric, critical awareness studies could attend more to how rhetoric works. Below are some common rhetorical devices (after Sornig, 1989) that can serve powerful purposes:

(1) Announcements to introduce argumentative steps appearing in discourse:

'I'll begin by outlining my case...'

'I'll explain this to you, shall I?'

'You (really) must admit...'

'Look here...'

'The facts of the matter are these...'

'I have only (two) points to make in reply...'

(2) Strategic phrases that listeners often use to interrupt arguments or to get the floor:

'Keep to the point, please'
'What are you trying to say?'
'What's the idea...'
'So what!'
'I appreciate your point but...'

(3) Strategies that speakers often use to draw their listeners into an unwilling consensus:

using the first names of listeners as a signal of solidarity;

using the 'pronouns of solidarity' that appear in some languages (e.g. the French 'tu');

using in-group phrases to show solidarity (e.g.'us men'; 'fellow members of the master race');

using first person plural pronouns as a signal of solidarity;

using phrases like 'Let's be reasonable' [which Sornig calls 'the nurse's plural'].

(4) The use of nicknames and caricatures, to praise or condemn: this was a favourite tactic of Cicero and Demosthenes. Nicknames and caricatures need not be justified and they cannot be contradicted or disproved. Hitler and Churchill were expert in using both in their speeches.

These four examples of the use of rhetoric suggest the range of material that rhetoric can draw from. Rhetoric is the art of the politician, in either the literal or the figurative sense. Bourdieu's 'magisterial discourse' is most often heard in a political context. For example the sentence 'all the necessary steps will be taken' coming from a politician who is addressing constituencies with a range of interests and opinions, can convey everything, anything or nothing to the listeners. If they add their own meanings to this message and if it is spoken with sincerity and the right non-verbal language, its rhetorical effect can be more reassuring than a list of specific promises.

Mundane Discourse and Discrimination

Informal language is often used in discriminatory ways. One of the aims of education is to help children learn sensitivity to the feelings of others. Critical language awareness can be very helpful in meeting this aim. Much of the discrimination in everyday language arises because people tend to take discriminatory usages for granted if they are in the company of others who are similar in social, gender, or ethnic background. When used to exclude or include other individuals or groups, mundane discourse expresses the speakers' membership of a currently dominant group, even if that group only lasts for the duration of the discourse itself.

By exchanging and stressing group norms and values, speakers in an in-group reinforce its solidarity and reproduce those values. Any discourse expressing group solidarity tends to caricature, ironicize, and recast out-group values or characteristics. This often happens unintentionally, simply because language is an inadequate instrument for expressing meaning in highly complex values areas. Often the discourse reformulates out-group values and attributes, in handy expressions that are readily identifiable and re-usable for group reference; these expressions can become a basis for more formal acts of discrimination against the out-group itself; and these acts can be rationalized by the in-group, since the discourse referring to those values and norms has become the taken-for-granted account of how things are. Small and large ideologies of discrimination are created in this way on a daily basis.

In similar ways, everyday talk can provide the vehicle by which personal prejudices become the views of an entire group. Opinions put into words permeate, define, and redefine social situations until the out-group members as the objects of the opinions, are translated into a threat to the dominant group. At the same time in their own discourse, the members of the dominant group become the objects whose rights seem to be threatened by the out-group members. Various pedagogies are helpful in exploring these complex powers that mundane discourse possesses: role play, improvisation, and film studies are among these. But the best place to start is in the language practices modelled by teachers in the classroom.

Critical Awareness of Classroom Discourse Practices

When teachers encourage their students to reflect critically on the language practices used within the school itself, this is an important step towards implementing the discourse ethic in the school. It is also a statement by teachers that this is the way they would like the world of discourse outside the school to be. By looking at real acts of discourse in the school's own context rather than at abstract examples, students are empowered by the activities rather than just informed and perhaps demoralized by them. If mundane discourse practices in schools are not tied in children's minds to a critical awareness of that discourse set in its wider context, then the discourse conceals the structures of domination within which it is located. In doing so, it creates a deceitful illusion of freedom which is clearly miseducative.

Gender imbalances in communication offer a guide here. The unequal power relations in many male–female conversations often force females into conceding to the world view of males in their conversations, which are then conducted so as to favour the male's style of operating often with unwelcome consequences for the females. For example, young women as a routine part of their educational experience in many institutions have to develop discursive tactics for dealing with unwelcome forms of harassment from male students and teachers. This continues in spite of the best phrased anti-harassment policies, because even to engage with harassment at a verbal level often means that females have to recognize and accept the discourse used by males as natural and normal, thus accepting at the same time complicity in the harassment itself and thereby reinforcing sexual harassment as a legitimate attribute of masculinity.[3] Those of lesser power are often drawn into supporting the practices of the powerful, thereby reinforcing the structures of power that allowed those practices to develop in the first place. I think this point can be reapplied with equal force to the situation that confronts all children in schools.

Young children engaging in dialogue with powerful adults like teachers almost always accept that discourse on the adult's terms. Habermas talks about the 'strategic' communication that adults engage in with children. Usually there is some further purpose behind an adult's discourse with children, and the talk is only instrumental to that end. When teachers are bent on reaching some curriculum or personal goal through their interactions with children, the imbalance in the power relationship gives many children a distorted view of the purposes of language. They often develop perceptions of their own powerlessness in school which reinforce their sense of powerlessness outside the school. Many girls are routinely disempowered in this way. School experiences finish off a long process of discursively distorted socialization for many young women who go on to accept roles which they perceive to be their lot in life because most of the structural narratives that they have encountered leave them with no alternative. Nor are girls the sole victims of this process of disempowerment. Chapters 3 and 5 argued that many children from minority social groups and from cultural minorities are in great need of empowering classroom practices.

One way to reform school discourse practices is to study practices in the wider community and bring conclusions back as a basis for changing the school reality. David Graddol and Joan Swann (1989: 184–7) set out some aims and classroom activities for strengthening children's critical awareness of discourse in society and promoting their practice for change. They suggest that in helping students correct misinformation and bias, teachers need to develop or extend student skills in observing, analyzing, interpreting, and judging; and that in helping students cope with group and individual manifestations of prejudice and discrimination, teachers need to encourage the development of a range of response strategies that children can apply in their own lives. The authors go on to give classroom examples of what they mean.

As part of their work in one classroom, students discuss images they hold of themselves and other people. These include: gender images; images of other social groups, such as young and old people; images of people from different ethnic groups and different religious backgrounds; and images of disabled and able-bodied people. Students are asked to think critically about the sources of positive and negative images and to challenge popular stereotypes. While the class examines many other forms of representation (music, pictures, and clothing), language is the focus of this work. The pupils think about the language used to describe other people, such as terms of abuse. As evidence, they collect and analyze written texts (newspapers, magazines, comics, textbooks). They develop a checklist to detect bias and the methods used to perpetuate unjust stereotypes. They 'brainstorm' their own stereotypes about women and minority people, to retrieve words often used to label these groups; and they also look critically at books that challenge stereotypes. The authors report that both boys and girls respond favourably to books that provide positive images of girls.

Also mentioned in Chapter 6, the literacy practices of the school are the source of many assumptions about the world at large for children. A critical language awareness curriculum addressing the context of the school itself would also encourage children to look critically at their own literacy practices and at the texts that they encounter both inside and outside school: to engage in acts of critical literacy. Below is a list of questions to ask about the language of children's books. This is an expanded version of a list provided by Rosemary Stones (1983: 16ff):

(1) Does the book use 'man' or 'men' to mean 'people' or does it use 'men and women' instead (e.g. the inclusion of Boadicea and Joan of Arc in a book titled *Fighting Men*)?

(2) Does the book caricature the members of racial or ethnic groups by giving them unfairly stereotyped roles, attributes, or personalities?

(3) Is the book imbalanced in giving heroic and other leading roles to actors from elite backgrounds while putting ordinary individuals in the background?

(4) Does the book use sexist or racist terminology?

(5) Does the book use the pronoun 'he' generically?

(6) Does the book use a 'two-value system' in the language it applies to female and male characters (e.g. girls 'giggling' while boys 'laugh')?

(7) Does the book use a 'two-value system' in the way it characterizes people from different cultures (e.g. 'brave colonists' struggling against

'bloodthirsty savages'; 'hard-praying ancestors' versus 'troublesome renegades')?

(8) Are females and the members of minority cultures described in demeaning terms (e.g. 'the women and children'; 'a hen party'; 'jabbering away in their language')?

(9) Are females described as male appendages rather than in their own right (e.g. 'the clever wife'; 'the wise daughter')?

(10) Is the female member of a partnership presented as unequal (e.g. 'the farmer' and 'the farmer's wife')?

(11) Does the resolution of the story depend on whether a character is 'pretty', 'ugly', 'strong', 'handsome', 'rich', 'titled'?

(12) Are the problems of the characters set against a real background of social inequality and social problems?

If critical language awareness is to find a place in classrooms, teachers may have to reduce their heavy reliance on several favoured approaches to teaching. In concluding this section, I mention just two of these as examples of the kinds of critical changes that may be needed. The first 'pedagogy of disempowerment' spans and affects the entire process of education. The conventional classroom questioning technique of the 'initiation — feedback — response' cycle (IRF) is the basis of most teaching acts, yet the IRF cycle actually excludes the possibility of students responding rationally to the validity claims that teachers make, since in the context of whole class teaching the presuppositions present in the teacher's initiations have to be taken-for-granted by students if their feedback is to be validated in the teacher's responses (Young, 1987, 1992). The second 'pedagogy of disempowerment' is often popular among teachers of younger children or ESL teachers. The use of whole class or group recitations is an ancient practice that often goes uncriticized because of its antiquity. In research studies discussing the fit between discourse and aim in maths and social studies lessons with children of different socioeconomic backgrounds, more recitations are used for maths than for social studies and more in schools for children from low-income backgrounds (Cazden, 1988). While recitation may have a positive impact in topics that are algorithmic and factual through its emphasis on the public practice of reviewing and checking details, Cazden also alerts her readers to the negative side of recitation. It depends on questionable assumptions about the nature of school knowledge since it encourages students to see knowledge as linear and dogmatic. It also requires students to approach the content of the curriculum uncritically with their powers of analysis and synthesis untapped. Its common use as a pedagogy in some schools, for some children rather than for others, raises questions about the 'control' function that recitation activities can serve.

Conclusion

This chapter makes many controversial recommendations. Like any conclusions in the human sciences, my recommendations need to be accepted tentatively and critically. Even when the premises are true and the reasoning is correct, the conclusions are still only probable. I hope that none of the many points comes across as a dogmatic prescription. In every case I have tried to fit the recommendations to the argumentation, the theory, and the research evidence presented in this book, rather than to advance my educational preferences. An analogy from a cognate field may help here. In studies of syntax, there are two contrasting forms of prescriptivism: there is the kind of illiberal prescriptivism that proscribes certain usages as categorically ungrammatical and does so in the interests of elite users of the language; and then there is the kind of prescriptivism that lays down ethical guidelines such as 'anti-sexist' guidelines and does so in the interests of social justice (Graddol & Swann, 1989). Mindful of these varieties of prescriptivism, I try to present 'prescriptions' in this book that are not at all like the grammatical, but very like the ethical. In other words, the text tries to model an exercise in moral reasoning, not an exercise in power. Although 'social justice and language' has been my sub-text since beginning the project, there has been much talk of 'power' throughout the book and on balance perhaps less talk of 'social justice'. But this imbalance has come about because of the nature of social justice itself: it can really only be served by identifying and constraining the powerful within certain circumstances, and then empowering the less powerful after consulting their expressed interests.

A just language policy adopted across an educational system would begin with principles as norms for use at system level; it would elaborate on the ways in which these principles can be related to one another; and it would study what makes different principles appropriate to different situation types. Having done all this, it would devolve language policy decision making and power to schools themselves so that just compromises could be reached appropriate to local contexts and consistent with the original normative principles. In their turn, schools could then address many of this chapter's recommendations directly. By doing so, they could help to reproduce an educated citizenry capable of articulating and clarifying principles for just social policies in general. All of these things seem fundamental to the liberating and critical ends that formal education serves.

Notes to Chapter 7

1. As well as drawing on Habermas (1970; 1971; 1985), I also use the work of interpreters of his ideas (Ottmann, 1982; McCarthy, 1984; Thompson, 1984; R. Bernstein, 1985; Giddens, 1985; Carr & Kemmis, 1986; Rizvi & Kemmis, 1987; Rasmussen, 1990; and R. Young, 1992). Some see a tension between Bourdieu and Habermas in their use of the insights reached by speech-act theorists. While Bourdieu's project is to show that whatever power resides in speech acts comes from the social institution in which those acts are produced, Habermas sees a 'rationally motivating force' involved in communicative interaction. For Bourdieu, the very idea of producing an ideal speech situation unhindered by social constraints as Habermas recommends, is contrary to what is possible in the real world. Although I cannot remove the tension between the two views, I can lessen it by saying that Bourdieu describes the way that the world of speech acts actually is, while Habermas is describing how it should be, given the validity claims that he says underlie human communicative action. While Bourdieu describes a state, Habermas offers an ethical ideal that we should pursue. Like perfect justice, his discourse ethic can never be reached but it is no less worth striving for than justice itself.

2. The origin and early development of the idea of school language policies is linked with the 'language across the curriculum' movement. In 1966, members of the London Association for the Teaching of English began to develop their interest in language across the curriculum by preparing a Discussion Document entitled 'Towards a Language Policy Across the Curriculum' (Rosen in Barnes *et al.*, 1969). This Discussion Document provided a catalyst for action; schools in various places within Britain, in other countries of the British Commonwealth, and in the United States began to develop their own language policies, using the original document as a reference point. In 1975, the aim and value of language policies for British schools received official endorsement in *A Language for Life* (The Bullock Report) (DES, 1975). Subsequently, several influential texts addressed the need for a whole-school language policy especially at secondary level, and discussed its implementation (Marland, 1977; Torbe, 1980; Schools Council, 1980). As the idea of having school language policies spread, practitioners and theorists began to see potential in them for small-scale but important acts of educational reform. For example, Knott (1985) presents novel ideas for researching pupil language use and discovering the attitudes of school staff to language issues; and Maybin (1985) provides practical approaches for working towards a school policy in a culturally pluralist setting. My own work integrates these ideas with concerns for gender, the needs of minority cultures, and with the process itself of administration and policymaking in schools.

3. Clearly most young women learn appropriate strategies and become more successful in verbally combating male harassment. As Beverley Skeggs (1991) confirms, older female students refuse to be rendered powerless in the process; they resist the verbal harassments of innuendo and double meanings with considerable success. This often happens when young women become more aware of their powerful role in legitimating masculinity and in guarding the male ego. When the educational, cultural, or economic context does not require them to show support for masculine power by conforming to male discursive practices, they withdraw consent and reconstitute the power relationships.

References

Albert, M. and Obler, L. (1979) *The Bilingual Brain.* New York: Academic Press.

Ammon, U., Dittmar, N. and Mattheier, K. (1987) *Sociolinguistics.* Berlin: Walter de Gruyter.

Andersson, L. and Trudgill, P. (1990) *Bad Language.* Oxford: Basil Blackwell.

Appel, R. (1988) The language education of immigrant workers' children in The Netherlands. In Skutnabb Kangas and Cummins, *op. cit.*

Appel, R. and Muysken, P. (1987) *Language Contact and Bilingualism.* London: Edward Arnold.

Apple, M. (1982) *Education and Power.* London: Routledge.

Arnot, M. and Weiner, G. (eds) (1987) *Gender and the Politics of Schooling.* London: Unwin Hyman.

Aronowitz, S. (1981) Preface. In Giroux, *op. cit.*

Au, K. (1978) Participation structures in a reading lesson with Hawaiian children: Analysis of a culturally appropriate instructional event. *Anthropology and Education Quarterly* 11, 91–115.

Au, K. and Jordan, C. (1981) Teaching reading to Hawaiian children: Finding culturally appropriate solutions. In H. Truba, G. Guthrie and K. Au (eds) *Culture and the Bilingual Classroom: Studies in Classroom Ethnography.* Rowley, MA: Newbury House.

Au, K. and Mason, J. (1983) Cultural congruence in classroom participation structures: Achieving a balance of rights. *Discourse Processes* 6, 145–67.

Baetens Beardsmore, H. (1986) *Bilingualism: Basic Principles.* Clevedon: Multilingual Matters.

Baker, C. (1988) *Key Issues in Bilingualism and Bilingual Education.* Clevedon: Multilingual Matters.

Baker, C. (1990) The effectiveness of bilingual education. *Journal of Multilingual and Multicultural Development* 11, 269–77.

Bakhtin, M. (1981 [1975]) *The Dialogic Imagination: Four Essays.* Austin: University of Texas Press.

Baran, G. (1987) Teaching girls science. In M. McNeil (ed) *Gender and Expertise.* London: Free Association Books.

Barnes D., Britton J. and Rosen H. (1969) *Language, the Learner and the School.* London: Penguin Education.

Barry, B. (1989) *A Treatise on Social Justice: Volume 1 — Theories of Justice.* Berkeley: University of California Press.

Bentham, J. (1789) [1970 edn] *An Introduction to the Principles of Morals and Legislation.* New York: Hafner.

213

Berko-Gleason, J. (1975) Fathers and other strangers: Men's speech to young children. In D. Dato (ed.) *Developmental Psycholinguistics: Theory and Applications.* (pp. 289–97). Georgetown University Press.

Bernstein, B. (1975) On the classification and framing of educational knowledge. In B. Bernstein (ed) *Class, Codes and Control Vol. 3: Towards a Theory of Educational Transmissions.* London: Routledge and Kegan Paul.

Bernstein, R. (1985) *Habermas and Modernity.* Cambridge: Polity Press.

Bettoni, C. (1985) *Tra Lingue Dialetto e Inglese.* Leichhardt: FILEF Italo-Australian Publications.

Bhaskar, R. (1979) *The Possibility of Naturalism: A Philosophical Critique of the Contemporary Human Sciences.* Brighton: Harvester Press.

Bhaskar, R. (1986) *Scientific Realism and Human Emancipation.* London: Verso.

Bhaskar, R. (1989) *Reclaiming Reality: A Critical Introduction to Contemporary Philosophy.* London: Verso.

Biggs, A. and Edwards, V. (1991) 'I treat them all the same': Teacher–pupil talk in multi-ethnic classrooms. *Language and Education* 5, 161–76.

Bolinger, D. (1980) *Language — The Loaded Weapon: The Use and Abuse of Language Today.* London: Longman.

Bourdieu, P. (1966) L'École conservatrice. *Revue Française de Sociologie* 7, 225–26; 330–42; 346–47.

Bourdieu, P. (1977) *Outline of a Theory of Practice.* London: Cambridge University Press.

Bourdieu, P. (1981) *Ce Que Parler Veut Dire: L'Économie des Échanges Linguistique.* Paris: Fayard.

Bourdieu, P. (1984) *Distinction: A Social Critique of the Judgement of Taste.* Cambridge, MA: Harvard University Press.

Bourdieu, P. (1988) *Homo Academicus.* Cambridge: Polity Press.

Bourdieu, P. [& Passeron, J-C]. (1977) *Reproduction in Education, Society and Culture.* Los Angeles: Sage.

Bourdieu, P. and Wacquant, L. (1992) *An Invitation to Reflexive Sociology.* Chicago: University of Chicago Press.

Brandl, M. (1983). A certain heritage: Women and their children in north Australia. In F. Gale (ed.) *We Are Bosses Ourselves: The Status and Role of Aboriginal Women Today* (pp. 29–39). Canberra: Australian Institute of Aboriginal Studies.

Branson, J. (1991) Gender, education and work. In D. Corson (1991d) *op. cit.*

Branson, J. and Miller, D. (1993) Sign language, the deaf and the epistemic violence of mainstreaming. *Language and Education* 7, 21–41.

Bray, D. and Hill, C. (1973) *Polynesian and Pakeha in New Zealand Education.* Palmerston North: Bennetts.

Brekle, H. (1989) War with words. In Wodak, *op. cit.*

Brophy, J. (1985) Interactions of male and female students with male and female teachers. In L. Wilkinson and C. Marrett (eds) *Gender Influences in Classroom Interaction* (pp. 115–42). Orlando, FL: Academic Press.

Brouwer, D. (1982) The influence of the addressee's sex on politeness in language use. *Linguistics* 20, 697–711.

Brouwer, D., Gerritsen, M. and De Haan, D. (1979) Speech differences between women and men: On the wrong track? *Language in Society* 8, 33–50.

Bruck, M. (1985) Consequences of transfer out of early French immersion programs. *Applied Psycholinguistics* 6, 39–61.

Bryk, A.S. and Driscoll, M.E. (1988) *The High School as Community: Contextual Influences and Consequences for Students and Teachers.* Madison: National Center on Effective Schools.

Buchanan, A. E. and Mathieu, D. (1986) Philosophy and justice. In Cohen, *op. cit.*

Bullivant, B. (1984) *Pluralism: Cultural Maintenance and Evolution.* Clevedon: Multilingual Matters.

Burns, J. and Bird, L. (1987) Girls' cooperation and boys' isolation in achieving understanding in chemistry. *GASAT Conference Proceedings* (pp. 16–25). Wellington: Victoria University of Wellington.

Burns, J., Clift, C. and Duncan, J. (1991) Understanding of understanding: Implications for learning and teaching. *British Journal of Educational Psychology* 61, 276–89.

Cameron, D. (1984) Sexism and semantics. *Radical Philosophy* 36, 14–16.

Cameron, D. (1985) *Feminism and Linguistic Theory.* London: Macmillan.

Cameron, D. and Bourne, J. (1988) No common ground: Kingman, grammar and the nation. *Language and Education* 2, 147–60.

Cameron, D. and Coates, J. (1985) Some problems in the sociolinguistic explanation of sex differences. *Language and Communication* 5, 143–51.

Cameron, D., McAlinden, F. and O'Leary, K. (1988) Lakoff in context: The social and linguistic functions of tag questions. In Coates and Cameron, *op. cit.*

Campos, S. and Keatinge, H. (1988) The Carpinteria language minority student experience: From theory, to practice, to success. In Skutnabb-Kangas and Cummins, *op. cit.*

Canale, M. (1984) A communicative approach to language proficiency assessment in a minority setting. In Rivera, *op. cit.*

Carr, W. and Kemmis, S. (1986) *Becoming Critical: Knowing Through Action Research.* Geelong: Deakin University Press.

Cazden, C. (1987) Enhancing teachers' interactions with Maori children in New Zealand. *Language and Education* 1, 69–70.

Cazden, C. (1988) *Classroom Discourse: The Language of Teaching and Learning.* Portsmouth, NH: Heinemann.

Cazden, C. (1989) Richmond Road: A multilingual/multicultural primary school in Auckland, New Zealand. *Language and Education* 3, 143–66.

Cazden, C. (1990) Differential treatment in New Zealand: Reflections on research in minority education. *Teaching and Teacher Education* 6, 291–303.

Chalk, F. and Jonassohn, K. (1990) *The History and Sociology of Genocide: Analyses and Case Studies.* New Haven: Yale University Press.

Chamot, A. (1988) Bilingualism in education and bilingual education: The state of the art in the United States. *Journal of Multilingual and Multicultural Development* 9, 11–35.

Chandler, J., Argyris, D., Barnes, W., Goodman, I. and Snow, C. (1986) Parents as teachers: Observations of low-income parents and children in a homework-like task. In Schieffelin and Gilmore, *op. cit.*

Cheshire, J. (1984) The relationship between language and sex in English. In P. Trudgill (ed) *Applied Sociolinguistics* (pp. 33–49). London: Academic Press.

Cheshire, J., Edwards, V. and Whittle, P. (1988) Survey of British Dialect Grammar: An unpublished report. ESRC Project: Birkbeck College, University of London.

Cheshire, J. and Jenkins, N. (1991) Gender differences in the GCSE Oral English Examination: Part 2. *Language and Education* 5, 19–40.

Christie, M. (1985) *Aboriginal Perspectives on Experience and Learning: The Role of Language in Aboriginal Education.* Geelong, Victoria: Deakin University Press.

Christie, M. (1988). The invasion of aboriginal education. In Institute of Applied Aboriginal Studies, *Learning My Way (Waikaru* 16) (pp. 5–19). Perth: Western Australia College of Advanced Education.

Churchill, S. (1986) *The Education of Linguistic and Cultural Minorities in OECD Countries.* Clevedon: Multilingual Matters.

Churchill, S., Frenette, N. and Quazi, S. (1986) *Éducation et Besoins des Franco-Ontariens: Le Diagnostic d'un Systeme d' Éducation.* Toronto: Le Conseil de l'Éducation Franco-Ontarienne.

Clark, R., Fairclough, N., Ivanic, R. and Martin-Jones, M. (1990) Critical language awareness. Part 1: A critical review of three current approaches to language awareness. *Language and Education* 4, 249–60.

Clark, R., Fairclough, N., Ivanic, R. and Martin-Jones, M. (1991) Critical language awareness. Part 2: Towards critical alternatives. *Language and Education* 5, 41–54.

Coates, J. (1986) *Women, Men and Language.* London: Longman.

Coates, J. and Cameron, D. (1988) *Women in Their Speech Communities: New Perspectives on Language and Sex.* London: Longman.

Cobarrubias, J. and Fishman, J. (1983) *Progress in Language Planning.* Berlin: Mouton.

Cohen, R. (ed.) (1986) *Justice: Views from the Social Sciences.* New York: Plenum.

Comer, J. P. (1984) Home/school relationships as they affect the academic success of children. *Education and Urban Society* 16, 323–37.

Connors, B. (1984) A multicultural curriculum as action for social justice. In Shapson and D'Oyley, *op. cit.* pp. 104–11.

Cooper, R. (1989) *Language Planning and Social Change.* Cambridge: Cambridge University Press.

Corson, D. (1985) *The Lexical Bar.* Oxford: Pergamon Press.

Corson, D. (1987) *Oral Language Across the Curriculum.* Clevedon: Multilingual Matters.

Corson, D. (1988) Language policy across the curriculum (LPAC). *Language and Education* 2, 61–3.

Corson, D. (1990a) *Language Policy Across the Curriculum.* Clevedon: Multilingual Matters.

Corson, D. (1990b) Three curriculum and organisational responses to cultural pluralism in New Zealand schooling. *Language, Culture and Curriculum* 3, 181–93.

Corson, D. (1991a) Educational research and Bhaskar's conception of discovery. *Educational Theory* 41, 189–98.

Corson, D. (1991b) Bhaskar's critical realism and educational knowledge. *British Journal of Sociology of Education* 12, 223–41.

Corson, D. (1991c) Realities of teaching in a multiethnic school. *International Review of Education* 37, 7–31.

Corson, D. (ed.) (1991d) *Education for Work: Background to Policy and Curriculum.* Clevedon: Multilingual Matters.

Corson, D. (1993a) Restructuring minority schooling. *Australian Journal of Education* 37, 46–68.

Corson, D. (1993b) Discursive bias and ideology in the administration of minority group interests. *Language in Society* 22, 165–91.

Crosby, F. and Nyquist, L. (1977) The female register: An empirical study of Lakoff's hypotheses. *Language in Society* 6, 313–22.

Crystal, D. (1987) *The Cambridge Encyclopedia of Language.* Cambridge: Cambridge University Press.

Cummins, J. (1981) *Bilingualism and Minority Language Children.* Toronto: OISE Press.

Cummins, J. (1984) *Bilingualism and Special Education: Issues in Assessment and Pedagogy.* Clevedon: Multilingual Matters.

Cummins, J. (1986) Empowering minority students: A framework for intervention. *Harvard Educational Review* 56, 18–36.

Cummins, J. (1988) From multicultural to anti-racist education: An analysis of programmes and policies in Ontario. In Skutnabb-Kangas and Cummins, *op. cit.*

Cummins, J. *et al.* (1984) Linguistic interdependence among Japanese and Vietnamese immigrant students. In Rivera *op. cit.*

Cummins, J. and Swain, M. (1986) *Bilingualism in Education: Aspects of Theory, Research and Practice.* London: Longman.

Daniels, N. (ed.) (1976) *Reading Rawls.* New York: Basic Books.

Dahrendorf, R. (1978) *Life Chances.* Chicago: University of Chicago Press.

de Castell, S., Luke, A. and Egan, K. (eds) (1986) *Literacy, Society and Schooling: A Reader.* Cambridge: Cambridge University Press.

Dannequin, C. (1987) Les enfants bâillonnés: The teaching of French as mother tongue in elementary school. *Language and Education* 1, 15–31.

Department of Education (1988) *Administering for Excellence: Effective Administration in Education* (The Picot Report). Wellington.

Department of Education (1989) *Assessment for Better Learning: A Public Discussion Document* (The ABLE Report). Wellington.

DES (Department of Education and Science) (1975) *Language for Life* (The Bullock Report). London: HMSO.

DES (Department of Education and Science) (1985) *Education for All: Report of the Committee of Inquiry into the Education of Children from Ethnic Minority Groups* (The Swann Report). London: HMSO.

DES (Department of Education and Science) (1988) *Report of the Committee of Inquiry into the Teaching of the English Language* (The Kingman Report). London: HMSO.

Dittman, A. (1977) Developmental factors in conversational behaviour. *Journal of Communication* 22, 404–23.

Dworkin, R. (1978) *Taking Rights Seriously.* London: Duckworth.

Edelman, M. (1984) The political language of the helping professions. In Shapiro, *op. cit.*

Edwards, J. (1985) *Language, Society and Identity*. Oxford: Basil Blackwell.

Edwards, J. (1989) *Language and Disadvantage: Studies in Disorders of Communication* (2nd edn) London: Cole & Whurr.

Edwards, J. B. (1987) *Positive Discrimination, Social Justice, and Social Policy: Moral Scrutiny of a Policy Practice*. London: Tavistock.

Edwards, V. (1986) *Language in a Black Community*. Clevedon: Multilingual Matters.

Erickson, F. (1975) Gatekeeping and the melting pot. *Harvard Educational Review* 45, 44–70.

Erickson, F. (1984) Rhetoric, anecdote and rhapsody: Coherence strategies in a conversation among Black American adolescents. In Tannen, *op. cit.* pp. 81–154.

Esposito, A. (1979) Sex differences in children's conversation. *Language and Speech* 22, 213–20.

Fairclough, N. (1985) Critical and descriptive goals in discourse analysis. *Journal of Pragmatics* 9, 739–63.

Fairclough, N. (1989) *Language and Power*. London: Longman.

Fairclough, N. (ed.) (1992) The appropriacy of 'appropriateness'. In *Critical Language Awareness*. London: Longman.

Fairweather, H. (1976) Sex differences in cognition. *Cognition* 4, 231–80.

Fargher, R. and Ziersch, R. (1981) What happened at Hermansburg? *Set No. 2*. Wellington: NZCER.

Fasold, R. (1984) *The Sociolinguistics of Society*. Oxford: Basil Blackwell.

Fasold, R. (1990) *The Sociolinguistics of Language*. Oxford: Basil Blackwell.

Fennema, E. and Peterson, P. (1985) Autonomous learning behaviour: A possible explanation of gender-related differences in mathematics. In L. Wilkinson and C. Marrett eds *Gender Influences In Classroom Interaction* (pp. 17–36) Orlando, FL: Academic Press.

Ferrara, A. (1985) A critique of Habermas' 'diskursethik'. *Telos* 64, 45–74.

Fichtelius, A., Johansson, I. and Nordin, K. (1980) Three investigations of sex-associated speech variation in day school. *Women's Studies International Quarterly* 3(2), 219–25.

Fishman, J. (1967) Bilingualism with and without diglossia: Diglossia with and without bilingualism. *Journal of Social Issues* 23, 29–38.

Fishman, J. (1969) *Readings in the Sociology of Language*. The Hague: Mouton.

Fishman, J. (1973) Language modernization and planning in comparison with other types of national modernization and planning. *Language in Society* 2, 23–42.

Fishman, J. (1990) What is reversing language shift (RLS) and how can it succeed? *Journal of Multilingual and Multicultural Development* 11, 5–36.

Fishman, P. (1983) Interaction: The work women do. In Thorne, Kramarae and Henley, *op. cit.*

Fisk, M. (1976) History and reason in Rawls' Moral Theory. In Daniels, *op. cit.*

Fitzpatrick, F. (1987) *The Open Door*. Clevedon: Multilingual Matters.

Foucault, M. (1972) *The Archaeology of Knowledge*. London: Tavistock.

Foucault, M. (1977) *Discipline and Punish: The Birth of the Prison*. New York: Pantheon.

Foucault, M. (1980) *Power/Knowledge: Selected Interviews and Other Writings 1971–1977*. New York: Pantheon.

Fowler, R., Hodge, B., Kress, G. and Trew, T. (1979) *Language and Control*. London: Routledge.

Frank, F. W. and P. A. Treichler (1989) *Language, Gender and Professional Writing: Theoretical Approaches and Guidelines for Nonsexist Usage*. New York: Modern Language Association of America.

Frazer, E. and Cameron, D. (1989) Knowing what to say: The construction of gender in linguistic practice. In Grillo (1898a), *op. cit.*

Furby, L. (1986) Psychology and justice. In Cohen, *op. cit.*

Gadd, B. (1976). *Cultural Differences in the Classroom: Special Needs of Maori in Pakeha Schools*. Auckland: Heinemann.

Garcia, O. and Otheguy, R. (1987) The bilingual education of Cuban-American children in Dade County's ethnic schools. *Language and Education* 1, 83–95.

Gee, J. (1990) *Social Linguistics and Literacies*. Basingstoke: The Falmer Press.

Giddens, A. (1979) *Central Problems in Social Theory*. Berkeley: University of California Press.

Giddens, A. (1985) Jürgen Habermas. In Q. Skinner (ed.) *The Return of Grand Theory in the Human Sciences*. London: Cambridge University Press.

Giles, H. *et al.* (1987) Research on language attitudes. In Ammon, Dittmar and Mattheier, *op. cit.*

Gilligan, C. (1982) *In a Different Voice: Psychological Theory and Women's Development*. Harvard: Harvard University Press.

Giroux, H. (1981) *Ideology, Culture and the Process of Schooling*. Philadelphia: Temple University Press.

Gleason, J. B. (1987) Sex differences in parent–child interaction. In Philips *et al., op. cit.*

Graddol, D. and Swann, J. (1989) *Gender Voices*. Oxford: Basil Blackwell.

Graham, A. (1975) The making of a non-sexist dictionary. In B. Thorne and N. Henley (eds) *Language and Sex: Difference and Dominance* (pp. 57–63). Rowley, MA: Newbury House.

Gramsci, A. (1948) *Opere di Antonio Gramsci (Quaderni Del Carcere)*. Turin: Einaudi.

Greenberg, P. (1989) Parents as partners in young children's development and education: A new American fad? Why does it matter? *Young Children* 44, 61–75.

Greenfield, T. (1976) Bilingualism, multiculturalism, and the crisis of purpose. *Canadian Society for the Study of Education Yearbook* 3, 107–36.

Grillo, R. (ed.) (1989a) *Social Anthropology and the Politics of Language*. London: Routledge.

Grillo, R. (1989b) *Dominant Languages: Language and Hierarchy in Britain and France*. Cambridge: Cambridge University Press.

Gumperz, J. (1976) Language, communication and public negotiation. In P. Sanday (ed.) *Anthropology and the Public Interest*. New York: Academic Press.

Gumperz, J. (1977) Sociocultural knowledge in conversational inference. In M. Saville-Troike (ed.) *Twenty-Eighth Annual Roundtable Monograph Series in Language and Linguistics*. Washington: Georgetown University Press.

Gumperz, J. (1982) *Discourse Strategies*. Cambridge: Cambridge University Press.

Gumperz, J., Kaltman, H. and O'Connor, M. (1984) Cohesion in spoken and written discourse: Ethnic style and the transition to literacy. In Tannen, *op. cit.* pp. 3–19.

Gupta, A. and Lee, A. (1990) Gender representation in English language textbooks used in the Singapore primary schools. *Language and Education* 4, 29–50.

Haan, N., Bellah, R., Rabinow, P. and Sullivan, W. (1983) *Social Science as Moral Inquiry*. Columbia: Columbia University Press.

Habermas, J. (1970) Towards a theory of communicative competence. *Inquiry* 13, 360–75.

Habermas, J. (1971) *Knowledge and Human Interests*. Boston: Beacon Press.

Habermas, J. (1979) *Communication and the Evolution of Society* (translated by T. McCarthy). London: Heinemann.

Habermas, J. (1982) A reply to my critics. In Thompson and Held, *op. cit.*

Habermas, J. (1985) *The Theory of Communicative Action: Volume 1, Reasoning and the Rationalisation of Society* (translated by T. McCarthy). London: Heinemann.

Hagman, T. and Lahdenperä, J. (1988) Nine years of Finnish-medium education in Sweden: What happens afterwards? The education of minority children in Botkyrka. In Skutnabb-Kangas and Cummins, *op. cit.* pp. 328–25.

Hamilton, B. (1989) Giving effect to the Treaty in schools: A guide for teachers. *National Education* 71(4), 129–31.

Hamilton, M. *et al.* (1993) *Worlds of Literacy*. Clevedon: Multilingual Matters.

Hare, R. M. (1963) *Freedom and Reason*. Oxford: Clarendon Press.

Harker, R. (1990) Bourdieu: Education and reproduction. In R. Harker, C. Mahar and C. Wilkes (eds) *An Introduction to the Work of Pierre Bourdieu*. London: Macmillan.

Harley, B. (1986) *Age in Second Language Acquisition*. Clevedon: Multilingual Matters.

Harris, L. J. (1977) Sex differences in the growth and use of language. In E. Donelson and J. Fullahorn (eds) *Women: A Psychological Perspective* (pp. 79–94). New York: Wiley.

Hastings, W. K. (1988). *The Right to an Education in Maori: The Case from International Law*. Wellington: Institute of Policy Studies.

Haugen, E. (1983) The implementation of corpus planning: Theory and practice. In Cobarrubias and Fishman, *op. cit.*

Haynes, N. M., Comer, J. P. and Hamilton-Lee, M. (1989) School climate enhancement through parental involvement. *Journal of School Psychology* 27, 87–90.

Heath, S. (1982) What no bedtime story means: Narrative skills at home and school. *Language in Society* 11, 49–76.

Heath, S. (1983) *Ways With Words: Ethnography of Communication in Communities and Classrooms*. Cambridge: Cambridge University Press.

Heath, S. (1986a) The functions and uses of literacy. In de Castell *et al.*, *op. cit.*

Heath, S. (1986b) Critical factors in literacy development. In de Castell *et al.*, *op. cit.*

Heath, S. (1986c) Taking a cross-cultural look at narratives. *Topics in Language Disorders* 7, 84–94.

Heath, S. and Branscombe, A. (1986) The book as narrative prop in language acquisition. In Schieffelin and Gilmore, *op. cit.*

Hewitt, R. (1989) Creole in the classroom: Political grammars and educational vocabularies. In Grillo (1989a), *op. cit.*

Hewstone, M. and Giles, H. (1986) Social groups and social stereotypes in intergroup communication. In W. Gudykunst (ed.) *Intergroup Communication*. London: Edward Arnold.

Hingangaroa Smith, G. (1986). Taha Maori: A pakeha privilege. *Delta* 37, 11–23.

Hingangaroa Smith, G. (1990). Taha Maori: Pakeha capture. In J. Codd, R. Harker and R. Nash (eds) *Political Issues in New Zealand Education* (2nd edn) (pp. 183–97). Palmerston North: The Dunmore Press.

Holm, A and Holm, W. (1990) Rock Point, a Navajo way to go to school: A valediction. In C. Cazden and C. Snow (eds) *English Plus: Issues in Bilingual Education* (pp. 170–84). Newbury Park: Sage.

Horvath, B. (1980) The education of migrant children: A language planning perspective. *ERDC Report No. 24*. Canberra: AGPS.

Hospers, J. (1982) *Human Conduct: Problems of Ethics*. New York: Harcourt Brace Jovanovich.

Hyltenstam, K. and Pienemann, M. (eds) (1985) *Modelling and Assessing Second Language Acquisition*. Clevedon: Multilingual Matters.

Hymes, D. (1966) Two types of linguistic relativity. In W. Bright (ed.) *Sociolinguistics*. The Hague: Mouton.

Hymes, D. (1971) On linguistic theory, communicative competence and the education of disadvantaged children. In M. Wax, S. Diamond and F. Gearing (eds) *Anthropological Perspectives in Education*. New York: Basic Books.

Iglesias, A. (1985) Cultural conflict in the classroom. In D. Ripich and F. Spinelli (eds) *School Discourse Problems*. London: Taylor & Francis.

Ingram, D. (1985) Assessing proficiency: An overview of some aspects of testing. In Hyltenstam and Pienemann, *op. cit.*

Jenkins, N. and Cheshire, J. (1990) Gender issues in the GCSE Oral English Examination: Part 1. *Language and Education* 4, 261–92.

Jones, A. (1987) Which girls are 'learning to lose'? In S. Middleton (ed.) *Women and Education in Aotearoa* (pp. 143–52). Wellington: Allen and Unwin.

Jordan, C. (1985) Translating culture: From ethnographic information to educational program. *Anthropology and Education Quarterly* 16, 105–23.

Jordan, D. (1988) Rights and claims of indigenous people: Education and the reclaiming of identity. The case of Canadian Natives, the Sami and Australian Aborigines. In Skutnabb-Kangas and Cummins, *op. cit.* pp. 189–222.

Kelly, A. (1988) Gender differences in teacher–pupil interactions: A meta-analytic review. *Research in Education* 39, 1–23.

Khosroshahi, F. (1989) Penguins don't care, but women do: A social identity analysis of a Whorfian problem. *Language in Society* 18, 505–25.

Klann-Delius, G. (1987) Sex and language. In U. Ammon, N. Dittmar and K. Mattheier (eds) *Sociolinguistics* (pp. 767–80). Berlin: De Gruyter.

Knott, R (1985) *The English Department in a Changing World*. Milton Keynes: Open University Press.

Kohlberg, L. (1976) Moral stages and moralization. In T. Lickona (ed.) *Moral Development and Behaviour*. New York: Holt, Rinehart and Wilson.

Kozol, J. (1986) *Illiterate America*. New York: Anchor & Doubleday.

Kramarae, C. (1981) *Women and Men Speaking: Frameworks for Analysis*. Rowley, MA: Newbury House

Kramarae, C., Schulz, M. and O'Barr, W. (1984) *Language and Power*. Beverley Hills: Sage.

Kress, G. and Hodge, R. (1979) *Language as Ideology*. London: Routledge.

Kymlicka, W. (1989) *Liberalism, Community and Culture*. Oxford: Clarendon Press.

Labov, W. (1966) Finding out about children's language. *Working Papers in Communication* 1, 1–30.

Labov, W. (1970) The logic of non-standard English. In F. Williams (ed.) *Language and Poverty*. Chicago: Markham.

Labov, W. (1971) The notion of system in creole studies. *Pidginization and Creolization of Language*. New York: Cambridge University Press.

Labov, W. (1972) *Language in the Inner City*. University of Pennsylvania Press.

Labov, W. (1982) Objectivity and commitment in linguistic science: The case of the Black English trial in Ann Arbor. *Language in Society* 11, 165–201.

Labov, W. (1987) Are black and white vernaculars diverging? *American Speech* 65, 5–12.

Lakoff, R. (1975) *Language and Women's Place* New York: Harper & Row.

Lambert, W. (1975) Culture and language as factors in learning and education. In A. Wolfgang (ed.) *Education of Immigrant Students: Issues and Answers*. Toronto: Ontario Institute for Studies in Education.

Lees, S. (1987) The structure of sexual relations in school. In Arnot and Weiner, *op. cit*. pp. 175–86.

Levine, R. and White, M. (1986) *Human Conditions: The Cultural Basis of Educational Development*. New York: Routledge & Kegan Paul.

Lobban, G. (1987) Sex roles in reading schemes. In Weiner and Arnot, *op. cit*. pp. 150–4.

Locke, J. (1690) [1973 edn].*Two Treatises of Government*. Cambridge: Cambridge University Press.

Lukes, S. (1974) *Power: A Radical View*. London: Macmillan.

Lukes, S. (1982) Of gods and demons: Habermas and practical reason. In Thompson and Held, *op. cit*.

Macaulay, R. (1977) *Language, Social Class and Education: A Glasgow Study*. Edinburgh: University of Edinburgh Press.

Macauley, R. (1978) The myth of female superiority in language. *Journal of Child Language* 5, 353–63.

Maccoby, E. and Jacklin, C. (1974) *The Psychology of Sex Differences*. Stanford: Stanford University Press.

Macpherson, C.B. (1973) Rawls' models of man and society. *Philosophy of Social Science* 3, 341–7.

Macshane, D. (1978) *Black and Front: Journalists and Race Reporting*. London: National Union of Journalists.

Malcolm, I. (1979) The West Australian Aboriginal child and classroom interaction: A sociolinguisitc approach. *Journal of Pragmatics* 3, 305–20.

Malcolm, I. (1982) Speech events of the aboriginal classroom. *International Journal of the Sociology of Language* 36, 115–34.

Maltz, D. and Borker, R. (1983) A cultural approach to male–female miscommunication. In J. Gumperz (ed.) *Language and Social Identity* (pp. 195–216). Cambridge: Cambridge University Press.

Marland, M. (1977) *Language Across the Curriculum*. London: Heinemann Educational Books.

Marsh, H. (1989) Sex differences in the development of verbal and mathematics constructs: The High School and Beyond Study. *American Educational Research Journal* 26, 191–225.

Martin-Jones, M. (1989) Language, power and linguistic minorities: The need for an alternative approach to bilingualism, language maintenance and shift. In Grillo (1989a), *op. cit.*

Martyna, W. (1978) What does 'he' mean? Use of the generic masculine. *Journal of Communication* 28, 131–8.

Martyna, W. (1983) Beyond the he/man approach: The case for nonsexist language. In B. Thorne, C. Kramarae, and N. Henley (eds) *Language, Gender and Society*. Cambridge, Mass: Newbury House.

Marx, K. (1974) *The Early Writings*. Harmondsworth: Penguin.

Marx, K. and Engels, F. (1976 [1846]) *The German Ideology*. Moscow: Progress Publishers.

Masemann, V. (1984) Multicultural programs in Toronto schools. In J. Mallea and J. Young (eds) *Cultural Diversity and Canadian Education* (pp. 349–69). Ottawa: Carleton University Press.

May, S. (1992). The relational school: Fostering pluralism and empowerment through a 'language policy across the curriculum'. *New Zealand Journal of Educational Studies* 27, 35–51.

May, S. (1994) *Making Multicultural Education Work*. Clevedon: Multilingual Matters.

Maybin, J. (1985) *Every Child's Language: An In-Service Pack for Primary Teachers*. Clevedon: Open University Press/Multilingual Matters.

McCarthy, T. (1984) *The Critical Theory of Jürgen Habermas*. Cambridge: Polity Press.

McConnell-Ginet, S., Borker, R. and Furman, N. (eds) (1980) *Women and Language in Literature and Society*. New York: Praeger.

McDermott, R. (1977) Social relations as contexts for learning in schools. *Harvard Educational Review* 47, 198–213.

McDonald, M. (1989) The exploitation of linguistic mis-match: Towards an ethnography of customs and manners. In Grillo (1989a), *op. cit.*

McLaughlin, B. (1986) Multilingual education: Theory east and west. In Spolsky, *op. cit.* pp. 32–52.

McPherson, J. (1990) Gender, language and education. In Corson (1990a), *op. cit.* pp. 237–46.

Mehan, H. (1984) Language and schooling. *Sociology of Education* 57, 174–83.

Michaels, S. (1981) 'Sharing time': Children's narrative styles and differential access to literacy. *Language in Society* 10, 423–42.

Michaels, S. and Cazden, C. (1986) Teacher/child collaboration as oral preparation for literacy. In Schiefflein and Gilmore, *op. cit.*

Michaels, S. and Collins, J. (1984) Oral discourse styles: Classroom interaction and the acquisition of literacy. In Tannen, *op. cit.* pp. 219–44.

Mills, C.W. (1940) Situated actions and vocabularies of motive. *American Sociological Review* 5, 904–13.

Milroy, J. and Milroy, L. (1978) Belfast: Change and variation in an urban vernacular. In Trudgill, *op. cit.*

Ministry of Education and Training (1993) *Antiracism and Ethnocultural Equity in School Boards: Guidelines for Policy Development and Implementation.* Queen's Printer for Ontario.

Moffatt, S. (1991) Becoming bilingual: A summary report of a sociolinguistic study of the communication of young mother-tongue Panjabi-speaking children. *Language and Education* 5, 55–71.

Moi, T. (1985) *Sexual/Textual Politics: Feminist Literary Theory.* London: Methuen.

Moorfield, J. (1987) Implications for schools of research findings in bilingual education. In W. Hirsh (ed.) *Living Languages.* Auckland: Heinemann.

Morse, L. and Handley, H. (1985) Listening to adolescents: Gender differences in science class interaction. In L. Wilkinson and C. Marrett (eds) *Gender Influences in Classroom Interaction.* Orlando, FL: Academic Press.

Murphy, J. (1980) School administrators besieged: A look at Australian and American education. *American Journal of Education* 88, 1–26.

Nader, L. and Sursock, A. (1986) Anthropology and justice. In Cohen, *op. cit.*

Nemetz Robinson, G. (1978) *Language and Multicultural Education: An Australian Perspective.* Sydney: ANZ Book Co.

Nielsen, K. (1978) Class and justice. In J.A. and W.H. Shaw (eds) *Justice and Economic Distribution.* Englewood Cliffs, NJ: Prentice Hall.

Northam, J. (1987) Girls and boys in primary maths books. In Weiner and Arnot, *op. cit.* pp. 155–9.

Nozick, R. (1974) *Anarchy, State and Utopia.* Oxford: Blackwell.

NUJ (1982) *Non-Sexist Code of Practice for Book Publishing.* London: National Union of Journalists.

Oakes, J. (1985) *Keeping Track: How Schools Structure Inequality.* New Haven: Yale University Press.

O'Barr, W. (1982) *Linguistic Evidence: Language, Power and Strategy in the Courtroom.* New York: Academic Press.

O'Barr, W. and Atkins, B. (1980) 'Women's language' or 'powerless language'? In McConnell-Ginet *et al., op. cit.*

Ogbu, J. (1983) Minority status and schooling in plural societies. *Comparative Education Review* 27, 168–90.

Ogbu, J. (1987) Variability in minority school performance: A problem in search of an explanation. *Anthropology and Education Quarterly* 18, 312–34.

Okano, K. (1992) *School to Work in Japan: A Bilingual Ethnography.* Clevedon: Multilingual Matters.

Okin, S. M. (1989) *Justice, Gender and the Family.* New York: Basic Books.

Oliner, S.P. and Oliner, P.M. (1988) *The Altruistic Personality: Rescuers of Jews in Nazi Europe*. New York: The Free Press.

OPCS (1992) *1991 Census*. London: Office of Population Censuses and Surveys.

Osborne, B. (1991) Towards an ethnology of culturally responsive pedagogy in small-scale remote communities: Native American and Torres Strait Islander. *Qualitative Studies in Education* 4, 1–17

Ottmann, H. (1982) Cognitive interests and self-reflection. In Thompson and Held, *op. cit.*

Ozolins, U. (1991) National language policy and planning: Migrant languages. In Romaine, *op. cit.*

Pascal, C. (1987) Democratised primary school government: Relevant theoretical constructs. *Oxford Review of Education* 13, 321–30.

Pauwels, A. (1991) Gender differences in Australian English. In Romaine, *op. cit.*

Peal, E. and Lambert, W. (1962) The relation of bilingualism to intelligence. *Psychological Monographs* 76 (Number 546), 1–23.

Pecheux, M. (1982) *Language, Semantics and Ideology: Stating the Obvious*. London: Macmillan.

Penetito, W. (1986) Towards social justice: Curriculum, culture and context. A paper presented to the Wellington Institute for Educational Research, Education House, Wellington.

Pettit, P. (1980) *Judging Justice: An Introduction to Contemporary Political Philosophy*. London: Routledge & Kegan Paul.

Philips, S. (1972) Participant structures and communicative competence: Warm Springs children in community and classroom. In C. Cazden, V. John and D. Hymes (eds) *Functions of Language in the Classroom* (pp. 370–94). New York: Teachers College Press.

Philips, S. (1975) Literacy as a mode of communication on the Warm Springs Indian Reservation. In E.H. and E. Lenneberg (eds) *Foundations of Language Development: A Multidisciplinary Approach* (pp.367–82). New York: Academic Press.

Philips, S. (1980) Sex differences and language. *Annual Review of Anthropology* 9, 523–44.

Philips, S. (1983) *The Invisible Culture: Communication in Classroom and Community on the Warm Springs Indian Reservation*. New York: Longman.

Philips, S., Steele, S. and Tanz, C. (eds) (1987) *Language, Gender, and Sex in Comparative Perspective*. Cambridge: Cambridge University Press.

Plomin, R. and Foch, T. (1981) Sex differences and individual differences. *Child Development* 52, 383–5.

Potter, M. and Wetherell, M. (1987) *Discourse and Social Psychology*. London: Sage.

Ramsey, F. (1978) *Foundations*. London: Routledge & Kegan Paul.

Randall, G. (1987) Gender differences in pupil–teacher interaction in workshops and laboratories. In Weiner and Arnot, *op. cit.* pp. 163–72.

Rasinski, T. V. and Fredericks, A. D. (1989) Dimensions of parent involvement. *Reading Teacher* 43, 180–2.

Rasmussen, D. M. (1990) *Reading Habermas*. Cambridge, MA: Basil Blackwell.

Rawls, J. (1972) *A Theory of Justice*. Oxford: Oxford University Press.

Rawls, J. (1980) Kantian constructivism in moral theory: The Dewey Lectures. *Journal of Philosophy* 77, 515–72.

Reay, D. (1991) Intersections of gender, race and class in the primary school. *British Journal of Sociology of Education* 12, 163–182.

Reed, C. (1981) Teaching teachers about teaching writing to students from varied linguistic social and cultural groups. In Whiteman, *op. cit.*

Rehbein, J. (1984) Diskurs und Verstehen: Zur Role der Muttersprache bei der Textverarbeitung in der Zweitsprache. Hamburg: University of Hamburg.

Reid, E. (1988) Linguistic minorities and language education: The English experience. *Journal of Multilingual and Multicultural Development* 9, 181–91; 220–3.

Rivera, C. (ed.) (1983) *An Ethnographic/Sociolinguistic Approach to Language Proficiency Assessment*. Clevedon: Multilingual Matters.

Rivera, C. (ed.) (1984) *Communicative Competence Approaches to Language Proficiency Assessment*. Clevedon: Multilingual Matters.

Rizvi, F. and Kemmis, S. (1987) *Dilemmas of Reform*. Geelong: Deakin University Press.

Romaine, S. (1978) Postvocalic /r/ in Scottish English: Sound change in progress?. In P. Trudgill (ed.) *Sociolinguistic Patterns in British English*. London: Edward Arnold.

Romaine, S. (1984) *The Language of Children and Adolescents: The Acquisition of Communicative Competence*. Oxford: Basil Blackwell.

Romaine, S. (1989) *Bilingualism*. Oxford: Basil Blackwell.

Romaine, S. (ed.) (1991) *Language in Australia*. Cambridge: Cambridge University Press.

Rorty, R. (1983) Method and morality. In Haan *et al., op. cit.*

Sachdev, I. (1991) Oral assessment and accent evaluation. Unpublished paper.

Sadker, M. and Sadker, D. (1985) Sexism in the schoolroom of the '80s. *Psychology Today* (March), 54–7.

Sanchez, G. (1934) Bilingualism and mental measures: A word of caution. *Journal of Applied Psychology* 18, 765–72.

Sandel, M. (1982) *Justice and the Limits of Liberalism*. Cambridge: Cambridge University Press.

Saville-Troike, M. (1979) Culture, language and education. In H. Trueba and C. Barnett-Mizrahi (eds) *Bilingual Multicultural Education and the Professional: From Theory to Practice*. Rowley, MA: Newbury House.

Schieffelin, B. and Gilmore, P. (eds) (1986) *The Acquisition of Literacy: Ethnographic Perspectives*. Norwood, NJ: Ablex.

Schieffelin, B. (1987) Do different worlds mean different words? An example from Papua New Guinea. In Philips *et al., op. cit.* pp. 249–62.

Schools Council Working Paper No. 67. (1980) *Language Across the Curriculum*. London: Methuen.

Scollon, R. and Scollon, S. (1979) *Linguistic Convergence: An Ethnography of Speaking at Fort Chipewyan*. New York: Academic Press.

Scollon, R. and Scollon, S. (1981) *Narrative Literacy and Face in Inter-Ethnic Communication*. Norwood, NJ: Ablex.

Scollon, R. and Scollon, S. (1984) Cooking it up and boiling it down: Abstracts in Athabaskan children's story retellings. In Tannen, *op. cit.* pp. 173–97.

Scribner, S. and Cole, M. (1981) *The Psychology of Literacy.* Harvard: Harvard University Press.

Shakeshaft, C. (1987) *Women in Educational Administration.* Newbury Park, CA: Sage.

Shapiro, M. (ed.) (1984) *Language and Politics.* Oxford: Blackwell.

Shapson, S. and D'Oyley, V. (eds) (1984) *Bilingual and Multicultural Education: Canadian Perspectives.* Clevedon: Multilingual Matters.

Simich-Dudgeon, C. and Rivera, C. (1983) Teacher training and ethnographic/sociolinguistic issues in the assessment of bilingual students' language proficiency. In Rivera, *op. cit.*

Skeggs, B. (1991) Challenging masculinity and using sexuality. *British Journal of Sociology of Education* 12, 127–39.

Skilbeck, M. (1984) *School-Based Curriculum Development.* London: Harper & Row.

Skutnabb-Kangas, T. (1981) *Bilingualism or Not: The Education of Minorities.* Philadelphia: Multilingual Matters.

Skutnabb-Kangas, T. (1988) Multilingualism and the education of minority children. In Skutnabb-Kangas and Cummins, *op. cit.* pp. 9–44.

Skutnabb-Kangas, T. and Cummins, J. (1988) *Minority Education: From Shame to Struggle.* Clevedon: Multilingual Matters.

Slavin, R. (1983) *Cooperative Learning.* New York: Longman.

Smith, D. (1985) *Languages, the Sexes and Society.* Oxford: Blackwell.

Smith, D. (1986) The anthropology of literacy acquisition. In Schieffelin and Gilmore, *op. cit.*

Smitherman, G. (1977) *Talkin' and Testifyin': The Language of Black America.* Boston: Houghton Mifflin.

Smitherman, G. (1992) Black English, diverging or converging?: The view from the National Assessment of Educational Progress. *Language and Education* 6, 47–61.

Smitherman-Donaldson, G. and van Dijk, T. (1988) *Discourse and Discrimination.* Detroit: Wayne State University Press.

Smolicz, J. (1984) Multiculturalism and an overarching framework of values. *European Journal of Education* 19, 11–24.

Soltan, K. (1986) Public policy and justice. In Cohen, *op. cit.*

Sornig, K. (1989) Some remarks on linguistic strategies of persuasion. In Wodak, *op. cit.*

Spender, D. (1980) *Man Made Language.* London: Routledge & Kegan Paul.

Spolsky, B. (1986) *Language and Education in Multilingual Settings.* Clevedon: Multilingual Matters.

Stanworth, M. (1983) *Gender and Schooling: A Study of Sexual Divisions in the Classroom.* London: Hutchinson.

Starratt, R. (1991) Building an ethical school: A theory for practice in educational leadership. *Educational Administration Quarterly* 27, 185–202.

Stockard, J. and Johnson, M. (1981) The sources and dynamics of sexual inequality in the profession of education. In P. Schmuk, W. Charters and R. Carlson (eds) *Educational Policy and Management: Sex Differentials.* New York: Academic Press.

Stones, R. (1983) *'Pour Out the Cocoa, Janet': Sexism in Children's Books*. York: Longman for Schools Council.

Swann, J. (1988) Talk control: An illustration from the classroom of problems in analysing male dominance of conversation. In Coates and Cameron, *op. cit.*

Swann, J. and Graddol, D. (1988) Trapping linguists: An analysis of linguists' responses to John Honey's pamphlet 'The Language Trap'. *Language and Education* 2, 95–111.

Tajfel, H. (ed.) (1984) *The Social Dimension* (Volumes 1 & 2). Cambridge: Cambridge University Press.

Tannen, D. (ed.) (1984) *Coherence in Spoken and Written Discourse*. Norwood, NJ: Ablex.

Tanz, C. (1987) Introduction. In Philips *et al.*, *op. cit.* pp. 163–77.

Taylor, O. and Matsuda, M. (1988) Storytelling and classroom discrimination. In Smitherman-Donaldson and van Dijk, *op. cit.*

Thompson, J. (1984) *Studies in the Theory of Ideology*. Cambridge: Polity Press.

Thompson, J. and Held, D. (1982) *Habermas: Critical Debates*. London: Macmillan.

Thorne, B. (1986) Girls and boys together ... but mostly apart: Gender arrangements in elementary schools. In W. Hartup and Z. Rubin (eds) *Relationships and Development* (pp. 167–84). Hillsdale, NJ: Lawrence Erlbaum.

Thorne, B., Kramarae, C. and Henley, N. (eds) (1983) *Language, Gender and Society*. Rowley, MA: Newbury House

Todd, R. (1978) Social policies towards Gypsies. In M. Brown and S. Baldwin (eds) *The Year Book of Social Policy in Britain 1977*. London: Routledge & Kegan Paul.

Tollefson, J. (1991) *Planning Language, Planning Inequality*. London Longman.

Torbe, M. (ed.) (1980) *Language Policies in Action: Language Across the Curriculum in Some Secondary Schools*. London: Ward Lock.

Tosi, A. (1984) *Immigration and Bilingual Education*. Oxford: Pergamon.

Tosi, A. (1988) The jewel in the crown of the modern prince: The new approach to bilingualism in multicultural education in England. In Skutnabb-Kangas and Cummins, *op. cit.* pp. 79–102.

Treichler, P. (1989) From discourse to dictionary: How sexist meanings are authorized. In Frank and Treichler, *op. cit.* pp. 51–79.

Treichler, P. and Kramarae, C. (1983) Women's talk in the ivory tower. *Communication Quarterly* 31, 118–32.

Troike, R. (1981) A synthesis of research on bilingual education. *Educational Leadership* 14, 498–504.

Troyna, B. (1993) *Racism and Education*. Buckingham: Open University Press.

Trudgill, P. (1974) *The Social Differentiation of English in Norwich*. Cambridge: Cambridge University Press.

Trudgill, P. (1978) *Sociolinguistic Patterns in British English*. London: Edward Arnold.

Trujillo, C. (1986) A comparative examination of classroom interactions between professors and minority and non-minority college students. *American Educational Research Journal* 23, 191–200.

UNESCO (1953) *The Use of Vernacular Languages in Education*. Paris: UNESCO.

Valdes, G., Lozano, A. and Garcia-Moya, R. (eds) (1981) *Teaching Spanish to the Hispanic Bilingual: Issues, Aims and Methods*. New York: Teachers College Press.

Vallen, T. and Stijnen, S. (1987) Language and educational success of indigenous and non-indigenous minority students in the Netherlands. *Language and Education* 1, 109–24.

Vogt, L., Jordan, C. and Tharp, R. (1987) Explaining school failure, producing school success: Two cases. *Anthropology and Education Quarterly* 19, 276–86.

Vygotsky, L. (1962) *Thought and Language*. Wiley: New York

Wagner, D., Messick, B. and Spratt, J. (1986) Studying literacy in Morocco. In Schieffelin and Gilmore, *op. cit.*

Wald, B. (1984) A sociolinguistic perspective on Cummins's current framework for relating language proficiency to academic achievement. In Rivera, *op. cit.*

Walkerdine, V. (1987) Sex, power and pedagogy. In Arnot and Weiner, *op. cit.* pp. 166–74.

Watson, K. (1975) Transferable communicative routines: Strategies and group identity in two speech events. *Language in Society* 4, 53–72.

Weiner, G. and Arnot, M. (eds) (1987) *Gender Under Scrutiny: New Inquiries in Education*. London: Unwin Hyman.

White, J. (1990) On literacy and gender. In F. Christie (ed.) *Literacy for a Changing World*. Hawthorn, Victoria: ACER.

Whiteman, M. (1981) Dialect influence in writing. In Whiteman, *op. cit.*

Whiteman, M. (ed.) (1981) *Writing: The Nature, Development and Teaching of Written Communication. Volume 1. Variation in Writing: Functional and Linguistic–Cultural Differences*. Hillsdale, NJ: Lawrence Erlbaum.

Whyld, J. (ed.) (1983) *Sexism in the Secondary Curriculum*. London: Harper & Row.

Whyte, J. (1983) *Beyond the Wendy House: Sex Role Stereotyping in the Primary School*. York: Longmans.

Wilkinson, L and Marrett, C. (eds) (1985) *Gender Influences in Classroom Interaction*. Orlando: Academic Press.

Winch, C. (1989) Standard English, normativity and the Cox Committee Report. *Language and Education* 3, 275–93.

Winch, C. (1993) Dialect interference and difficulties with writing: An investigation into St Lucian primary schools. *Language and Education* 7 (in press).

Wodak, R. (ed.) (1989) *Language, Power and Ideology: Studies in Political Discourse*. Amsterdam: John Benjamins.

Wolff, R.P. (1977) *Understanding Rawls*. Princeton: Princeton University Press.

Wright, C. (1987), The relations between teachers and Afro-Caribbean pupils: Observing multiracial classrooms. In G. Weiner and M. Arnot (eds) *Gender Under Scrutiny* (pp. 173–86). London: Hutchinson.

Wrong, D. (1979) *Power: Its Forms, Bases and Uses*. Oxford: Blackwell.

Yeakey, C., Johnston, G. and Adkison, J. (1986) In pursuit of equity: A review of research on minorities and women in educational administration. *Educational Administration Quarterly* 22, 110–49.

Young, I. M. (1981) Towards a critical theory of justice. *Social Theory and Practice* 7, 279–302.

Young, R. E. (1987) Critical theory and classroom questioning. *Language and Education* 1, 125–34.

230   LANGUAGE, MINORITY EDUCATION & GENDER

Young, R. E. (1992) *Critical Theory and Classroom Talk*. Clevedon: Multilingual
Matters.
Yu, V. and Atkinson, P. (1988) An investigation of the language difficulties experi-
enced by Hong Kong secondary school students in English-medium schools.
Journal of Multilingual and Multicultural Development 9, 267–84.
Zinsser, C. (1986) For the Bible tells me so: Teaching children in a fundamentalist
church. In Schieffelin and Gilmore, *op. cit.*

Index